COURT ART OF THE TANG

Patricia Eichenbaum Karetzky

University Press of America, Inc.
Lanham • New York • London

Copyright © 1996 by

of America,® Inc.

ston Way

iryland 20706

etta Street

E 8LU England

s reserved
Printed in the United States of America
British Cataloging in Publication Information Available

Library of Congress Cataloging-in-Publication Data

Karetzky, Patricia Eichenbaum.
Court art of the Tang / Patricia Eichenbaum Karetzky.
p.   cm.
Includes bibliographical references and index.
1. Art, Chinese--Tang--Five dynasties, 618-960.   2. China-Kings
and rulers-Art patronage. I. Title.
N7343.3K37   1995   709'.51 --dc20   95-25357 CIP

ISBN 0-7618-0115-4 (cloth : alk: ppr.)
ISBN 0-7618-0201-1 (pbk: alk: ppr.)

⊖™The paper used in this publication meets the minimum
requirements of American National Standard for information
Sciences—Permanence of Paper for Printed Library Materials,
ANSI Z39.48—1984

Dedicated to my Mother,
who taught me to love beauty.

Acknowledgments:

Sincere thanks to Duan Wen-jie, Director of the Dunhuang Research
Institute; Wang Shi-ping, Curator, Shaanxi Province Historical
Museum, Xian; Zhou Yue, Vice-President of Education, Shaanxi
Province Historical Museum, Xian; Zhang Fang, Chief Curator
Shaanxi Provincial Museum, Xian; Han Jin-Ke, Museum Chief,
Famen Temple, Xian; Liu Ding, Shaanxi Provincial Famen Museum;
Xian; Yang Ziu-sha, Sichuan Provincial Museum, Chengdu; and in
general to the Shanghai Museum of Art; Zhaoling Museum, Xian;
Xinjiang Autonomous Region Province Museum, Urumqi; Gansu
Provincial Museum, Lanzhou; Ding Liang, Patrick Coleman, Chief
Librarian Metropolitan Museum of Art Library, Alexander Soper,
Harry Karetzky, and Ellen Levine.

CONTENTS

List of Illustrations

Preface

Acknowledgments

Introduction

ILLUSTRATIONS

EARLY TANG (618-711)

CHAPTER VII EMPEROR SUZONG 756-762

CHAPTER VIII EMPEROR DAIZONG 763-779

LATE TANG 805-907

PREFACE

This book, compared with other art historical texts, is organized in an unusual fashion. First, as a study of the arts of the Tang, it is not based on connoisseurship but rather on archeological data. Second, because so much has been recently discovered from this period, which only ten years ago would have been cited for a dearth of dated material, the well-known landmarks of Tang style (often the centerpieces of other art books) have been purposefully omitted. Only objects that have been recently unearthed, most of which bear a date, are discussed, in an effort to create a concrete body of knowledge of this newly discovered material. In addition, although there are broad introductions to the general divisions of early, middle, and late Tang, archaeological finds are not described as part of a general discussion of the art of the era but rather are entered under the specific emperor. This type of chronological format has been used with great success in other disciplines,[1] and its use is due in part to the fact that the historical records themselves are now for the first time, arranged in this way.[2] To be sure, one difficultly with this type of organization is that some eras are much better represented by archaeological remains than others; the problem of disparate amounts of data for the various emperors is also encountered in the historical annals.[3] Some emperors' reigns were brief; others lived during the late Tang when the histories were no longer written by contemporary annalists. Moreover, some rulers were highly esteemed by the official historians and are thus granted greater and more favorable attention. Similarly, the strong rulers showing a Confucian interest in didactic art, and in art in general, are afforded greater coverage by Chinese art historians.

There are several reasons for a presentation of the multitude of new finds in a strict chronological framework. First, materials that address the problem of Tang chronology are rare; most books, both Western and Chinese, only place the art objects within the broad, 300-year framework with the general divisions of early, middle, and late. This type of organization has serious shortcomings. For one, although these terms are used uniformly in the West and in China, they are rarely defined, and the chronological parameters vary greatly in the different sources. For example, Chinese scholars at the research center at Dunhuang propose four periods of Tang art, in part to distinguish the period of Tibetan occupation; this system has not been adopted elsewhere. More importantly, undated materials are relegated to periods in accordance with certain prejudicial attitudes. One such viewpoint is that the late Tang (or mature Tang) was an inferior epoch when little of quality was produced. As it has long been held that the climax of Tang aesthetic achievement was attained under the Emperor Xuanzong (712-756),[4] much excellent material is attributed to that reign, without question. However, new dated materials prove that much exquisite workmanship was produced under the later Tang after the cataclysmic An Lu-shan rebellion that temporarily shattered the empire in 750. Even a cursory view of the names of artists active after the mid-eighth century dispels the untenable theory that the late-Tang was artistically barren. Though many famous painters worked under the Emperor Xuanzong, they flourished beyond his reign. They included Wang Wei (d. 759), Wu Dao-zu (active to 760), Han Gan (d. 781), and Zhou Fang (d. 800). Many great poets wrote during the era of the brilliant Emperor Xuanzong; but the high level of prose, prose-poems, and narrative fiction[5] did not occur until the ninth century with Liu Zong-yuan (d. 819), Han Yu (d. 824), and Yuan Zhen (d. 831), and poets like Li Ho (d. 816), Bai Ju-yi (d. 846), and Li Shang-yin (d. 858).

Another common presumption was that Buddhist art ended with the persecutions of the mid-ninth century. All too many excellent books on the subject of Tang Buddhism and its art venture no further than the great proscription of 850. However, this destructive rage was quite short in duration, less than four years, and although it was ferocious in its intensity and successful in destroying a great deal of Buddhist art and architecture, much was immediately reconstructed. In the aftermath of the destruction, popular and imperial efforts were directed to rebuilding temples and monastic establishments. As a result of this restoration of Buddhist monuments, there was a renaissance of Buddhist art. There are several sources for the study of Buddhist material: Some Buddhist sites, like Dunhuang and Sichuan, were supported throughout the Tang era and thus allow for study of their art over a long and continuous period of time. These rock-cut caves, more impervious to destruction, were relatively unaffected by the proscription. There are also new archaeological discoveries and studies that have been recently published in China. One outstanding example is the cache of glorious objects found in the temple of Famen, which does much to restore our opinion of late Buddhist art.

This book is much indebted to the scholars of Chinese history and art who contributed to the formulation of a chronological body of knowledge. They provided the historical context in which the archaeological materials could be organized.

NOTES

1. For example Stanley Weinstein's *Buddhism under the Tang* (New York, 1987) which is organized chronologically by emperor.
2. Denis Twitchett, *The Writing of Official History Under the T'ang* (New York, 1992): 119, the official account of the *Shilu*, which treats each emperor's reign individually, was an innovation of the Tang record keepers.
3. Twitchett, 1992: 202.
4. This evaluation of artists under Xuanzong began with the mid-ninth-century art historian Zhang Yan-yuan in his *Li Dai Ming Hua Ji*, translated by William Acker, *Some T'ang and pre T'ang Texts on Painting* (Leiden, 1954): 146: "In the K'ai Yuan and Tien Pao eras there were more such men (of rare ability) than at any other time."
5. Y. W. Ma and J. Lau, *Traditional Chinese Stories* (New York, 1978).

INTRODUCTION

The Tang dynasty has long been characterized as glorious and magnificent because of the extraordinary artistic accomplishments in the secular arts of literature, painting, sculpture, ceramics, and Buddhist art. China's prosperity sustained three large cosmopolitan centers: Chang-an, the main capital, in modern Shaanxi, with a population of nearly two million residents, was the largest and most lively metropolis in the world; Luoyang, in present day Henan, figured as the second capital; and in the later Tang, Yangzhou, in modern Zhekiang, was an extremely important commercial center. There were many great innovations in science and technology: The first pharmacopoeia was written in 643, *Old, New, Tried and Tested Prescriptions*, by Zhen Chuan.[1] Woodblock printing was invented, as was gunpowder,[2] and polychrome porcelain was perfected.

For the most part the period of approximately 300 years from 618 to 906 was marked by the reigns of capable emperors whose efforts to create and sustain a centralized government led to the foundation of a political and social bureaucracy that was the model for succeeding dynasties. Military and commercial exploits resulted in the expansion of the empire to its greatest territorial extent.

Interestingly, the Tang was a period of dramatic contrasts. At this time the frequency of cultural exchanges with the West reached an apex: Tang cities were host to large foreign populations and housed their temples, churches, and mosques, but in 845 rampant xenophobia led to the expulsion of nonnationals. Although Buddhist art of the Tang was celebrated as the apogee of aesthetic and spiritual expression, the severe proscription against Buddhism in 845 resulted in the wholesale destruction of temples and icons in and around the capital cities and the relaification of hundreds of thousands of monks. And, finally, while the first half of the Tang saw the empire at its strongest, in part because of its military supremacy over the neighboring peoples and territories that included the Uighur Turks, Tibet, Korea, and Champa (Vietnam), it was this militarism that later led to the rebellious insurgencies that threatened the government's stability and seriously weakened it during the later half of the Tang.

Many of the accomplishments of the early Tang period actually had their origins in the previous era, that of the Sui dynasty. After the post-Han period--400 years of disunion that saw the rise and fall of two dozen small dynasties--the country was finally unified under Yang Qian, Emperor Sui Wendi (541-605). A series of military conquests reunited the disparate regimes of the northern territories and central and southern China. The Sui empire now extended beyond its traditional borders south to Fukien, Annam (Yunnan), and Champa, west to the Turkish empire of Central Asia and, more tenuously, east to Manchuria and Korea.

The first Sui emperor and his successor sought to unify the country and consolidate their power through ambitious building campaigns, which included city structures, large-scale engineering projects, and luxurious palaces. During the early Sui the repair of the Great Wall was undertaken and a capital city was established at Daxingheng, later known as Chang-an. The second emperor, Yangdi, moved the capital to Luoyang and established a third capital in Yangzhou. These large, walled cities followed a gridlike pattern of intersecting broad avenues. Districts were designated for aristocratic residences, imperial quarters, an administrative center, and commercial markets. At Luoyang opulent palaces and lush gardens teeming with exotic wildlife and flora were under the direction of the architect Yang Xu, who is also remembered for his design of enormous naval junks.[3] A large imperial art collection was amassed; the famed connoisseur Ho Tiao was not only an expert on paintings and art but a military engineer.[4] These cities, with their magnificent residences and opulent settings, were symbols of the power of the Yang ruling family.

Major undertakings to link the empire internally led to the building of canals and waterways in eastern China, they facilitated commerce and administration by connecting the metropolitan centers.[5] The capital was linked to the Yellow River, the Han River with the Yangze, and later the Huai River was joined to the Yellow River; in the end, a water route led from the south at Hangzhou to the north and encircled modern Beijing. Upon its completion Emperor Yangdi took a pleasure cruise along the Grand Canal. One of the great engineering feats of the Sui was the construction of the Anchi Bridge, outside the south gate of Zhaoxian in Hebei. The engineer Li Chun built a segmental arched bridge from 605 to 616 that spanned more than 30 meters by reinforcing the construction with iron; it is still in use today.[6] Although the Grand Canal was a boon to grain transport, communication, and commerce, the means by which these and other large-scale efforts were accomplished was forced labor. It is estimated that nearly four million men, in addition to family members who were needed to care for them, were conscripted upon pain of death.

Despite the military expansion, bureaucratic organization, and monumental constructions, the Sui was a short-lived dynasty. Military defeat in Korea, the insurgence of the Turks in the northwest, famines, and the burden of forced labor led to unrest and disloyal factions.

Li Yuan, a Sui official, came out of one of the rebellious groups that sought to put an end to the Sui dynasty. His sons were of considerable help in the conquest and consolidation of the empire. The designated crown prince gained control in the northwest, and another son, Li Shi-min, was particularly effective in unifying the eastern plain. After a rival faction staged a coup and murdered the Sui emperor, the Li faction captured the capital at Chang-an and took the throne. Through a subsequent series of brilliant military stratagems, the Tang dynasty was established and became an empire. Attempts were made to encompass and control the peripheral regions, including Tibet, that of the northern Uighur Turks, Korea, and Assam in the south, but dominion over these distant territories was inconstant, and for centuries, these regions were in continuous turmoil.

The first Tang emperors consolidated their empire through effective administrative organization. They adopted and adapted the bureaucratic divisions of the government and the legal code employed by the Sui. The examination system, based on a knowledge of Confucian literature, was reinstituted. Officials selected on the basis of the exam system joined the ranks of the nobility to assist the imperial ruling body. Although in the early Tang the exam-selected candidates were of little threat to the official bureaucracy, by the late Tang the examination was one of the primary means of gaining a position in government. The legal code, rewritten first in 653 and again in 737, was a notable and lasting achievement.[7] The vast territories were organized into governable entities ruled over by provincial ministers. Such large geographic divisions facilitated administration and tax collection; these provincial designations are still in part preserved today. In addition, early Tang rulers redistributed the land and there were sweeping changes in the ranking of bureaucrats, imperial family members, and provincial landholders in an effort to increase tax collection. A census facilitated tax assessments and helped to identify the tax-paying populace. Large-scale construction projects, both civil and residential, continued.

By the middle Tang an overhaul of the canal systems was necessitated to keep Chang-an adequately stocked with essential goods, especially food. The improved transportation led to a boom in commercial trade that revitalized the capital city, long depressed by insufficient provisions. Canton, dominated by a large foreign settlement, was a busy commercial center owing to the thriving commerce along the sea routes. Yangzhou, situated as it was on the Yangze and the Grand Canal, prospered in the eighth century. It was a banking center and gold market and monopolized the salt and tea trade.[8]

THE TANG COURT AND ITS ART

The court of the Tang emperors, divine rulers of the largest realm in the world, was conspicuous in its pomp and splendor. Their palaces were replete with magnificently wrought furniture and art objects, and the walls were painted with illustrations of famous rulers and heroes of the past as well as images of themselves and their families. Collections of art and antiquities were culled from preceding imperial treasures like those of the Sui and added to through the system of tribute and requisition. The court drank wine made from rice and from newly imported grapes in gold, silver, and porcelain cups. During this era tea drinking, introduced with Buddhism as an aid in meditation, became a popular custom, and, as a result, new types of ceramic vessels--cups, saucers, and pots--were produced in regional kilns. A variety of firing and glazing techniques heralded the invention of porcelain and other ceramic types, such as celadon, white, black, and polychrome wares. Some of these vessels are characterized by austere simplicity and refinement in shape; others are ornately decorated with three-dimensional or engraved designs. Gold and silver plates, bowls, and cups became fashionable; and complex techniques evolved for their design and manufacture, whether delicately inlaid, engraved, or three-dimensionally decorated.

In addition to the archaeological excavations in recent decades that have provided a remarkable amount of information about Tang art, art historians of that era are a primary source. Zhang Yan-yuan, active in the period 815-880, wrote his *Record of Famous Painters, Lidai Minghuaji;*[9] Zhu Ching-xuan composed his *Celebrated Painters of the*

Tang, Tang Chao Ming Hua Lu in the 840s.[10] Visiting the capital after the destruction of Buddhist monuments in 845, Duan Zheng-shi wrote his *A Vacation Glimpse of the Tang Temples of Chang-an, Sidaji.*[11] Late Tang art was recorded by Guo Ruo-xu in his *Experiences in Painting, Tu Hua Jianwen Zhi,* written in the 1070s.[12] These men gave vivid descriptions of the Tang artists called to court to design the various gardens or to oversee the building and decoration of new halls. Court artists painted pictures of foreign ambassadors (with their strange physiognomies and odd costumes) bearing exotic gifts of tribute; prized horses in the imperial stables; the birds and wildlife that inhabited the imperial parks; the renowned beauties at court; and the courtiers at their aristocratic pastimes such as horseback riding, polo, singing, dancing, music-making or playing games of chance. These themes are often found in paintings on the walls of excavated tombs.

These works were done in the monumental figure style. Large-scale figures, painted on horizontal scrolls, fill the entire height of the silk. The nearly empty backgrounds include only a few props necessitated by the narrative content. One hallmark of Tang style is the naturalistic and meticulously rendered details of the silk embroidered garments, delicate hair jewels, and other personal articles. These portraits provide a rich contrast of figures of different social positions, age, and sex; not only is there a keen appreciation of the particularities of individual physiognomy but psychological makeup and mood is evident as well. Figures are shown in a variety of postures ranging from rear, three-quarter, profile, and front view, seated, standing, kneeling, and stooped. The Tang is known for its celebration of women; the court lady is a favorite subject in poetry, painting, tomb figurines, and short stories.

Although virtually no examples survive, the art of landscape painting enjoyed its first flowering during the Tang. Two distinct styles were practiced. The ornate blue and green style, which was often adorned with gold, rendered the natural forms with outlines that were filled in with polychrome. The celebrated monochrome ink style is attributed to the mid-eighth century artist, scholar-official, and poet Wang Wei, whose landscape scrolls were said to have demonstrated calligraphic grace and deft control of washes. Wang is credited with the method of using wash alone in the broken ink or "po mo" technique. By the later Tang, landscape painting achieved true autonomy from figure painting: a subject like trees and rocks was a sufficient theme for an artist such as Wang Zai (ca. 785-805).[13]

Sculpture was never considered a fine art in China, yet the large-scale funeral carvings from the imperial tombs reached their grandest in the Tang and set the style for the *shendao*, or tomb path, for the remaining dynasties.[14] Long processional paths leading to the imperial tombs were flanked by numerous matching pairs of oversize, free-standing animals, attendants, and court dignitaries.

In the early Tang the cities of Chang-an and Luoyang were filled with foreigners, selling their wares in markets that boasted a wide variety of imports from the distant corners of the known world, much of which was under Chinese suzerainty. Roman and Near Eastern glass, Sasanian silver, Central Asian and Persian rugs, exotic silks and embroidery, musical instruments, pottery, jewels, and all manner of spices, exotically prepared foods, and rare fruits were the source of great delight and profit. These foreigners were welcomed, though many lived in areas designated for non-Han residents, and allowed to worship their own faiths. They built Islamic mosques, Zoroastrian temples, and Nestorian churches in the metropolitan areas. Central Asian dancers and musicians, jugglers, acrobats, magicians, and storytellers performed for the court while west Asian singing girls, in local bars, played their strange airs with lyrics written by prominent poets.

IMPERIAL CITY

The Tang appropriated the surviving cities, palaces, and administrative centers that had been established by the preceding dynasty of the Sui. Excavations in the ancient capitals reveal that Chang-an occupied an area 9,721 meters east to west and 8,651.9 meters south to north; it was surrounded by a rammed earth wall and a moat. Each of the four side walls, oriented to the cardinal directions, had three formal entranceways of which the middle one was the largest; the main entrance was the south gate. The city was divided into three major parts. At the northern end were the palatial quarters and the administrative sector; princely residences were located at the south. The inner city was further subdivided into 111 streets, each with ditches dug along its side; 108 wards were demarcated by avenues and enclosed by walls. There were two principal markets in the east and west districts, each being the area of two wards. Three canals linked the districts. Located in the outer city were Buddhist and Taoist temples and an Islamic mosque.

The Daming Palace was unusual in that it was built outside the city walls and was not rectangular in plan.[15] Set on a hill facing south, it was dominated by three state halls; this palace city had over 30 buildings, halls, towers, terraces, and a small lake. The Daming Palace was built in 634 by Taizong as a residence for his father, the retired emperor, Gaozu, who died before its completion in 635. Later, in 662, Emperor Gaozong transformed it into Penglaigong, where he retreated to recuperate from his ill health. But after his death, his wife, Empress Wu, neglected it and chose to live in Luoyang. During the reign of Xuanzong (ca. 712-756), the Daming remained the seat of the imperial government and the permanent residence of the emperor until it was destroyed at the end of the dynasty. The most important of the three main state halls, the throne hall, or Hanyuandian, in the front half of the palatial area, was recently excavated. Flanking the main building were two pavilions connected to the main hall by flying galleries; a path of stairways was at the rear. According to historical sources, it was used for imperial audiences and ceremonies, such as those that marked the winter solstice, the investiture of a new emperor, and the emperor's birthday.[16]

As yet unstudied are Xuanzheng Hall and Zhichen Hall; these state halls, known from literary records, were located immediately north and far north, respectively, of the Hanyuandian. One of the largest structures, the Linde Hall, situated in the northwestern part of the palace compound, was also unearthed. It was the site of feasts held for courtiers, and historical annals report it could accommodate 3,500 men at one time.[17] The imperial area in the northeastern part of the city included Taiye Pond which was actually two semicircular bodies of water connected by a narrow canal. Several pavilions were situated near the pond, one of which was a well-known site for poetry readings.[18]

Great festivals were celebrated with lavish imperial processions. It was at these times that the masses could catch a glimpse of members of the court, who were carried in their palanquins through the crowded streets.[19]

BUDDHISM

From its inception in India around the sixth century B.C.E., Buddhism underwent a dramatic evolution that resulted in the formation of diverse sects having different doctrinal points and ritual practices. As a result of improved travel and commerce along the silk roads of Central Asia, monks of different schools bringing their scriptures and icons, arrived continuously in Tang China as they had since the opening of these routes in the post-Han era. Monks from

Indian and Central Asian Buddhist centers who ventured along the overland and sea routes were welcomed at the Tang court and feted at the great temples. In turn Chinese monks traveled to India as an act of pilgrimage to the sites important in the life of the Buddha and to get instruction, and acquire scriptures and icons. Xuan Zang, who embarked in 629 via the overland Central Asian silk route, returned in 645 with an extraordinary amount of scriptures and religious artifacts. Yi Jing, who made the journey to the West by sea, returning in 689, recorded having met over 50 Asian monks in residence at one of the great Buddhist universities, Nalanda, in eastern India.[20] As a result, several new sects of Buddhism blossomed during the Tang.

Primal Buddhism was based on the teachings of the Buddha, who lived around the sixth century B.C.E. His doctrine encompassed the Four Noble Truths: All life is suffering; suffering is caused by attachment; the means to end suffering is to achieve nonattachment; the means to nonattachment is to follow the Eight-fold Path. The Eight-fold Path included moral conduct--the right words, actions, and livelihood; mental discipline--the right concentration, mindfulness, and effort; and wisdom--the right intention and outlook. Gradually, over the ensuing centuries, the philosophy evolved into a religion: The Buddha was deified, a pantheon of divine attendants appeared, and anthropomorphic icons of the Buddha became the primary focus of worship. By the time Buddhism was introduced into China, it was a mixture of the earlier school, Hinayana,[21] which stressed the effort of the individual to achieve enlightenment that had as its ideal the monk, and Mahayana, which stressed universal salvation. In Mahayana Buddhism the individual could look to a number of deities for help in achieving salvation; the ideal was the Bodhisattva, a deity far advanced on the path to enlightenment, who delays his personal salvation to assist others.

Early Buddhist art in China drew heavily upon images of the historic Buddha, who lived and preached, and of his disciples and attendant Bodhisattvas. The Buddha of the Future, Milo (Maitreya), was also venerated; his worship reached a peak during the last quarter of the seventh century, when the widowed Empress Wu was proclaimed his incarnation. Beginning in the early Tang, the cult of the Western paradise was prevalent; it promised devotees rebirth in the Paradise of the West under the direction of the Buddha of Infinite Life, Amitofu (Amitabha). By the middle Tang, the cult of Amitofu had spread quickly and dominated Buddhist art. Grand murals presented panoramas of this paradise, which included large lotus pools, jeweled terraces, and multiple towers with their divine inhabitants. The Buddhist pantheon with its multiplicity of musical angels, divine orchestras and dancers, and celestial attendants surrounded the central preaching Buddha, much as the imperial courtiers gathered around the emperor.

The middle-Tang also saw the propagation of a newly developed school, Tantric Buddhism, which relied upon sacred incantations, magnificent ritual implements, and cosmic diagrams of the divine forces and their personifications, male and female, benevolent and horrible, to impart the difficult doctrine of Esoteric Buddhism. One of its most appealing tenets was that enlightenment could be achieved in this lifetime. The Chenyan sect--True Word--was promulgated by the Indian monks Vajrabodhi, who was active from 719 until 732, and Amoghavajra, active until 774. This sect was especially popular at the court of Xuanzong (r. 713-755) and thereafter. In the late Tang, Chan, or Zen Buddhism, was recognized and patronized by the court. Its influence on the pictorial arts and literature was considerable near the end of the era. These three schools, Amidism, Esotericism, and Chan, continued to flourish in the late Tang.

Under imperial and aristocratic patronage, as well as receiving popular support, Buddhist temples were built in great numbers. Colossal images of the Buddhist pantheon were carved into stone mountains, and smaller stone sculptures were fashioned into freestanding icons and steles. On altars located in the rear of the temples were large gilt figures of the Buddha and his attendants. Bronze, a material associated with the most ancient ritual objects of China, was a favored medium for small images. Clay, lacquer, and wood sculptures were less expensive alternatives for icons, especially during periods of metal shortage. In addition, temples housed splendid ritual objects wrought from luxurious materials like bronze, gold, and silver, some of which were encrusted with semiprecious stones. Historical records of the temples' magnificent wall paintings preserve at least an inventory of what was once a thriving spiritual art, remains of which are still visible in the remote caves at Dunhuang in the Gobi desert and other archaeological sites. Metropolitan temples, often formerly great mansions donated by the wealthy, vied to win imperial or aristocratic patronage and to enjoy the lavish benefits bestowed among them, much to the chagrin of Confucian court officials and the Taoist church.

Taoist and Confucian temples dedicated to their doctrines were well supported by the many court officials who found solace in the more traditional native systems of thought. It was under Emperor Xuanzong that Taoism underwent considerable development. Following prototypes of its rivals, the Taoist church expanded its literature and developed an iconography.

NOTES

1. Robert Temple, *The Genius of China* (New York, 1985): 133. One of the
Tang advances in medical treatment recorded in the book of prescriptions
was the use of thyroid hormones in the treatment of goiter.
2. Temple, 1985: 224-229.
3. Laurence Sickman and A. C. Soper, *Art and Architecture of China*
(Maryland, 1987): 399.
4. Sickman, 1987: 399.
5. L. P. Van Slyke, *Yangtze* (Stanford, 1988): 67ff.
6. Andrew Boyd, *Chinese Architecture* (London, 1962): 155.
7. L. Carrington Goodrich, *A Short History of the Chinese People* (New
York, 1969): 119.
8. Edward Schafer, *The Golden Peaches of Samarkand* (Berkeley, 1962): 17-
18.
9. William Acker, *Some Tang and Pre-Tang Texts* (Leiden, 1954).
10. Translated by A. C. Soper, "T'ang Ch'ao ming hua lu of the T'ang
Dynasty by Chu Ching-hsuan of T'ang," *Artibus Asiae*, 1958, vol. XXI: 212.
11. Translated by A. C. Soper, "A Vacation Glimpse of the T'ang Temples
of Ch'ang-an," *Artibus Asiae*, 1960, vol. XXIII: 15-38.
12. Translated by Alexander Soper, *T'u Hua Chien-wen Chih, Kuo Jo-hsu's
Experiences in Painting* (Washington, D. C., 1951).
13. Soper, 1958: 219.
14. Ann Paludan, *The Chinese Spirit Road* (New Haven, 1991): 120.
15. S. P. Chung, "A Study of the Daming Palace: Documentary Sources and
Recent Excavations," *Artibus Asiae*, 1990, vol. L: 23ff.
16. Chung, 1990: 35.
17. The Linde, one of the largest halls, measured 130.41 meters south to
north and 77.77 meters east to west; pillar holes offer evidence that it had
three adjoining halls with aisles separating them. (See Chung, 1990: 38.)
18. One pond measured 500 meters east-west, 320 meters north-south; the
other body of water was 220 meters east-west and 150 meters north-south.
19. The historical novel written by Eleanor Cooney and Daniel Altieri, *The
Court of the Lion* (New York, 1989), recreates these processions.
20. Latika Lahiri, *Chinese Monks in India* (New Delhi, 1986).
21. There have been many objections to this term, Hinayana or "smaller
vehicle," as it is considered derogatory, having been coined by its
successors--the Mahayana ("greater vehicle") sects. Recent attempts to give
a new term to this form of Buddhism are also problematic. The suggested
name Theravada, for example, describes a specific form of Buddhism rather
than the state of pre-Mahayanist Buddhism.

PART ONE

EARLY TANG (618-712)

Early Tang life was characterized by an exuberance resulting from the stability of the empire. Her suzerainty maintained, tribute came in from many neighbors as well as distant countries and states. Tang glory won by military expansion was enhanced by the great success of commercial trade along the silk roads that traversed Central Asia to the West. The creation of a stable and strong central government was accomplished by building on and adapting the statecraft of the Sui--utilizing and adjusting their bureaucratic divisions, law code, land boundaries, and tax collection methods. Moreover, many Sui officials serving under the Tang facilitated the transition.[1] Cultural life was no less influenced by Sui precedents; the capital cities, palaces, imperial trappings, and lifestyle as well as mode of burial were all based on Sui achievements. Adherence to the Buddhist religion and grand-scale imperial sponsorship reflected Sui practice, which had the beneficial effect of unifying a disparate population under a spiritual banner, as once accomplished under King Asoka.[2]

Prosperity and optimistic enthusiasm were present in the arts, the imperial tombs, the animals of the *shendao* or funeral path, as well as in the secondary tombs of followers. All disciplines of pictorial expression--painting, sculpture and ceramics--reflected a growing interest in naturalistic depiction. In the early part of the era, however, mural paintings of farming activities, funeral entertainment (music-making and dancing), or attendants were still rendered rather stiffly, and distinctions among the individuals portrayed or their poses were few. The figures were fairly contained and did not explore space either in their individual postures or in group dispositions. By the end of the seventh century and the first decade of the eighth century, artists achieved the first stage in naturalistic portraiture with their rendering of the varied characters, physiognomies, and poses. Advances in compositional organization resulted in a greater sophistication in the portrayal of complex groups and in spatial definition.   Mural themes also changed; agricultural activities, depicted in early Tang tombs, were replaced by aristocratic pastimes, such as hunting and polo.

Ceramics underwent a dramatic evolution during the early Tang. Figures were executed with the same aesthetic concerns manifested in other media. Even early Tang figurines presented more diversity than in the assemblage of Six Dynasties tomb figures (*mingqi*). Though in this early stage the figures were treated as generic types--young maid, soldier, official, or supernatural guardian--by the end of the era, the figures became more individualistic, with attention given to particularities of portraiture.   Within groups of figures, various characters differed from one another in physical appearance and in pose. The figures, which up until now had been static forms, began to move with a slight hip sway and tentatively extended their limbs into the surrounding space.

Early Tang tomb figurines tended to be hand-painted. By the last decade of the seventh century the glazing technique previously used for utilitarian stoneware was adapted for figurines. Clear and lightly tinted glazes were used for the bodies of figurines, but the faces remained hand-painted. There was also some experimentation with colored glazes on vessels and figurines, but only for monochrome effects.

It was only gradually that gold and silver utilitarian and ornamental objects became popular. At first vessels were modeled closely on Western prototypes and technologies, but eventually their shapes and decorative themes were adapted to Chinese aesthetic preferences.

Owing to the thriving commerce along the silk routes, Western influences were prevalent.   Most clearly seen in Buddhist art, heterogeneous races of India and Central Asia were included in the great entourages of the Buddhas.   Since contact with India was frequent, there was an influx of Indian sutras and deities; these influenced Chinese Buddhist art and thought. Several Buddhist schools were introduced at this time, but judging from the extant art, the Historic Buddha, the Buddha of the Future, and the Buddha of the Western Paradise were among the most frequently depicted. The iconography was dominated by a large-scale central Buddha with his attendants; one popular convention, a pentad, comprised the central Buddha flanked by two monks and two Bodhisattvas. Resplendent of the might and wealth of the imperial court were the several colossal icons cut into mountains. In addition, Guanyin, Bodhisattva of Compassion, once an attendant to the Buddha of the West, became an autonomous deity. Later in this period Guanyin assumed many guises: for the first time the 11-headed icon appeared. Of secondary importance was the theme of the debate between Vimalakirti and the Bodhisattva of Wisdom, Wenshu. As the popular sutra narrates, the sage Vimalakirti was ill. Shakyamuni Buddha wanted one of his disciples to call on the ailing sage, but his monks demurred, knowing that sick or not Vimilakirti would engage in a discussion on the most difficult topics. In the end Wenshu visited with Vimilakirti. Their debate demonstrated knowledge of and respect for the Confucian doctrine as represented by the sagacious sick man, who came to recognize the superiority of universal salvation offered by Buddhism. In depictions of the great debate the audience surrounding the Bodhisattva was Chinese; those with Vimalakirti were a heterogeneous assemblage of devotees. Imperial sponsorship was also afforded to the Zen or Chan sect of Buddhism, which was introduced at this time.

Thus the art of the early Tang reflects the imperial pride, commercial prosperity, and cosmopolitan character of life in the seventh-century capital.

NOTES

1. Like Yuchi Jingde (d. 658) and Yang Wen (d. 639), both of whom were awarded attendant tombs in Taizong's mausoleum, Zhaoling. See Han Wei, *Zhaoling Wenwu Qinghua* (Shaanxi Bowuguan: Shaanxi, 1991).
2. King Asoka, who lived in the third century B.C.E., was the first emperor of India. Unifying his empire under the banner of Buddhism, he became renowned in Asia as a universal sovereign. His building program for the glory of Buddhism, greatly exaggerated in China, was the paradigm for later Buddhist emperors of the Sui and Tang dynasties.

CHAPTER I

EMPEROR GAOZU

In the historical annals of the Tang, the short reign of Li Yuan, or Gaozu (618-626), the first emperor, is often overshadowed by the brilliance of his son and successor, Li Shi-min.[1] Li Yuan had three sons who helped him establish the new dynasty during the political turmoil that marked the end of the Sui. Li Shi-min, whom Chinese annals cite as the most daring of the three, was only 16 years old at the time of the founding of the Tang.[2] It has been suggested that Tang historians were much impressed with Li Shi-min's brilliant military exploits, his close affiliation with Confucian scholar-officials, and his long reign, and as a result, attributed much of the early success of the dynasty to him.[3] Recent studies, however, have made it clear that Li Yuan was a dominant figure in establishing the new dynasty and its institutions.[4] Li Yuan was a Sui official, Duke of Tang, whose base of authority was in Taiyuan. In contrast to the portrait of his son, Li Yuan is described in the historical texts as a cautious man, reluctant to act. Yet it may have been these very characteristics of moderation and thoughtfulness that enabled him, in the struggle for dominance, to win confidence as a leader. At the end of the Sui, floods and crop failures led to insurrections instigated by local leaders. At such times of political uncertainty, poems and songs commonly circulated prophesying new heroes and happier times. Several messianic songs at the end of the Sui celebrated the name Li. Historians have found that there were at least four leaders named Li who were competing for power.[5] In the end, Li Yuan, perhaps because of brilliant military strategy and astute statesmanship, emerged successful among the various rebellious factions.[6] Li's most important victory was the conquest of the Sui capital of Chang-an, where, even before the declaration of the new dynasty, he inaugurated a bureaucratic structure for legal and administrative functions.[7] Soon schools with Confucian curricula were founded, temples to Confucius dedicated, the exam system was reestablished, and historians were engaged in writing up the events of the preceding dynasties.[8] These political institutions that Gaozu established were the foundation for the accomplishments of his son, Emperor Taizong.[9] Despite his role as an ideal Confucian ruler, the personal excesses and luxurious tastes of Gaozu's later life were subject to condemnation by his Confucian advisers.[10]

In addition to the Confucian influence at court, Taoism was awarded a primary place in the new dynasty. The portents that encouraged Li Yuan's assumption of power were understood to be Taoist.[11] Thus the Li family, claiming to be descendants of the Taoist patriarch Laozu, selected Taoism as the dominant religion. Ever after, the Tang maintained close relations with the Taoist church, which advised the court in political as well as spiritual matters. But it was not until the rule of Xuanzong in the eighth century that Taoism achieved high status. The association of the court with the Taoists, particularly those of the Shang-qing school, date to this early period and continue through the reign of Xuanzong.[12] Buddhism, the state religion under the Sui, was reduced to the status of a foreign religion by Gaozu, who declared Taoism and Confucianism the twin pillars of the state.

ARCHAEOLOGY

In the vicinity of Gaozu's imperial mound are numerous secondary tombs. According to historical documents, the most valued officials were awarded the honor of being buried in the vicinity of the imperial mound. Though 25 such tombs are described, the number of accompanying tombs so far reported exceeds 67.[13] Since Gaozu's mound has not been opened, these satellite tombs, which represent contemporary mortuary art, are a reliable source for archaeological study.   For example, the tomb belonging to Li Shou (577-630) contains an abundance of painted murals. Cousin to Gaozu, Li Shou was also active in the Sui court; surviving the first emperor, he served as a general under the second Tang emperor, Taizong. His tomb, dated 632, was found in 1973.[14] The tomb's spirit path, or *shendao*, originally had two columns and three pairs of stone mortuary sculptures of rams, officials, and tigers. Interspersed along the tomb's long, sloping path, which measures 44 meters in length, are with alcoves that housed pottery figurines (of which over 300 were found), an offering room for tomb articles, and a coffin chamber. Murals on the walls of the sloping passageways show scenes of farming, deer and boar hunting, family life, music-making, and dancing. Additionally, seven halberds on a rack and 12 guards of honor are depicted. One hunting composition has over 42 horses and 48 people arranged in four major groups. Agricultural depictions, characteristic of both earlier Han and post-Han tomb art, show ox-ploughing and sowing with a mechanical device for distributing the seed, the releasing of steers from their pen, and an animal herding scene. The drawing, done in a rigid and unchanging line technique called iron wire, is not masterful; the draftsmanship is surely competent but it lacks the naturalism of later times. As a result the figures appear stiff and cartoonlike. (FIGURE 1) There is a noticeable attempt to render each person's status, size, and physical type, but these are still generic rather than specific portraits. A large brick tomb of this era, located far from the emperor's tomb mound, in Changsha, Hunan, yielded numerous pottery figurines.[15] Though treated in a regional style, stiffly modeled, and somewhat stereotypical in their representations, these figurines are distinguished by a variety of characterizations: officials, guardians, female musicians, grooms, and calendrical animals. Additionally, there is a horse, chimera, and one of the earliest Tang ceramic camels, though its modeling is perfunctory.

GAOZU'S TOMB

The brevity of Gaozu's reign and his emphasis on acquiring territory and unifying the Tang empire perhaps explain the meager art attributed to Gaozu's reign. In accordance with Confucian doctrines of modesty, Gaozu, considerate of the time and materials wasted on lavish imperial burials, refused to construct his tomb at all. This stance was a dramatic contrast to the usual extravagant imperial burial preparations inaugurated with the ascent of a new reign. Furthermore, Gaozu specified that he wanted a frugal burial.[16] Thus the preparations for his interment were left until after his death. In 635, his son and successor, Li Shi-min, ordered the famed architect-painter Yen Li-de to build the monument, which was to be 40 miles northeast of the capital. Although the size of the tomb disregards Gaozu's modest wishes, it was a fitting memorial to the founder of the dynasty. It may well be that the decorative plan was carried out with an attempt to respect the prudent wishes of its inhabitant. Unfortunately, because of the late start, construction was undertaken with great speed and as a result the builders suffered hardships; memorials written by officials protested the harsh treatment of the harried workers. In all, completion of the monument was achieved within five months of Gaozu's death.

Gaozu's tomb has many features common to subsequent Tang tombs. The precinct was surrounded by a square wall, with four towers at the corners and gates on its four sides. Because in court ritual the emperor sits with his back to the north and faces south, it has been suggested that the imperial tombs were therefore often oriented to the south. This is certainly true for Gaozu's tomb, where the south gate is the functional one and is marked by a shendao. Despite the fact that the site has been identified (as so many Tang and pre-Tang tombs have been), it has not been excavated. The tomb itself is believed to be a subterranean construction comprising a central coffin chamber with dual side rooms that act as a repository for funerary articles. Aboveground, the location of the tomb is marked by a large earth mound.[17] Originally, Tang tombs had several palatial structures built aboveground at some distance from the tomb, but none has survived. One such structure, which functioned as a place for memorials and offerings, was also the site for an important court ritual--the visit of the current emperor to pay his respects to his predecessor and to report on the state of the empire.

Monumental stone sculptures were erected around the tomb. Originally, there were stone tigers placed inside each of the four gates. The shendao leading to the tomb was marked by large paired stone sculptures of animals and men. At one time the tomb had a tall column with a lion capital that resembled the famous columns erected by Asoka, the Indian Buddhist king.[18] Such allusions to Asoka must be considered Buddhist as well as political in connotation, for Asoka, who conquered ancient India, built an empire, and united the disparate population under Buddhism, was the paradigm of a universal sovereign.

At the site, one of the tigers remains; a second tiger and a rhinoceros from the tomb path are now housed in the Shaanxi Provincial Museum. Both animals are noted for their fierceness and independence. The rhinoceros, an animal known only in the south of China and thus a tribute from southern countries,[19] was symbolic of the size and political power of the Tang domain. The composition of these over-life-size sculptures in the round is still limited by the size and shape of the boulders from which they were carved. (FIGURE 2) Sculpturally defined features do not boldly project from the stone and there is only surface articulation of its physical attributes--the head, chest, legs, and flanks. These creatures functioned beyond mere guardians, as their majestic magnitude also expressed the high rank of the tomb occupant. Moreover, judging from other, better-preserved tomb paths, the stone sculptures of cavalry, civil and military officials, and foreign dignitaries which stood in two rows lining the shendao replicated the funeral procession of the deceased and were expected to stand in attendance forever.

BUDDHISM UNDER GAOZU

Although Buddhist thought and art reached its peak during the Tang, the early decades of the dynasty were marked by a fierce rivalry between the Taoist and Buddhist churches. Suspicion of Buddhist insurrection was based on jealousy of the church's tax-exempt lands and industries, disapproval of the Buddhist disregard for the perpetuation of the family, and nonallegiance to the state. Moreover, there was a general distrust of those who sought refuge in the church. Thousands of people were able to avoid corvee labor, military conscription, taxation, and the wrath of the authorities by joining the brotherhood. Throughout the reigns of the early Tang emperors, Buddhism was mistrusted and envied for its spectacular riches; frequent attempts were made to control the number of the temples and monasteries and their wealth. Officials in this early period often advocated the extirpation of Buddhism, but they were largely unsuccessful. No doubt there was ample awareness of the widespread and profound influence of Buddhism on the population of China; wholesale destruction of the religion would only result in a divisiveness at a time when unity was important for solidification of the empire. Fear of reprisal from devotees stayed the hand of antagonist factions seeking to establish their own primacy at Buddhism's expense. However, Gaozu sought to limit both the number of Buddhist monasteries and of monks; these restrictions were also meted out for Taoism as well. He ordered that there be a limit of three monasteries and two Taoist temples in each prefecture; all others were to be closed. Since there were many more Buddhist temples, the edict most adversely affected the Buddhist establishment. It would have meant a reduction to one fortieth the number of temples and monasteries.[20] Other controls on the Buddhist clergy were effected by several administrative changes. Replacing the single monk, who traditionally was chosen to oversee the administration of the Buddhist church, Gaozu selected ten monks to supervise church business. Moreover, he placed a government representative in both Buddhist monasteries and Taoist temples to act as an observer. Despite these restrictive measures, Gaozu also had new Buddhist temples built. Soon after taking the Sui capital of Chang-an, he established a temple in memory of his 14-year-old son, who was slain in the uprising that led to the Tang victory.[21]

NOTES

1. For example, one of the legends surrounding Li Shi-min was celebrated in the mid-ninth-century story, "The Curly Beard," which relates Shi-min's destiny to found the empire and describes his aura, a sign of heavenly mandate, with no mention of Li Yuan. See Lin Yutang, *Famous Chinese Short Stories* (London, 1953): 1ff.
2. Several studies of Tang Taizong by Arthur Wright discuss his relationship with his father: "T'ang T'ai Tsung: The Man and the Persona," *Essays of the T'ang Society,* ed. Perry, 1976: 22, and "T'ang T'ai Tsung and Buddhism," *Perspectives of the T'ang* (New Haven, 1973): 243. Woodbridge Bingham, *The Founding of the T'ang* (New York, 1970), has drawn an excellent portrait of Li Yuan and the events that led up to the founding of the dynasty.
3. Modern scholars caution taking Tang history too literally without questioning the political motivation of historians and their biases. Taizong's direction of the writing of the dynastic histories has also been pointed out. (See the next chapter.) One interesting proposal suggests that key advisers to the throne may have been the guiding lights of the anti-Sui faction led by Li Yuan but preferred to give him the credit of founding the empire. (See Bingham, 1970: 122.)
4. Dennis Twitchett and John Fairbanks, *The Cambridge History of China* (Cambridge, 1979) 10 vols., vol. 3, part I: 155.
5. Bingham, 1970: 118.
6. Wright, 1973: 243.
7. Bingham, 1970: 108.
8. Howard Wechsler, "The Confucian Impact on Early T'ang Decision-Making," *T'oung Pao*, 1980, vol. LXVI: 3.
9. Twitchett and Fairbanks, 1979: 187.
10. Wechsler, 1980: 16, mentions the promotion of a favorite dancer to high official rank and excessive drinking as some of the many actions criticized by his advisers. (See p. 26 for a description of his extravagances.)
11. Howard Wechsler, *Offerings of Jade and Silk* (Yale, 1985): 61-72, gives an extensive description of these numerous portents and their interpretations. Portents such as the vision of a man in white robes who appeared as a messenger for the gods of Mt. Huo or another later divine emissary from Mt. Yang Chia accompanied Li Yuan's rise to power. See Stanley Weinstein, *Buddhism Under the T'ang* (New York, 1987): 6-7.
12. J. Russell Kirkland, "The Last Grand Master at the T'ang Imperial Court: Li Han-kuang and T'ang Hsuan-tsung," *T'ang Studies*, 1986.4: 43-67. See also Holmes Welch, *Taoism* (Boston, 1967): 153.
13. Wechsler, 1985: 151.

14. The tomb is situated in Jiao Cun village, San Yuan county, Shaanxi Province. Parts of the frescoes have been removed and are on display at the new Shaanxi Provincial Historical Museum in Xian. *Han Tang Pihua* (Beijing, 1974): pl. 59; Jan Fontein and Wu Tung, *Han Tang Murals* (Boston, 1976): 78-89. These paintings are preserved by hand copies reproduced in *Tangmu Pihua Jijin* (Shaanxi Provincial Museum: Xian, 1988). See also *Wenwu*, 1974.9.

15. Hunan Bowuguan, "Hunan Changsha Xianjiahu Tangmu Fajue Jianbao," *Kaogu*, 1980.6: 506ff. Over 36 figurines and over two dozen utilitarian pottery objects were found. On the basis of stylistic evidence this tomb was attributed by the Hunan Provincial Museum to the early Tang (618-626).

16. Wechsler, 1985: 149ff, for specific details of Gaozu's tomb.

17. The mound measures over 21 meters high with a rectangular base measuring around 168 x 147 meters.

18. Associations between Gaozu and Asoka were later made by Empress Wu, who is said to have ordered an image made of Asoka with Gaozu's features; see Stanley Weinstein, "Imperial Patronage in T'ang Buddhism," *Perspectives on the T'ang,* ed. A. Wright (New Haven, 1973): 298.

19. Schafer, 1963: 83.

20. Weinstein, 1987: 9.

21. Wright, 1973: 241.

CHAPTER II

EMPEROR TAIZONG

Li Shi-min was born of Chinese and non-Chinese parentage: his maternal grandmother was from the Tuku clan of the Xianbei tribe and his father was a Sui dynasty official and army general. The youthful Li Shi-min, who excelled in the military arts, is often credited with important military victories that led to the establishing of the new dynasty.[1] It was said that because the youth was a charismatic leader, his popularity and power threatened the crown prince, his brother, who made an attempt on his life. Shi-min retaliated with the assassination of both the crown prince and a younger brother: They were ambushed at the Xuanwu gate of the palace. At the age of 27, Shi-min's father, Gaozu, left the throne (some say by coercion) to his son. Military conquests marked Taizong's reign. In an effort to expand and secure the borders, he defeated the Turks in 632, Tibet in 641, and Annam (Vietnam) in 648. And though the attempted conquest of Korea led to Chinese defeat in 645, victory was eventually won by his successors. Taizong saw his role as leader not only as subjugator of the Turks but as ruling them as a Heavenly Khan. This may have been a reflection of his mixed parentage.[2] Tang historians portray Shi-min as a man of swashbuckling valor and charismatic charm. He was celebrated as a romantic hero in the popular literature of the late Tang, when there was nostalgia for his reign and for the former era of Tang glory.[3]

Taizong (r. 627-649) was not only a military genius but an able administrator credited with strengthening the foundations of the empire, thus enabling it to survive for hundreds of years (even in less capable hands). This was achieved by establishing important bureaucratic institutions in the areas of military, court, and public administration. One of the major concerns was the adjustment of land distribution; another important consideration was the administration of the provincial areas. Thus political entities were created out of geographic territories--delineated by natural boundaries and common concerns.[4] The tax rate and method of collection were reassessed, the legal code continued to be revised, and, in 628, the relief granary system was instituted to provide for years of bad crops.[5] Moreover, the burden of corvee labor and taxation caused by large public works was limited.[6] Because of these accomplishments as well as the expansion of the empire and its consolidation into a unified political entity, Tang historians laud Emperor Taizong as a model Confucian ruler, responsive to his well-chosen officials among whom, during the earlier years, Wei Zheng was eminent. During Taizong's reign, many Confucian institutions were supported; the Wen Xue Guan and Hung Wen Guan, colleges of Confucian scholars, were established, and Taizong himself presided over the compilation of Confucian texts and commentaries.[7] But Arthur Wright has shown how Taizong's personality underwent a great change, after the death of his father and queen, in his fortieth year.[8] It was after this time that he exerted his authority in defiance of his ministers' advice. Court officials admonished him, disapproving of his pleasure-seeking pursuits such as hunting and womanizing. They were particularly wary of his plan to build a palace in Luoyang. Their fears proved true: After a vast expenditure of time and money, the effort was an acknowledged fiasco and the building was dismantled.[9] Taizong's concern for the historical accounts of his reign led him, in an unprecedented manner, to demand to read and censor these records.[10] Thus modern historians, aware of his role in the editing of the dynastic history, are cautious about the accuracy of the chronicles of both his and his father's reign.[11]

ART AT TAIZONG'S COURT

The ideal of a Tang emperor was a complex one: It encompassed universal power and dignity in several domains. This role comprised not only military prowess and administrative savvy, but as for earlier empire builders such as King Asoka of India and Alexander the Great before him, it also involved being a sponsor of massive building projects and patron of the arts. Taizong, as emperor of China, had artistic talents: He is remembered for his poetry, calligraphy, and collection of art and antiquities. Recent studies of his literary efforts show him an adept, if not original, poet celebrating his military exploits as well as describing weather conditions and landscapes.[12] Records of his aesthetic interests are also preserved in Chinese histories of art. One Song art historian recalled:

> His Imperial Majesty T'ai Tsung, awesome in brilliance and profoundly wise, was richly (endowed in) the arts and manifold in talents. In his time all pretenders returned to the true (Imperial sway) while the far corners of the earth (communicated by) interpretation. (His Majesty) (in hours of) fruitful relaxation from his myriad cares, often purchased the rare and curious.[13]

According to the *Li Dai Ming Hua Chi* (History of Famous Painters), written by Zang Yan-yuan in 847, Taizong acquired objects from the Sui imperial collection.[14] This collection was augmented by the booty of his many military conquests and yearly tribute from subjugated realms. He had these exotic gifts catalogued and recorded by court administrative offices as well as artists. One anecdote related that Taizong possessed the most famous piece of calligraphy, *The Orchid Pavilion Preface*, by Wang Xi-zhi (fourth century).[15] Perhaps his most extraordinary command was that the writing be interred with him.[16]

At court Taizong maintained a coterie of artists--painters, architects, and artisans--who waited upon his aesthetic needs. Among the famous artists in attendance were the painter Yen Li-ben (Li-pen) (600-674) and his brother, Yen Li-de, a painter and architect, who was in charge of both the building of the ill-fated palace at Luoyang and the construction of the imperial tombs. Li-ben, the younger brother, was lauded in the art historical texts for his skills at painting. Near-contemporary records, like that of Zhu Qing-xuan's *Tang Chao Ming Hua Lu*, rank the Yen brothers as artists of the inspired class, well above the merely talented. Several anecdotes from that source help describe the artistic achievements at Taizong's court.[17]

> Yen Li-pen rose in office under T'ai Tsung to be Vice-president of the Board of Justice, with the rank of a member of the Council of State. He and his elder brother were equally renowned in their day. He once received a command to paint the august countenance of T'ai Tsung. Later the portrait was expertly copied on a front bay of the east hall of the Hsuan tu kuan to hold in check the emanations from

the Nine Mountains. Thus one can still gaze in reverence at the heroic majesty of the god-like warrior.

.... At one time there was a wild beast on the Southern Mountain that was killing people. T'ai Tsung despatched a party of brave men to capture it, but they were unsuccessful. Thereupon the Prince of Kuo, Yuan-feng, was stirred by his loyalty to go and shoot it, killing the creature with a single shaft. T'ai Tsung, in appreciation of his gallantry, sent the younger Yen, Li-pen, to depict the exploit. He rendered the scene, complete with saddle-horses and members of the prince's troop, in so life-like a way that no one who saw it could fail to be struck with admiration at the artist's inspired subtleties.

.... At another time, when T'ai Tsung was paying a visit to the Hsuan-wu Lake and saw some mandarin ducks at play, he summoned Li-pen to depict them. The attendants were so tactless as to shout: "Summon the master painter." Li-pen was so deeply chagrined by this that he finally gave up painting and warned the junior members of his family against making any study of the art.

.... Prior to that time, he had depicted the "Eighteen Scholars at the Court of the Prince of Chin" and the twenty-four Meritorious Subjects of the Ling yen Pavilion: works that truly are among the glories of our time. Only in pictures of tribute-bearers and in designing imperial insignia and the like did he always work in collaboration with Li-te ....

Paintings of distinguished scholars, foreigners, and Buddhist subjects have also been credited to Li-ben based on the historical accounts. Extant portraits claimed to have been painted by Yen include *Emperor Taizong in a Sedan Chair Greeting Three Envoys from Tibet*, which is in the Peking Palace Museum.[18] Despite the title, the attribution to Yen and to the Tang era have been questioned. *The Emperors of the Past,* in the Boston Museum of Fine Arts, ascribed to Yen (ca. 627-649), is one of the rare paintings whose Tang attribution has been considered, though only a few portraits of the emperors remain. Done in the traditional medium of a silk hand scroll, the composition is not a continuous depiction of the emperors but rather an independent series of portraits of the rulers with their attendants. These subjects, characteristic of the Tang monumental style, occupy the entire height of the silk, without scenery or background. The brush is the primary means of pictorial realization; it exhibits limited variety in thickness. While broad contour lines define the figures, their drapery, and accoutrements, a fine line articulates the facial features and other details. In the rendering of the garments, reverse shading, a technique

imported from the West, is evident. For the most part, this foreign
artistic technique is common only to Tang painting. Subdued
coloration typical of the modulated palette of Chinese art dominates in
the delicate tones of the pale red garments. Of the 13 emperors shown
on the scroll, the first six are believed to be a later replacement. In the
remaining portraits individual characterizations are accomplished
through a variety of poses. Particular attention is given to not only
the unique physiognomies but also to psychological makeup, which is
conveyed through body gesture and facial expression. Contrasts
between good and incompetent rulers are intended, as well as
comparisons between rank, age, and sex.[19] Another painting loosely
attributed to Yen Li-ben is *Western Barbarians Bringing Tribute to
the Emperor*, in the Taipei Palace Museum. Here the descriptive
brush is directed to the portrayal of the odd appearance, character,
and dress of the foreigners and their extraordinary gifts of tribute.

Zhu Qing-xuan's anecdotes of Yen's service at court reveal a
formative stage in the evolution of the status of the artist during the
Tang. With few exceptions, artists of the pre-Tang did not achieve
high rank and favor, and certainly possessed no degree of
independence. Artistic and personal freedom were only won by
complete withdrawal from court life; this model of the recluse was
found among the poets of the Han and post-Han periods. It is clear
from Yen's distress at being rudely summoned that he felt more like
an entertainer than an artist. This same account, however, also related
that Yen won even higher rank under the succeeding Gaozong's reign.
Yen Li-ben achieved true eminence later in his career when he
attained the offices of Senior Secretary of the Peerage Bureau, Grand
Architect, and President of the Board of Works (657), and when he
became one of two state ministers (668). But few scholars believe
these honors involved much actual administrative power or
responsibility.[20] It does not seem likely that painters won entry into
the upper echelons of power through artistic efforts. It was not until
the fifth century that artists like Gu Kai-zhi, who navigated the
unstable politics of his time by means of a combination of his divine
talent and buffoonery, achieved true renown. The first essayist of art
history, the sixth-century Xie He, wrote a brief preface on the theory
of excellence in art; then he listed, by rank and title, the noted
practitioners of the day and of the recent past.[21] By the ninth century
art historical criticism evaluated artists by merit, not only social
position; moreover, artists were commonly recognized for their
individual talents and thematic specializations. Still, it is clear in these
histories that artists were not independent of the court but an integral

component of its hierarchy and dependent on it for artistic commissions.

ARCHAEOLOGY

The Zhaoling area is over 30 kilometers in circumference, within which over 185 satellite tombs have been discovered. It was a distinct honor to be buried there. Over two dozen tombs of important military commandeers of the northwest have been identified, in addition to members of the imperial family (several of the emperor's daughters)[22] and high officials, notably Wei Zheng. The tombs were marked aboveground with small mounds, usually two, memorial steles (up to 20 at a single tomb have been found), and several sculpted animals placed along the spirit path, usually pairs of rams and tigers.[23] Excavated tombs have yielded painted mural decorations and burial objects of precious materials and clay. One such tomb, which was discovered in 1975, is that of Yang Gong-ren, who served under the Sui and was Chief Governor of Liang Chou district in 640. Despite extensive damage to the murals, several paintings of palace ladies have survived. In many ways these compositions anticipate those in the Tang tombs of the beginning of the eighth century. Slim, youthful girls are dressed in demure, high-waisted gowns, with scarves covering their shoulders. They walk in procession holding a variety of objects, including fans, musical instruments, a stick, or a deep bowl. Characteristic of early Tang funerary murals, the figures are not clearly differentiated in physical type, age, or status. With their garments and tender age, these young ladies are quite different from the women of later Tang tomb paintings, who are older, more voluptuous and wear deep-cut garments. In addition, the arrangement of the figures in Yang Gong-ren's tomb is not convincingly three-dimensional; later, the placement of figures will create complex spatial relationships.

TAIZONG'S CHARGERS

The most famous extant monument commissioned by Taizong consisted on the large stone relief panels depicting six of the chargers that had served him in his military campaigns. Taizong's reputation as a great warrior and his deep love of horses are reflected in these portraits of individual steeds; according to tradition, they were named and eulogized by him. Each horse's individual spirit and beauty is captured through the detailed naturalistic rendering of its poses, physiognomy, and trappings. These skilled representations are evidence of the high level of animal portraiture in the Tang. It is said that Yen Li-ben made the sketches upon which the bas-reliefs were based. Five of the horses are shown in rapid movement--full gallop or trotting--but Saluhsi, on the bas-relief now in the University of Pennsylvania Museum in Philadelphia, stands with the famous commander, Ji Xing-gong.[24] (FIGURE 3) This is a story of exemplary valor: Ji saved Taizong when, as a young prince, he was surrounded by the enemy during a scouting expedition. The prince, suddenly isolated from his attendants, was in grave danger, but his mount, though shot by many arrows, continued to charge. Ji approached, pulled the arrows from the prince's mount, gave him his own horse, and pursued the enemy on foot, allowing the prince to break free. In the relief, the general calms the mount, whose reins he holds in his hand. The communion between the two is expressed by the head-to-head posture and the responsive stance of the horse as he submits to the general's ministrations. These six horses are beautifully groomed, with ornamentally knotted tails and combed manes. This treatment of the manes is relatively significant, for not since the Han were horses groomed in this manner. The resumption of this practice indicates that the animals and their trainers are from the West.[25] Horses, one of the most desirable gifts of foreign tribute,[26] were a prime necessity for military defense. They were so prized for hunting and polo by the aristocracy that a 667 edict forbade artisans and tradesmen from riding horseback at all.[27] Of the many Western nations who sent horses as tribute, the main source was from the Uighur Turks and Mongols. Obtaining the horses was important but training them was also a challenge; the foreign neighbors to the West were far better at horsemanship than the Chinese, and so became an increasingly important part of the military forces. Another group of horses associated with Emperor Taizong was the Ten Chargers, personally chosen from a herd of 100 sent by the Turks in 647. Although the emperor named them, there is no record of their depiction.[28]

TAIZONG'S TOMB

Unlike his father, Taizong was directly involved in the planning of his own funeral monument. The tomb was begun after his wife, the empress, died in 636. She was buried on the south side of a small mountain at Jaoling, in northwest Xian. Taizong built his monument on the north side--but, quite extraordinarily, inside the mountain--and was buried there in 649. His was the first imperial tomb constructed in this manner. This innovation lent the tomb a greater monumentality and longevity. Moreover, the monument now shared the symbolic connotations of the spirituality and immortality of mountains celebrated since pre-Han times. It was also claimed to be a more economical undertaking, requiring less material. However, judging by the scale of the project--it was the largest imperial tomb yet constructed--economy does not appear to have been a primary concern.[29] Taizong's father, Gaozu, was buried in a traditional underground chamber marked by an earth mound, and according to the historical records, Taizong's minister, Wei Zheng, soundly rebuked him for the less majestic scale of his father's monument.[30] Taizong's tomb was conceived of as being at the center of a walled city; his closest followers were allowed satellite tombs which were laid out in broad avenues.[31] The underground structure took 13 years to complete; 250 meters underground, it had three chambers.[32] Aboveground structures included an offering hall to the south, an altar shrine to the north in front of the tomb, and a spirit path marking the northern approach. Although the aboveground structures have been lost, the ruins of the altar and a section of the wall remain. In addition, numerous palatial buildings, now lost, were at the foot of the mountain to the south; they were intended as a "nether palace" for the entertainment of the spirit of the deceased.

Over-life-size, free-standing stone carvings of men and animals marked the spirit path, including representations of 14 sculptures of barbarian chiefs whom Taizong had vanquished during his reign. Of the original 14 sculptures, only the bases of a few remain--that of a Qarashar lord, a Turkish Khan, and a Tibetan leader.[33] It has been noted that this inclusion of figures of subjugated peoples was a non-Han funeral practice common among the Turks; thus its adoption by Taizong was an indication of his identification of himself not only as ruler over the Chinese empire but also as Heavenly Khan of the Turks.[34] In this regard, it is noteworthy that several of the satellite tombs belong to minority chieftains. In general, the Tang population comprised several heterogeneous minorities, predominantly of northern origins; Taizong himself was of Xianbei descent on his mother's side.

Not much is left of the shendao. A few of the large-scale stone sculptures have survived, including a sculpture of a standing horse at the site. According to a modern Chinese reconstruction of the tomb, the bas reliefs of the chargers were made as part of the funeral monument and set up in front of the entrance to the tomb.[35] In contrast to the sensitive and naturalistic portrayal of the six chargers in the reliefs, these free-standing sculptures of the shendao are relatively awkward and naively rendered. The reason for the disparity in quality is that three-dimensional sculpture belongs to an entirely different artistic tradition: Stone carving in the round was never considered a fine art in China, but relief carving was tied to the very highest aesthetic expression, calligraphy. Important historical and literary works as well as specimens of famous calligraphy were preserved by being inscribed in stone. Thus the renderings of the six chargers were probably based on two-dimensional drawings, reputedly by the famous Yen Li-ben, and translated into the more lasting medium of bas-relief sculpture, while the free-standing figures were made by artisans of funeral sculpture.

BUDDHISM UNDER TAIZONG

Taizong's sponsorship of Buddhism is complex: On the one hand, he was a grand patron who built large-scale temples and authorized the ordination of monks; and on the other, he enacted measures to control the growth of the Buddhist church and tap some of its ever-increasing wealth. Wright has written of Li Shi-min's relationship with Buddhism, noting that Li's mother was a devout Buddhist and that his affiliation with Buddhists began in 621 when he was aided in his struggle to take Luoyang by Shaolin temple martial monks.[36] The details of this conflict are the subject of modern murals and sculptures on view at the monastery in Dengfeng county outside of Luoyang. During the early years of his reign, Taizong was supportive of the church. Upon ascending the throne, he rescinded his father's edict to reduce the temples in the capital to one-fortieth their number; he celebrated the completion of his first year on the throne by inviting eminent monks to the capital for a seven-day service.[37] Meanwhile, he converted his father's residence into a nunnery, sponsored the construction of several temples, and fostered the ordination of monks and nuns. Certain days were commemorated by Buddhist services. One remarkable edict of 629 called for the construction of seven monasteries at the sites of different battles so that prayers could be offered for the repose of the dead soldiers. One of these structures, the Dafo, or Great Buddha Temple, located in the suburbs of modern Xian, is still extant.[38] In 634, Taizong had the Hongfu Temple, once a military noble's palace, grandly refurbished in his mother's memory. Additionally, he built her an enormous temple comprising a large compound with ten courtyards and 1,897 rooms to accommodate 300 monks.

But the court under Taizong by no means gave blanket support to Buddhism. Efforts were made to standardize the ordination of monks and to make them answerable to civil authority (previously the monastic community disciplined itself). Attempts were also made to eliminate the practice of parents of monastics making obeisance to their sons. Prior efforts to reverse this regulation had been unsuccessful for decades. In addition, several edicts examined the conduct and ordination of monks, and ultimately, in 637, Taizong established Taoism as the supreme religion.[39] It is often noted that a change took place at the end of Taizong's life, when he met the eminent monk Xuan Zang. The famous monk had returned to China from a long sojourn in India, where he had made a pilgrimage to the sites important in the life of the Buddha and studied the different savants' interpretations of Buddhism at the famous monasteries. He collected icons and scriptures that he carried back with him. Although Xuan Zang had left China surreptitiously, defying a state ban on exiting the country, he was heralded upon his return. Taizong, particularly eager for information about the West, summoned the monk to the palace to question him about his knowledge of Western lands. Throughout his later life, Xuan Zang was importuned to give up his religious career to become an adviser to the court. Taizong had Xuan Zang ensconced in the Hungfusi monastery in Chang-an, where he was subsidized to assemble a group of assistants to translate the Indian scriptures.

It was the Faxiang school of Buddhism that Xuan Zang brought into great prominence. His teachings, based largely on the Indian Yogacara school, were centered on the sutra he translated in 648, *Yogacara Bhumi*, for which Taizong himself wrote the preface. It has been suggested that the prominence this school saw was the result not of the appeal of its doctrine, but rather of Xuan Zang's espousal of it. Distinctions between the Faxiang school and the other Mahayanist sects popular in the early Tang can be only briefly presented here: Faxiang adherents believed that not everyone could become enlightened and that the achievement of enlightenment occurs only after complex and prolonged meditation over a very long period.[40]

One of the most popular Buddhist cults in the early Tang was that of the Pure Land. The sect believed in a Western Paradise, which all faithful devotees of the Buddha of Infinite Light, Amitabha, or Amitofu in Chinese, could enter. Calling on Amitofu's name and visualizing him and his Paradise were the main means of worship.

Images of this Buddha and his celestial environs were most predominant. Dissemination of the cult's belief's during the Tang was in part due to the propagation of its tenets and exegeses of its texts by Dao Chuo (562-645).[41] Another Buddhist master, Shan Dao (613-681), did much to popularize the sect by writing commentaries in simple language, addressing the important question of filial piety, and promulgating the use of paintings of the paradisiacal vision as an aid in the worship of Amitofu. It is also recorded that Shan Dao himself made hundreds of images of the Western realm.[42]

BUDDHIST ART

Although the art of Dunhuang is a far from the metropolitan centers of the Tang empire and is comprised of hybrid traditions, the murals and sculptures found there are representative of some of the trends and styles of Tang Buddhist art. The majority of themes painted in the early Tang caves at Dunhuang are visions of the Western Paradise. Several important caves ascribed to the early Tang, like 341 and 220, present the Paradise in all its glory. This image of the heavenly realm is not one of great antiquity; one of the earliest renditions is found in a sculpture at the cave site of Xiangtangshan, ascribed to ca. 550.[43] In comparison to that first and relatively simple depiction of the Western Buddha and his entourage, Tang renditions offer an architectural complex of celestial towers, pavilions, and stepped terraces laid out in a symmetrical plan in imitation of the palatial buildings of the capital cities of central China. For example, the top central area of a side wall mural in Cave 341 is occupied by an octagonal pavilion with two lateral semicircular wings in which heavenly dignitaries are seated. (FIGURE 4) Below are tiered terraces, jeweled pavilions, and towers; at center is an enthroned Buddha, and above his head is a jeweled canopy with long, pendant streamers. Surrounding him are Bodhisattvas and other celestials of various ranks. They fill every available space; some spiral down on eddying clouds. The most important part of the topography is the lotus pond in the foreground. (FIGURE 5) It is in this pool that devotees are reborn in the calyx of lotus buds; several can be seen here in varying degrees of rebirth.

A simpler treatment of Amitofu and his attendants is presented in the beautifully realized painting on the south wall of Cave 57. (FIGURE 6) Dominating the composition is Amitofu, seated on his hourglass-shape throne, with lotus-petal seat, under a jeweled canopy and flowering tree. He is dark-skinned, as are several other attendant figures. This marks a stage in Buddhist art when, owing to the close contact with the West via the silk routes, the prevailing aesthetic was to portray accurately the Indian origins of the Buddha and other deities. Moreover, this depiction of the racial heterogeneity of the Buddhist pantheon was common in India as well, notably at Ajanta. In Western fashion, the garment is drawn tightly across the Buddha's chest revealing the torso and exposing the right shoulder and arms; the drapery clings to his body as if it were wet. Gracefully, in a series of rhythmic folds, the skirt falls, covering the petals of his throne. The two flanking monks, the youthful Ananda on the left, and the older Kasyapa on the right, are lighter-skinned and clearly Chinese; their delicate features are highlighted with touches of pink pigment. (FIGURE 7) Contrasting light-and dark-skinned Bodhisattvas flank the Buddha; they are dressed in a lavish combination of scarfs in assorted patterns that are evidence of the rich textile trade that passed through the oasis city. The crown and the profusion of jewels, bracelets, necklaces, belts, and earrings are rendered with exquisite care, minutely recreating the variegated stones and their intricate settings. Identified by the seated Amitofu figure in his crown is Guanyin (Avalokitesvara in Sanskrit), the light-skinned figure on the left. Similarly painted but with different skin tones are the Guardian Kings, who kneel by the Bodhisattvas. In the Western mode, their muscular torsos are nearly uncovered, their scarves flutter with movement. Their animated, monstrous faces have piercing eyes and open mouths. These martial attributes of the Guardian Kings (Devaraja) are an excellent foil for the delicate beauty of the Bodhisattvas. Like the artists of the monumental figure style, the Buddhist painter emphasized the dramatic contrasts in physical characteristics and personalities among the different ranks of celestial beings.

Cave 220, dated 642, is magnificent. In addition to the paradisiacal scenes that are very similar to those of Cave 341, there is a mural depicting the popular theme of the great debate between Vimalakirti, the ailing Chinese scholar, and Wenshu, Buddhist God of Wisdom; they dispute the relative merits of their beliefs. In the painting, among the audience assembled around Wenshu is a Chinese ruler. (FIGURE 8) The stately procession of the dragon countenance and official courtiers is a marvel of figure painting, reflecting the achievements of Yen Li-ben's dynastic portraits. Much of the figural disposition and official regalia are dependent, if not on the work of Yen, then on a common source. Counterparts to Yen's lost works of foreign tribute bearers are seen in this composition's exotic racial types in the audience settled near Vimalakirti as well as in the guardian figures. (FIGURE 9) The inclusion of foreigners in the audience is a new feature, due no doubt to the intercourse along the Silk Road. It also attests to the universal appeal of the doctrine. Indian and Central Asian characters also play the harmonic music of the spheres for the four dancers who swirl and gyrate before the celestial hosts in the Paradise scenes. It is also interesting to note here the effective use of the Western technique of highlighting.

Buddhist sculpture of this era shares many of the stylistic characteristics seen in the paintings. The figure of the Buddha is dressed in Western style, with the chest area exposed. In this, the first stage of naturalistic representation, there are only vague allusions to anatomical details. Several limestone caves at Longmen, ascribed to the first half of the seventh century, herald the new Tang art. The once columnar figures of previous eras are now seemingly capable of movement; the cylindrical forms more closely approximate bodily forms. Though seated stiffly, the figure of the Buddha shows signs of greater naturalism in the modeling of the chest that is exposed to view; the portrayal of flesh is usually an anathema to the Chinese sensibility. As in Western art, there is a naturalistic treatment of the drapery in both the pattern of the folds and the suggestion of the texture of the cloth covering the shoulders, legs, and base. Similar sculptural treatment of the Buddha is found at Dunhuang, for example, in Cave 322. (FIGURE 10) Like the painted murals, these sculptural groups include a Buddha, pairs of Bodhisattvas, monks, and martial Guardian Kings. Of special interest are the Tianwang guardians, dressed in the armor of Chinese generals and standing stiffly on top of prone anthropomorphic representations of evil and ignorance, for these figures mirror most clearly the stylistic and iconographic changes that took place during the Tang. The warriors, clearly of Chinese descent, have dignified faces, with imperious expressions conveyed in part by highly arched brows. A slight hip sway in the guardian's stance suggests potential movement that is reinforced by the starched ribbons of the costume fluttering in a divine breeze. Over the centuries these guardian figures grow stouter and assume aggressive martial poses and fierce facial expressions--the increased belligerence of their appearance in concert with the growing militarism of the late Tang.

NOTES

1. Wright, 1976: 20, and Wright, 1973: 243.

2. Edwin G. Pulleyblank, "The An Lu-Shan Rebellion in Later T'ang China," *Essays on T'ang Society*: 38.

3. Lin Yutang: 1953: 6, from "The Curly Bearded Hero": *Li Shi-min was, of course, the man who was to found the great Tang Empire, to become the most beloved emperor in the last thousand years, brave and wise and kind, his reign marking a golden period in history.*

4. Denis Twichett, "Varied Patterns of Provincial Autonomy in the T'ang Dynasty," *Essays on the T'ang*: 90.

5. Wechsler, 1985: 39.

6. Wechsler, 1979: 191.

7. Wechsler, 1980: 4.

8. Wright, 1976: 25.

9. Wright, 1976: 26ff; Wright relates how the project amounted to nearly two million man-days, and that the artist-architect Yen Li-de was in charge.

10. Wright, 1976: 27: Taizong is recorded as saying: *I wish to view these records so that I may be guided in the future by my successes and my failures.* In anger at the historical accounts of the murder of his brothers, he said, p. 28: . . . *I acted to give peace to the country and to benefit the myriad people, nothing more. When the history officials take up their brushes why must they conceal the true meaning of my actions? They should at once remove the superfluous and give a straight account of this affair.* See also Wechsler, "T'ai Tsung the Consolidator," *Cambridge History of China*, vol. III (Cambridge, 1979): 189.

11. Denis Twitchett, *The Writing of Official History Under the T'ang* (New York, 1992): 41, believes the enhancing of the accounts of Taizong's contributions was to downplay his usurpation of his father's throne.

12. Hellmut Wilhelm and David R. Knechtges "T'ang T'ai-tsung's Poetry," *Tang Studies*, no. 5, 1987: 1-23; the best known of his military poems is "Watering Horses at a Great Wall Grotto," p. 6.

13. Soper, 1951: 7.

14. Acker, 1954: 127.

15. S. Goldberg, "Court Calligraphy of the Early Tang Dynasty," *Artibus Asiae*, 1989, vol. XLVIIII: 189-237, discussed the evolution of a Tang style of calligraphy, especially during Taizong's era.

16. Wright, 1976: 31.

17. Soper, 1958: 212ff. (See also Soper, "Yen Li-pen, Yen Li-te, Yen P'i, Yen Ch'ing: Three Generations in Three Dynasties," *Artibus Asiae*, 1991, vol. LI: 199-207.)

18. James Cahill, *An Index to Early Chinese Painters* (Berkeley, 1980): 23, considers this to be a Song copy.

19. K. Tomita, "Yen Li-pen's Portraits of the Emperor's Scroll," *Bulletin of the Museum of Fine Arts* (Boston), 1932, vol. 30, no. 177: 67; Cahill, 1980: 24, considers this to be the only genuine work attributed to Yen.

20. LTMHC, Soper, 1958: 212, Yen's qualification for this high office was "merely that he delighted in the pictorial art . . ."

21. Xie He's essay is translated by Acker, 1954: xiv-xliii.

22. For example, see Princess Linquan, Cultural Relics Committee of Shaanxi and the Zhaoling Cultural Relics Office, "The Grave Inscription and Imperial Proclamations Excavated from the Tomb of Princess Linquan of the Tang," *Wenwu*, 1977.10: 50-59, translated in Albert Dien, *Chinese Archaeological Abstracts: Post Han* (California, 1985), vol. III: 1643; over 300 ceramic figurines and other objects were found.

23. Yun, *Wenwu*, 1977: 33-40. This article identified and discussed 57 tombs. Mary Fong, "Antecedents of Sui Tang Burial Practices in Shaanxi," *Artibus Asiae*, 1991, vol. LI: 147-199, has shown that these early Tang tombs were derived from earlier pre-Sui models, with their long sloping, underground paths; chambers for funeral articles; domed coffin room; guardian figure "mingqi;" as well as aboveground sculptured tomb animals in pairs.

24. Wang Chonren, *Recent Discoveries in Chinese Archaeology* (Beijing, 1981): 27-31. C. W. Bishop, "The Horse of T'ang T'ai Tsung." *University of Philadelphia Museum Journal*, 1918, vol. IX: 244-73, discusses the sculptures and the circumstances of their acquisition.

25. Sun Ji, "Tangdai de Maju yu mashi," *Wenwu*, 1981.10: 82-88.

26. Herrlee G. Creel, "The Role of the Horse in Chinese History," *What is Taoism* (Chicago, 1970): 181.

27. Edward Schafer, *The Golden Peaches of Samarkand* (Berkeley, 1962): 69.

28. Schafer, 1962: 69. Their names included Frost Prancing White, Shining Snow Grizzle, Frozen Grizzle, Suspended Light Grizzle, Wave Plunging Bay, Sunset Flying Roan, Lightning Darting Red, Flowing Gold Yellow, Soaring Unicorn Purple, Running Rainbow Red.

29. Wechsler, 1985: 152.

30. Wright, 1976: 25, relates how Wei Zheng pointedly remarked on the small scale of his father's tomb in relation to his own.

31. Wright, 1976: 25. Wechsler says although there were 167 satellite tombs granted, over 200 were found; more recently over 300 have been estimated to exist. (See also Charles D. Weber, "The Spirit Path in Chinese Funerary Practice," *Oriental Art*, 1978, vol. XXIV, no. 2: 171ff.)

32. Yun Shi, Zhaoling Cultural Relics Office, "Report on a Survey of Attendant Tombs at Zhaoling," *Wenwu*, 1977.10: 33-40, translated by Dien, 1985: vol. III: 1645.

33. Yun, *Wenwu*, 1977.10: 33.

34. Wechsler, 1985: 152.

35. At present two of the six charger reliefs are in the University of Pennsylvania Museum in Philadelphia. Replications of these and the four still in China are in the Shaanxi Provincial Museum in Xian.

36. Wright, 1973: 244.

37. Taizong's actions in this regard are discussed at length in Weinstein, 1987: 5.

38. Carved into the living rock near the Jing River in Binxian county, Xian, the temple was first called Yingfosi and commemorated the soldiers who died in the battles of Wu Longban and Qian Shuiyuan in the ancient state of Bin.

39. Wright, 1973: 251.

40. Weinstein, 1973: 291ff.

41. David Chappell, "Chinese Buddhist Interpretations of the Pure Lands," *Buddhist and Taoist Studies I* (Hawaii, 1978): 23-50 (especially p. 36) offers an interpretative study of Tao Chuo's teachings.

42. Julian Pas, "The Life and Thought of Shan Tao," *Buddhist and Taoist Practice in Medieval Chinese Society, Buddhist and Taoist Studies II* (Hawaii, 1987): 65-84. Shan Dao painted over 200 works--both frescoes or scrolls.

43. From Hebei Province; currently in the Freer National Gallery in Washington, D.C.; Freer Gallery inv. no. 21.1.

CHAPTER III

EMPEROR GAOZONG
EMPRESS WU ZE-TIAN

Succession to Taizong's throne was problematic. Crown prince Cheng Qian was viewed with alarm. Historians condemn his fanatical espousal of Turkish culture and his relationship with a young dancing boy, whom his father had arranged to have assassinated. Cheng Qian's attempt to murder his half-brother Li Tai, because of the latter's designs on the throne, led to both their exile.[1] Thus the remaining heir mounted the throne in 649 as Emperor Gaozong (r. 649-683). Gaozong has been evaluated as a weak choice by historians because he was guided by his consort, Wu Ze-tian. During his reign, she was his closest adviser: They were called the Two Sages.[2] With his illness in 660, she took on the primary burden of rule until his death in 683. In 690, she usurped the throne, declaring a new dynasty.

Ancient and modern historians have delighted in vilifying Wu Ze-tian as a usurping, murderous tyrant, but some scholars, wary of the biases of Tang historians, have been more generous in their estimation.[3] Dynastic histories report that Wu began her career as a low-ranking concubine to Taizong, and that at his deathbed, she seduced his mourning son. Some historians maintain that, as was common practice, after the death of an emperor she and the other imperial consorts were sent to a Buddhist nunnery (that no other might enjoy what had once been the emperor's). Through the wiles of Gaozong's childless Empress Wang, who sought an ally against the

reigning imperial favorite and her progeny, Wu Ze-tian was allowed
to reenter the harem, where she soon received imperial favors. It was
recorded that she was not content as a high-ranking consort, and her
ambition led her to devise a plot to discredit the empress; shortly
thereafter, the empress and the previously highest-ranking consort
were imprisoned and sentenced to a horrible death. With intelligence,
cunning, and vaulting ambition, Wu mastered political court intrigue
by playing the various powerful factions against each other, thus
eliminating any opposition. Having begun her indirect rule during the
period of the emperor's illness, by the time of his death she openly
conspired against imperial princes, deposing and executing those who
prevented her direct control of the state. Empress Wu (r. 684-705)
named herself, in 690, sole ruler of the new Chao dynasty, which
lasted for over 15 years. Among the infamies of her reign were her
secret spies and a special box in which anonymous accusations could
be made against "disloyal" subjects. With one notable short-lived and
disastrous exception during the Han, no woman had presumed this
role in the male dominated hierarchy of China. Resistance to Wu was
particularly strong among the aristocrats holding high positions at
court.[4] Although her reign was grossly tainted by the execution of
many senior ministers and members of the imperial family who stood
in opposition to her, Wu has also been credited as an able
administrator.[5] To counter a lack of support among aristocrats and
high-ranking ministers, the empress turned to the lower members of
the bureaucracy and the common people to create a power base. It
was during her reign that the "professional bureaucrat," who had risen
through the examination system, began to share in the power.[6] Wu
won some measure of support because of the length of her largely
peaceful rule (excluding palace politics) as well as military victories in
Korea and Tibet. It can only be considered ironic that it was at this
time, under a woman's rule, that the Chinese empire reached its
greatest geographical extent. To deal with the ongoing hostilities
with the border states to the northwest in the Turkish arena of power,
in Tibet, and in Korea, a standing militia--the cost of which became a
burden for later rulers--was created to replace the old system of
military subscription. As a consequence of the success of the trade
route and territorial expansion by military conquest, a large
international population continued to reside at the capital. Among
these were the Persians led by Prince Firuz, who was allowed to build
a Zoroastrian temple.[7] In contrast to the preceding emperors who
maintained their capital at Chang-an, Empress Wu preferred Luoyang.
Some explain her choice by noting the presence of an entrenched

aristocracy at the old capital. In addition, the extreme difficulty of supplying Chang-an with grain from the south--a problem that was aggravated in subsequent eras--was also a factor in her decision.

In contrast to preceding rulers, Wu Ze-tian was wholly supportive of Buddhism. Certainly many excellent projects, notably some of the caves of Longmen, especially those in the eastern hills, were created under her direction. However, Wu also encouraged Confucian institutions. In 666, she and the sickly Gaozong performed the Feng Shan sacrifice at Mt. Tai in celebration of the pacification of the empire. The exorbitant cost of the sacrifice, despite the important symbolism of the ritual, had been avoided by imperial predecessors like Taizong. Among the foreign envoys who attended were Japanese and Koreans from the kingdom of Koguryo.[8] Another of Wu Ze-tian's dramatic efforts was the construction of the famous Ming Tang, a legendary structure with its origins in the ancient Zhou period. The Ming Tang Hall, completed in 688, was a three-story structure housing a shrine to the supreme deity and a state audience hall.[9] According to historical descriptions, the Ming Tang's two lowest levels were rectangular; the third was round. Rising to a height of over 89 meters, its decoration was symbolic: The first level had themes of the four seasons, the second had the 24 hours of the day, and the third had the 24 solar periods of the year. On top was a gilt phoenix, measuring over three meters in height. From the inception of the Ming Tang project, court ministers debated the correct architectural form and remonstrated against the extraordinary cost. In the end, rather than being honored for her efforts to sponsor Confucianism, Wu was condemned for the resultant extravagant waste. When the edifice was maliciously burned down in 695, an act of arson believed perpetrated by one of her rejected favorites, she had it rebuilt.[10] The Ming Tang functioned as a site for imperial sacrifices, for new year ceremonies, for announcing the calendrical laws, and for other state rituals.[11] Under Empress Wu's sponsorship, scholars simplified and added characters to the system of writing.[12]

The last years of Wu's rule were overshadowed by her unfortunate support of two young men, the Zhang brothers, whom she took as advisers and who, despite her advanced age, were reputedly her lovers. Her unqualified defense of them and not withstanding their abuses of power (misappropriation of land and funds and involvement in intrigues against a Tang restoration) led to her demise. One late-Tang art historian recorded how the Zhang brothers defrauded the imperial art collection:[13]

During the reign of the Heavenly Empress (her favorite) Chang I chih requested in a memorial that she should summon to court all the painter artisans (hua kung) in the empire and have them restore the paintings in the Inner Storehouse. The result was that he set these artisans to work, each working in his own line, industriously making copies and mounting these exactly as the old ones had been, so that they did not differ (from the originals) by a single hair. Most of the originals then found their way into I chih's hands. After I chih had been slain these were acquired by the Junior Guardian Hsieh Chi and after Hsieh's death they became the property of Prince Fan of Ch'i...

Near the end of her long life, Empress Wu's reign was dramatically terminated. Exasperated by their unbridled tyranny, a group of Tang loyalists captured and executed the Zhang brothers, marched into the empress's bedroom, and demanded her abdication in favor of Emperor Zhongzong.

ARCHAEOLOGY

Court art under Emperor Gaozong continued much in the fashion of Taizong. In fact, the artist Yen Li-ben was even more highly honored during this period. Historical records have scattered references to the many projects undertaken by Empress Wu. Court artists included Xie Ji and Wei-Chi Yi-Seng,[14] a foreigner who received high rank and favor. Unfortunately, nothing remains of Wei-Chi's paintings to illustrate how he may have used highlighting and shading, techniques associated with the West that he may have employed. The interest in naturalism characteristic of this era's art in general and realistic figure painting in particular that was heralded in the previous reign, may have been intensified by the presence of Western resident artists who used these effects. It may be that Wei-Chi was influential in introducing a new attitude toward painting; this trend was even more strongly felt in the following century.

Fortunately, the richness of the archaeological finds dating to the second half of the seventh century brings the evolution of figure painting to light. Gradual transitions in painting technique, including the use of line, whether the iron wire or a more soft and fluent contour, are all carefully documented. Changes in fashion--hairstyle, dress, and ideals of physical beauty--can be seen in the art. One prominent theme that serves comparative analysis well is the depiction of palace girls, dancers, and musicians. At first, the girls are stiff, thin shapes shown in a limited number of poses. Their limbs rarely extend or engage the space surrounding them; they are contained, columnar forms. Gradually, the figure types and poses vary; their movements relate to the space around them, and by 670, the whirling gestures of dance are captured in the wall paintings of Li Ji. In the earlier murals, the whole definition of the figure is determined by the unyielding iron-wire line, but by 670 the line exhibits a greater flexibility. Though still far short of calligraphic freedom, the contour lines become thicker and thinner both along the edges of the figure and in the interior definition of the drapery. Moreover, a variety of lines are employed--thick, dark lines for some of the drapery folds, more delicate ones for sleeves and scarves, and a very fine line for facial features. In addition, light colors are used to re-create the use of makeup: rosy cheeks, powdered brows, and red pursed lips.

The style of painting in the tombs of Yang Gongren (dated 640), Duan Jianbi (dated 651), and Li Shou is extremely similar.[15] All share a generic approach to portraiture, utilizing the inflexible and unvarying iron-wire line, limited poses that show little exploration of the figure in space. This style is also seen in the 668 tomb murals of Li Shuang that present a young woman standing stiffly. (FIGURE 11) But among the other figures depicted in this tomb--whether handmaids who hold a tray, cups, or a fan or a female dressed as a man--the postures, facial shapes, features, and gestures are all individualized. These figures are also distinguished by their hairstyles: Sometimes the long black tresses are pulled up into a central triple topknot or ornately looped on either side of the head. Many wear red-and-white boldly striped skirts, but their scarves no longer conceal their chests, and the necklines are deeply cut. The scarf falls below the shoulders, drapes over the upper arm and winds around the forearm, much as the Bodhisattva scarves do in Buddhist paintings. A more daring example of decollete was recently found in a tomb in Taiyuan. (FIGURE 12)[16] An emphatic portrayal of contrasting figure types is presented in a mural from Li Zhen's tomb:[17] Two young ladies with double hair knots stand close together and appear to be dancing in unison; both face front, and the rear figure extends her arm to hug the waist of her partner. Despite the similarity of dress--they each wear high-waisted, boldly striped and pleated gowns, long, monochrome aprons, and a shawl that is tucked in on the left side and hangs freely on the right-- their faces are quite different. One has a round, moon-shape face with a broad, flat nose; the other has a more aquiline nose and oval face. A depiction of a figure extending her arms into space is found in a fresco from Zhi Shi Geng-jie's tomb, dated 668.[18] As the young woman dances, her arms spread out at either side and she dips to the right. (FIGURE 13)

The acme of mural art during this period is reached in the extraordinary representation of the dancing maidens in Li Ji's tomb. Li Ji was an important official-general buried in 670 in Taizong's tomb area.[19] The stone sculptures of the spirit path--two men, three tigers, and three rams--are still extant. There is a large memorial stele as well, with an inscription that was written by Emperor Gaozong.[20] Among the remains of the tomb murals are fragments of female musicians, handmaidens, and male attendants. The women, slim and youthful, wear distinctive high-waisted garments with brocade cuffs, bodices, and hems; a scarf is draped over their shoulders, and their hairstyle is simple and low to the crown. Two girls swirl and dip as they perform the sleeve dance; their whirling movement is conveyed by their postures as well as the motion of the fabric of their skirts, sleeves, and delicate scarflike adornments. (FIGURE 14) Their hair is dressed in the most intricate fashion, with the tresses worked into arabesques that imitate bird and flower forms. A bronze sword and a very rare bronze ceremonial cap with brocade design, believed to have been Li Ji's, have also been found.[21]

The murals in the tomb of Princess Fang Ling, dated 673, offer a markedly changed ideal of feminine beauty. Some of the women are rounder, more portly; occasionally, several rings of flesh appear at the neck. Their garments, long-sleeved and high-waisted, are no longer striped, but monochrome, with scarves and sleeves in contrasting colors. Scarves demurely cover the plunging necklines by artful draping: Covering both shoulders, they crisscross in the front and wrap around both hands. Several of the women are dressed as Central Asian males. Some wear their hair piled up in a tall, lotus-bud-shape bun on the back of the head.

Allusions to Buddhist figures in the mural paintings during this period may not be accidental. One prominent similarity is the depiction of figures with triple rolls of flesh at the neck. This characteristic reflects the new image of the Buddha and his attendants now prevalent as a result of frequent travel along the Silk Road. Other similarities include the manner in which the scarf is worn by the palace ladies, crossing in front of the body, like the scarves of Bodhisattva images, and the lotus-bud-shape hairstyles. In a court that was deeply committed to Buddhism, ruled by an empress who was often likened to the Buddhist divinity Maitreya, or Milo in Chinese, the influence of Buddhist art and thought must have been pervasive. It seems highly likely that fashion trends reflect religious artistic activities sponsored by the court.

Several of the themes in the famous imperial tombs of 705 of Princess Yong Tai and her cousins are anticipated in murals dating to the last quarter of the previous century. For example, the tomb of Li Feng, buried in 674, has a representation of a camel, a prevalent theme in the next century. Also, a new figural format is used in this tomb: Two maidens stand in a minimal, gardenlike setting of tall flowering grasses.

CERAMICS

Ceramic manufacture was a growing industry during the Tang. Hundreds of pottery figurines of numerous kinds of animals and a variety of figure types filled important tombs. There also were plates, teapots, cups, dishes, and bowls made for practical and funeral use. A number of regional styles are identifiable.   With the succeeding reigns, kiln sites increased considerably so that by the mid-Tang period there were at least 30 sites in the ten provinces.[22]   With the development of ceramics came a variety of forms and decoration, different types of ceramic glazes, and new techniques for applying the glazes and constructing the vessels.

Most of the ceramic figurines found dated in the reign of Gaozong are unglazed.   These small-scale sculptures are simply modeled; the figures tend to be stiff, columnar forms, with limbs close to the body. One tomb, dated 637, yielded over two dozen clay figurines of guardians, officials, ladies-in-waiting, horses, and an ox-drawn cart, as well as utilitarian objects.[23] Such tomb furnishings are also found in imperial family tombs like the one ascribed to 653,[24] as well as in tombs of less elite members of the court. Typical is the tomb of Li Yanzhen who died in 685; tomb figures include, among others, a number of unglazed equestrian, camel, and guardian figurines.[25] The Shaanxi tomb dated in the Zhou dynasty of Empress Wu, with its several dozen unglazed figures of warriors, officials, ladies, and animals is also typical of the time.[26] In fact, Tang figurines of this sort have been found as far away as Changsha, Hunan.[27]

Empress Wu's reign was marked by the introduction of glazed polychrome pottery and advances in the experimentation with porcelain.   Porcelain came about as a result of the discovery that kaolin clay, when mixed with China stone or petunse, vitrified at high temperatures. Glaze, applied to the biscuit, melted during firing to form a glossy, glasslike surface. Sometimes the glaze was applied directly to the body or the biscuit, which was first coated with a slip made of liquid clay. The slip aided in the adherence of the glaze and thereby enriched the coating. During the Sui and early Tang period, the pottery was treated predominantly with a clear glaze that turned slightly yellow or green. Because the vessels were dipped in the glaze, the coating was uneven, with drip marks. From this period, there are only a limited number of vessels, all of which are rough in shape, large in size, and have incised or raised floral designs. One excellent example is the white-glazed porcelaneous footed bowl from a tomb in Hansenzhai, Xian, dated 667. Although white porcelaneous bowls had been produced since the Sui, this example is distinguished by a high foot that meets the bottom of the bowl to create a lotus flower design, and by the three-dimensional jewel and medallion motif. (FIGURE 15) Glazes were also applied to figures as seen in the sculptures found in the tomb of Zheng Ren-tai (dated 664) discovered in Liquan county, Shaanxi, in 1971. Among 352 ceramic pieces, there is ample evidence of the early stage of the development of glazing figurines, when the artist treated only the head or parts of the mount of equestrian figures with the clear glaze. All polychroming is done after firing by hand. One representative example is the female equestrian wearing a black traveling hat and scarf; the horse she rides is glazed, but she is not. Several of the ceramics of Zheng's tomb demonstrate the experimental phase for the faces were glazed and after firing the features were hand-painted, like the official who wears an elaborate court dress decorated with borders of rich floral designs. (FIGURE 16) Other figurines in this tomb that are also treated with clear glaze include a group of musicians and dancers, a dwarf, and a camel.[28]

Like the sculptures and murals of the Gaozong era, these figurines are not dramatically posed nor are the bodies well-defined; their limbs stay close to the trunk, evidence of the artist's reluctance to create boldly projecting forms. One rare exception to this is the recently discovered tomb figurines from Luoyang (dated 701). Although the majority of figurines in the tomb are hand-painted and typical of the time, the arms of the figure of the dancing lady are widely outstretched, and her hair is piled in high arabesques on top of her head.[29] The faces of ceramic figures of this era are not strongly individualized, but conform to a generalized category--beauty, foreigner, guardian--corresponding to the mural style of the middle of the seventh century. Their features as well as other decoration are painted in a rich combination of red, green, black, and, to a lesser extent, blue.

A second stage in the development of ceramics, the application of color to the glaze, is also seen in the figurines of Zheng Ren-tai's tomb, dated 664.[30] In the chromatic technique the glaze is melted down with other components into a glassy state that is then quenched in water, shattered, crushed, and finely ground; and finally, it is mixed with water and applied. The piece is then fired.[31] When minerals like copper oxide or iron oxide are added to the clear glaze, they make it green or brown, respectively. The earliest colored glazes are found on pilgrim flasks bearing impressed ornamentation, a type of vessel borrowed from the West. The colors range from dark brown to dark green.[32] Other early glazed vessels imitating Persian metal ewers have raised designs and sculpted caps in the form of a dragon or fanciful bird head.[33] (FIGURE 17)   In Zheng's tomb, several figurines are treated with a colored glaze, but these figures are still monochromatic. Only one color is applied--brown or green--and controlling the glaze was evidently problematic. Sometimes the effect is rather sloppy. In the next stage of development, several pigments are applied simultaneously to achieve a polychrome effect.[34] Combination of the clear or cream color with green and ochre is found on utilitarian vessels in tombs dated 684[35] and 689;[36] later, the technique is applied to figurines. An unusual blue glaze is splashed on a small tray unearthed in an imperial prince's tomb dated 664.[37]

GAOZONG'S TOMB

Gaozong's tomb, Qianling, was begun during his lifetime. Like his predecessor, he was interred within a mountain. In this case, it was actually three small mountains north of Xian. Although the tomb has been identified, it has not yet been excavated. The aboveground palace, it is said, had 378 rooms to serve the needs of the spirit of the dead emperor.[38] The funeral monument was enclosed by a wall with four gates, outside of which were stone lions, measuring four and one-half meters high. The shendao is one of the best preserved: Pairs of sculpted columns, no longer topped by a lion, but by a large, round, pearl shape, remain. Also still in situ are winged horses (twice life-size), paired ostriches, five pairs of saddled horses, each with a groom (whose heads were decapitated by vandals), ten pairs of officials (twice life-size), two large, stone, dragon-topped steles six meters high, and two brick pylons. The stele at the left of the shendao has a eulogy by Gaozong's son and successor. Inside the entrance are 60 figures of foreign ambassadors, their heads now missing. They are arranged into two groups--29 on one side, 31 on the other. (FIGURE 18) These represent the foreign officials who attended the funeral services. Records of etiquette indicate that foreign dignitaries were required to attend imperial funerals and other important ceremonies such as the Feng Shan ritual at Mt. Tai (see above). The sculpture of the Chinese official stands rigidly. His facial features, though suggestive of a portrait, are hard-edged and unconvincing. (FIGURE 19) The drapery falls close to the body, but does not reveal the form beneath, nor does the shallow carving of the cloth suggest actual material. The two extant relief carvings of ostriches are rather remarkable portrayals of a bird not native to China; its naturalistic representation must have been based on creatures sent as foreign tribute.[39] Similar to Taizong's chargers, the ostrich is not sculpted in the round, but is a low relief showing the profile view of the animal. The bird stands in an alert position, head held high, tail raised. The other creatures of the processional path, in contrast, are fully carved in the round. At this time, the animal sculptures are still relatively static: The winged lion's shape is restricted to the square of the stone from which it was carved. Exercising caution, the artist leaves the stone in the lower area between the legs, fashioning it into a shallow relief pattern of clouds. The lion stands rigidly, its wings are carved close to the body, and the mane is treated with a decorative pattern. Only its beautifully realized head and alert facial expression convey its life force. It was the function of these numerous majestic, over-life-size figures to not only mark the tomb path but to testify to the might and glory of the emperor.[40]

BUDDHISM UNDER GAOZONG AND WU ZE-TIAN

Although Emperor Gaozong was not an enthusiastic adherent of Buddhism, early in his reign he sponsored the construction of two temples. The Ximingsi, a grandiose building that was said to have 13 halls and 4,000 rooms, commemorated the recovery of the health of his heir (656-658).[41] A portion of the temple has recently been excavated.[42] Gaozong continued to support monk Xuan Zang and his efforts to translate the scriptures; the Dayen (Wild Goose) Pagoda was built in 652 to protect the 657 volumes of Buddhist writings brought back by the monk. Located in modern Xian's southern district, the Dayen Pagoda was 64 meters high and originally had five stories. Razed between 701 and 705, it was rebuilt with, probably, ten stories, of which only seven remain today. Despite Gaozong's high esteem for the monk, support for many of the causes Xuan Zang espoused was denied him. Until his death in 664, the eminent monk repeatedly sought to retire from attending the emperor in order to translate the scriptures. During this reign, the Faxiang school continued to be the one sponsored by the imperial court. By the Tang era, Buddhism had become an integral part of state ritual. The accession of a new emperor, birth of an imperial prince, and even ceremonies for ancestors involved the chanting of sutras, the casting of spells, and maigre feasts. Celebrations were held on Buddha's birthday, and a great banquet was held for All Souls. At these times, homage was paid to Buddhist deities; sutras were recited, and sermons preached.[43]

With the rise of Empress Wu, which began with Gaozong's paralytic stroke in 660, Buddhism flourished. In addition to whatever spiritual gratification and solace she was afforded, the empress's espousal of Buddhism was an effective means to challenge the established power structure of the Confucian hierarchy. Empress Wu was an outsider to the inner cliques of power and authority of the aristocracy. Any action of hers they deemed unmeritorious, they criticized within the context of the Confucian ideology of statehood and filial piety, whether it be her usurpation of power or the excessive expense she incurred in constructing the Ming Tang. Buddhism offered an alternate ideology by which, as a faithful devotee, she might hope to expiate the many crimes and murders committed in her name. More importantly, taking the precedent of Asoka, she established herself as *Cakravartin*, universal ruler over the political as well as the spiritual realm. With the aid of the monk Huai Yi, reputedly her lover, and the discovery of a specious text, the *Dayun Jing*, she attained this goal.[44] One chapter of this sutra concerns a female deity, who because of her devoted study of the *Mahaparinirvana sutra*, was born as universal monarch.[45] In another chapter, a woman was ruler of a prosperous kingdom owing to her devotion to Buddhism. Thus, on the basis of this sutra, her reign was prophesied and legitimized. In 695, Empress Wu was declared the living incarnation of Milo, Buddha of the Future.[46] In this same year, a colossal Milo figure, 33 meters tall was erected at Dunhuang, Cave 96, which has an inscription dated to her reign.[47] It was then ordered, in an unprecedented edict, that a Dayunsi monastery should be established in each of the prefectures of the empire as well as in the two capitals and that lectures on the sutra were to be given there. In this way, Empress Wu identified herself throughout the country, on a local level, with Buddhism and its observances; she thus attracted the support of the lower and middle classes under Buddhism. This broad-based endorsement gave her a means of establishing her power despite the prevailing influence of the Confucians and Taoists at court.

Empress Wu sponsored many Buddhist activities, among which were the construction and support of several temples, including Daqianfosi, built in Gaozong's memory.[48] In 659, the empress gave generous grants of cash and silk to the monks of Famensi, the temple outside of Chang-an that housed the famous, alleged finger-bone relic of the Buddha. Under her sponsorship, an image of Emperor Asoka with Emperor Gaozong's features was commissioned to be made at the temple, thus honoring the founding emperor of the Tang. In 660, the bone relic was brought to Luoyang where it was worshipped and carried in procession through the streets. The elaborate gold and silver case that Empress Wu had made for the relic has recently been discovered.[49] Under Wu Ze-tian, translations were undertaken on a large scale. In 695, when the monk Yi Jing returned to China from his 24-year Western sojourn via the sea route, he devoted himself, in Luoyang, to translating the scriptures, especially the Huayen Jing. Yi Jing is also credited with the compilation of a Sanskrit-Chinese dictionary of about 1,000 words, marking a definite stage in the translation process whereby Chinese loan words, appropriated for the strange new Buddhist expressions, became more standardized.[50] His account of eminent monks who went to India during the Tang is a fascinating document of the Chinese pilgrims of his time.[51] Western monks were welcomed at court: Divakara arrived in China in 676, and the empress had the eminent monk Siksananda brought to China from Khotan in 695. Under her sponsorship, a new catalogue of the canon was compiled in that same year.[52] Remarkable as it seems, it is also asserted that between the years 692 and 700, there were stern restrictions on the killing of animals for food.[53]

Several schools of Buddhism were favored during Wu's reign. The Tiantai sect, located on the renowned mountain of the same name, which had achieved prominence in the Sui dynasty under the brilliant monk Zhi Yi, had, since the end of the Sui, fallen out of favor until it was sponsored by the empress. Several disciples of the Chan school were treated with great regard by the court. One of the best-supported schools was centered on the *Huayan jing*. Characteristically, this scripture does not favor one sectarian tradition over another, considering such distinctions of the external world to be illusory.[54] More importantly, the Huayan concept of the universe as ruled by Vairocana, or Cosmic Buddha, found artistic expression in the sculpture of the period, notably at Longmen's Eastern Hill Grottoes. At Empress Wu's court the Huayan school was represented by the monk Fa Zang, who made a new translation of the sutra. Empress Wu's successor, her son, Emperor Zhongzong, continued to honor the monk Fa Zang. By imperial order, five temples were constructed for the study and propagation of Huayan Buddhism.[55]

BUDDHIST ART

The most spectacular evidence of Empress Wu's patronage of Buddhism is represented by the rock-cut temples at Longmen outside the new capital city of Luoyang. The best known, the Fengxian Temple, is commonly said to have been commissioned by Gaozong, but work on the central figure did not begin until 672, well after his stroke. In 675, according to the records, the empress planned to visit the site, but forewarned of an attempted coup, she demurred citing as an excuse the rainy weather; the insurgents, incidentally, were captured. The colossal sculptures include the Cosmic Buddha, flanked by two disciples of the Historic Buddha, Ananda and Kasyapa, two colossal Bodhisattvas, two Guardian Kings, and two Dvarapala guardians.[56] (FIGURES 20, 21) The iconographic arrangement of the figures, with the Buddha's earthly disciples placed nearest to the Buddha, was formulated in 500. This was an attempt to create a syncretic image that would reconcile the many disparate teachings of Buddhism, a religion with no closed canon and a proliferation of diverse scriptures. Thus the older school was represented by the two chief disciples: the youthful Ananda, personal attendant of the Buddha, who symbolized the path to enlightenment by means of the heart; and the elder Kasyapa, an eminent philosopher and ascetic, converted by the wisdom of the Buddha's teaching late in his career, who represented the path of the intellect. In contrast to these monks, the large-scale Bodhisattvas and guardian figures presage later developments in Buddhism, with its pantheon of deities. At the center of the group sits the colossal Cosmic Buddha, identified by the unique lotus-flower seat. Each petal of the base is decorated with a "Buddha world"--each is a cosmic universe replete with its own system of stars and planets, including an Earth. Shown seated atop a thousand of these petals, this figure is the embodiment of the universal Buddha, a concept central to the schools of Buddhism favored during the Tang era. Stylistically these carvings, based on prototypes imported from India, are harbingers of a new fashion in which naturalism in the depiction of the body, garments, and jewels is emphasized. The Buddha at Longmen sits majestically. He is full-bodied; his shoulders and torso, though not yet modeled with anatomical detail, echo the

Indian celebration of the physical form. His clinging garment falls in folds that reveal the body beneath; the drapery pattern of folds is a model of classic restraint, with no fussy details. While maintaining a Chinese appearance, the head of the Buddha has markedly new features: sensuous bow-shape lips, half-closed, meditative, almond-shape eyes, and triple rings of flesh around the throat. Many people today see the image of Wu Ze-tian in these features. Whether or not the Buddha was made to resemble the empress, the majesty and dignity of this figure, the all-important center of the Buddhist cosmic hierarchy, is clearly an allusion to the empress and her court. Treatment of the head halo and body mandorla behind the Buddha also reveal Indian influences. An inner ring of lotus petals, a zone of seated Buddhas, and an outer area of flame patterns create a hypnotic circular and linear rhythm; this visual movement is echoed in the loops of the folds of the garment. The resulting dynamic spiral pattern causes the viewer to concentrate on the meditative calm of the face, a still point in the midst of activity.

In contrast to the rather static figures of the Bodhisattva and monks who flank the Buddha, the Guardians Kings, with imperious faces, dressed as crowned Chinese generals, stand in pronounced hip-slung poses trampling the dark powers of ignorance and evil underfoot; their attributes are held in their outstretched hands. (FIGURE 21) The outermost pair of figures are Dvarapalas--muscular, seminaked athletic guardians. Their exposed, exaggerated anatomy is infrequently seen in native non-Buddhist art. Posed dynamically, their hip's swaying and limbs tensed indicate they are ready for action, assuring heroic protection of the faith. On the wall behind the sculptures are a series of holes that are visible along either side of the central Buddha; they once supported a large wooden, Indian-style facade that protected the images. Above the formal entranceway there probably was a large circular window that allowed in diffused sunlight. A large expanse of uncarved rock, seen also in Indian cave-chapels, frames the cave, providing a dramatic contrast to the skillfully articulated divine images.

Among the several Longmen caves commissioned during the reign of Empress Wu, one of the most remarkable is the Cave of a Thousand Buddhas.[57] (FIGURE 22) Amitofu is the focus of worship. He is flanked by two disciples, a pair of Bodhisattvas, and two celestial Guardian Kings. On the wall behind the icons, 54 beings emerge from lotus buds. The Thousand Buddha theme is represented by rows of identical small-scale, seated, meditating Buddhas carved on the northern and southern walls; below them are ten celestial musicians and two dancers.   These are delicately posed angelic figures; their divinity is indicated by the scarves that billow from a heavenly wind.   Carved in the early Tang style, the large central Buddha sits on a lotus-petal seat that is supported by an hourglass-shape base symbolic of the cosmic mountain of Buddhist mythology; small earth spirits uphold the throne.[58]

Many sites in north China are ascribed to the late seventh century. Although the cave chapels of Gongxian outside Luoyang in Henan are famous for Buddhist sculptures of an earlier period, pious works on a smaller scale continued to be undertaken during the Tang. A few small niches of triads found in Cave 4 conform to the Longmen style.[59] Another series of caves carved into a rock bluff in Junxian, Henan, were executed during three periods of Tang activity beginning with Gaozong, ca. 675, and ending with Xuanzong in the mid-eighth century. The iconography of the first period, contemporary to the work at Longmen, is built around Shakyamuni, the Historical Buddha; Milo (Maitreya), Buddha of the Future); Amitofu (Amitabha), Buddha of Infinite Light, and Guanyin (Avalokitesvara), the Bodhisattva of Compassion). Abundant epigraphical evidence provides specific dates for the sculptures. One unusual aspect of the iconography at these caves is found in Cave 1; the halo of the large, seated Buddha is filled with innumerable miniature seated Buddha images, foretelling the style of Todaiji Vairocana Buddha (Dainichi) in Nara, Japan.[60] Gansu Province was also the site of artistic undertakings dated to this reign, like the site of Qingyang not far northeast of the city of Tianshui. Of particular interest is Cave 32;[61] though not as finely carved, its sculptures correspond to the stylistic paradigm of this era; a naturalistic treatment of the body is most dramatically seen in the hip-slung pose of the flanking guardian figures. Their lively postures foreshadow the great martial figures of the eighth century. The Bodhisattva sculptures of Cave 222 are more finely carved; their drapery clings sensuously like wet cloth, delineating the mass of flesh beneath.[62] But, compared to the figures of the next century, their bodies are still relatively stiff and the folds of thin drapery only follow the contours of the body.

In Shansi Province in the city of Taiyuan, is a most unusual dragon-topped stele, with an inscription dated 692, in Empress Wu's reign. The title on the front face reads:

Great Zhou Great Cloud Temple; humbly on behalf of the Sacred and Divine Majesty one stele with scenes of the Nirvana has been Reverently made.

Another inscription on the back further states:

> The twenty-fourth day of the second month of the second year of
> Tianshou (691), the temple was renamed T'a yun ssu in conformity to
> law; while in the following year its title was again changed, in
> conformity to law to Jen shou ssu, the Temple of Mercy and
> Longevity.[63]

The renaming of the temple recorded here is part of the series of
events that ensued after the discovery and presentation of the
scripture, *Tayun sutra*. Steles crowned by intertwining dragons, a
native format employed since the Han to preserve historical
inscriptions, had long been appropriated by the Buddhists, but here
both the back and front surfaces are carved with small-scale
representations of the *Mahaparinirvana*, or death of the Historic
Buddha, and the preparations for his cremation. This is a rather
unusual theme, relatively unpopular and rare in China, where
depictions of death are eschewed, though several paintings and over-
life-size sculptures of the Parinirvana were found at Dunhuang and
elsewhere.[64] It is likely that these illustrations reflect the content of
the *Tayun sutra*, which stresses the piety of a female regent devoted to
the *Mahaparinirvana sutra*.

A clear concordance of stylistic characteristics can be seen among
the mural paintings of the late seventh century preserved at
Dunhuang, Maijishan, and Pinglingsi, and the sculptural icons of
Longmen and elsewhere. They all present the new image of the
Buddha that includes mature rather than youthful features, fleshy body
with its suggested definition of the chest, and naturalistic fall to the
drapery. Potential movement in the attendant celestials is also
suggested. The murals provide evidence of the Tang painting style;
some techniques, like highlighting and shading, reflect intercourse
with the West. This style was attributed to the Central Asian artist
Wei-Chi Yi-Seng (at Empress Wu's court), whose work did not
survive. Moreover, heavenly beings have a new variety of skin colors
that reveal their Indian origins, and iconographical innovations make
their appearance. For example, Cave 321 has one of the earliest
painted representations of the Eleven-headed, Six-armed Guanyin, the
Bodhisattva of Compassion, but it is painted in an archaic style that
seems anachronistic in comparison to its attendant Bodhisattvas.
(FIGURE 23) Guanyin, standing flat-footed, has a distinctly Indian
face; the garments are drawn with no suggestion of the fall and

movement of cloth observable in the other figures. The flanking dark-skinned Bodhisattvas are models of grace; bending slightly, their garments drape sensuously over their bodies. It seems clear that the new multiheaded image was closely copied from a Western source, and that the artist did not see fit to alter any of the characteristics to conform to contemporary Chinese style. Cave 335 at Dunhuang, dated 686 by inscription, also presents Indian deities. Such exotics as the god Asura are among the audience of the Vimalakirti and Wenshu debate. He stands on the extreme right; two of his four arms, holding the sun and moon, reach to the sky. (FIGURE 24) A more typical Bodhisattva may be seen in Cave 321, dated 705.[65] The deity stands gracefully, with hips swaying; the skin is painted a deep red. Contrasting hues highlight the triple rings of flesh at the neck and the celestial facial features, which approximate geometric forms. The drapery and jewels of the divinity are opulent, rendered with extreme fineness and variety; they cover the head, neck, waist, and arms. The scarves, seemingly of the finest silk, loop and wind around the waist and are tied in a complicated bow that cascades gently down the front of the skirt. In these celestial images the queenly refinement of Wu Ze-tian's court is seen.

NOTES

1. Raymond Dawson, *Imperial China* (London, 1972): 65.
2. R.W.L. Guisso, *Wu Tse t'ien and the Politics of Legitimization in T'ang China* (Western Washington, 1978): 20. Guisso maintains that Gaozong had an active role in government until 675, when owing to his illness, he offered his wife the regency.
3. Twitchett, 1992: 143, has pointed out that it was not until the ninth century that Tang historians first questioned Wu's legitimacy.
4. One such resister was a notable poet whose fame increased with time for having openly opposed the empress. Volker Klopsch, "Lo Pin-wang's Survival: Traces of a Legend," *T'ang Studies*, 1988, vol. 6: 77-97.
5. It is significant that Wu was thought of as a butcher because of the many people murdered during her reign, while both her predecessor, Taizong, and her successor, Xuanzong, who were both fratricides, were not remembered as a murderers.
6. Twitchett, "The Composition of the T'ang Ruling Class," ed. Wright, *Perspectives of the T'ang*: 65.
7. Twitchett and Wechsler, "Kao Tsung and the Empress Wu: the Inheritor and the Usurper," *Cambridge History of China* (Cambridge, 1979), vol. III: 280. Evidence of the Persian presence is provided by the numerous coins unearthed in Tang tombs, notably in that of Lady Yang. (See Xiaoga Dichu Bowuguan, "Anluwangzi Shantang Wuwangnu Yangshimu," *Wenwu*, 1985.2: 83-93.) This was the tomb of the consort of the third son of Taizong. The tomb also contained coins of the Kaiyuan era (712-756).
8. Dawson, 1972: 68.
9. Edward Schafer, *Pacing the Void* (Berkeley, 1977): 17ff, describes the structure and the courtiers' reactions. Xuanzang, in the early eighth century, is reported to have rebuilt it, but Schafer maintains this was just repair work. The structure was destroyed by fire in 740, and it was not rebuilt.
10. C. P. Fitzgerald, *Empress Wu* (London, 1968): 132, proposed that it was the monk Huai I, who had earlier enjoyed great favor and had been responsible for much of the hall's planning and construction, who burned it down.
11. William Soothill, *The Hall of Light* (London, 1951): 108.
12. Twitchett and Wechsler, 1979: 310. More recently Twitchett has attributed these efforts to the empress's cousin and trusted adviser. (See 1992: 131).
13. LTMHJ, Acker, 1954: 128.
14. LTMHJ, Soper, 1958: 216 and p. 213, respectively.

15. Shaanxisheng Bowuguan, "Tang Li Shou mu fachu Jianbao," *Wenwu*, 1974.9: 71-88. Shaanxisheng Bowuguan, *T'ang Mu Pihua Jinbu* (Xian, 1989): 30-36. Duan Wen-bi was buried in the Zhaoling; he died in 651. His tomb murals include serving women, a series of officials, and ceramic figurines. (See Han Wei, 1991: 37-9.) These murals are on view in the Zhaoling Museum.

16. Shanxisheng Kaogu Yanjiusuo, Taiyuan CPAM, "Taiyuan Jingshengcun 337 hao Tangdai Bihua Mu," *Wenwu*, 1990.12: 11-15 (see color plate).

17. Li Zhen, son of Li Ji, predeceased his father in 660. His tomb murals include depictions of ox-drawn carts in procession and several handmaids. (See *Tang Mu Pi Hua Jijin*: 58, figs. 23-24.)

18. Zhi Shi was Turkish and held an official post. His tomb was excavated in 1957 in Guodu, Chang-an county. Owing to water damage, only one mural is extant. (See *Tang Mu Pi Hua Jijin*: 37, fig. 22.)

19. These murals are on view in the Zhaoling Museum.

20. Yun, *Wenwu*, 1977: 38.

21. *Tang Mu Pihua Jinbu* (Xian, 1989): 94. His actual name was Xu Shuhi, but because of his important role in the founding of the empire he was given the imperial surname Li and a place in Taizong's funeral mound area. His tomb was later devastated by Empress Wu in retaliation for the rebellious plans of his grandson, Xu Jingye.

22. Much of this information can be found in Li Zhi-yan, "Tangdai Ciyao Gaikuang yu Tangci de Fenqi," *Wenwu*, 1972.3: 34-48, translated in Dien, 1985: vol. III: 1756-1766.

23. Changzhishi Bowuguan, "Changzhixian Songjiazhuang Tangdai Fancheng Fufu mu," *Wenwu*, 1989.5: 58-65.

24. Xiaoga diqu Bowuguan, Anluxian Bowuguan, "Anluwang dishan Tang Wuwang nu Yangshi mu," *Wenwu*, 1985.2: 83-93. This is the tomb of the wife of Prince Wu, who was the third son of Taizong. The brick tomb had, in addition to the usual forechamber and coffin room, four lateral chambers with a drainage system. Among the finds were 32 figurines, pottery, including three cups and 51 utensils, 139 pieces of gold jewelry and adornments, and 14 coins of the Persian king Peroz (r. 459-484).

25. Zhongguo Shehui Kexueyuan Kaogu Yanjiusuo Henan Dier Gongzuodui, "Henan Yanshi Xingyuancui de Liangzuo Tang mu," *Kaogu*, 1984.10: 904-908.

26. Changzhishi Bowuguan, "Shanxi Changzhishi Tangdai Fengkuo mu," *Wenwu*, 1989.6: 51-57.

27. Up to 90 early Tang figurines of warriors, officials, ladies, and horses, etc., were also found in Changsha, Hunan. (See Sheng Bowuguan, "Hunan Changsha Huojiahu Tangmu Fajue Jianbao," *Kaogu*, 1980.6: 506-511.)

28. *Shaanxi Taoyong Jinghua* (Xian, 1986): pl. 46-51; also *Wenwu*, 1972.7: 33-42.

29. 310 Guodao Mengjin Kaogusuo, "Luoyang Mengjin Shanxitou Tangmu," *Wenwu*, 1992.3: 1ff. The tomb had over 42 pottery figures and animals, including ten musicians, two female dancers, 19 guardian figures (some in Turkish dress), and female figures as well as utilitarian pottery pieces. A tomb record identified the deceased and gave his date of death.

30. Shaanxishen Bowuguan, "Tang Zheng Ren-tai mu Fachu Jianbao," *Wenwu*, 1972.7: 33-44.

31. Margaret Medley, *T'ang Pottery and Porcelain* (London, 1981): 24.

32. Medley, 1981: 36, says this type may be dated as early as the turn of the seventh century.

33. Now in the Shaanxi Provincial Museum. See *Chang-an Guibao* (Xian, 1985): pl. 39.

34. Another tomb, that of Li Shou dated 694, yielded several tricolor figurines of horses and male and female servants in addition to a high-quality lion-and-grapevine bronze mirror. (See Zhongguo Shehui Kexueyuan Kaogu Yanjiusuo Henan Dier Gongzuodui, "Henan Yanshi Xing yuancun de Liuzuo Jinan Tang mu," *Kaogu*, 1986.5: 429-431.) Unfortunately these figurines are not illustrated in the archaeological report.

35. Hupei Sheng Bowuguan, Yunxian Bowuguan, "Hupei Yunxian Tang Li Hui, Yan Wan Mu Fajue Jianbao," *Wenwu*, 1987.8: 30-42. Li Hui's tomb had 82 tomb objects, including a rhyton and eared cup with dragon as well as two other ceramics in the triglaze technique; remnants of wall paintings of serving persons also were extant, though in a poor state of preservation.

36. Wang Jinxian, Changzhishi Bowuguan, "Shanxi Changzhishi Beijiao Tang Cui Na Mu," *Wenwu*, 1987.8: 43-48 and p. 62. Tomb objects include unglazed, relatively simple, pottery figurines and other ceramic mingqi, two damaged bronze mirrors (one with a bird design), and a tomb record.

37. "Tang Li Fengmu Jianbao," *Kaogu*, 1973.6: pl. 12. This is the tomb of a son of Li Yuan; see also George Kuwayama, "The Sculptural Development of Funerary Figures," *The Quest for Eternity* (Los Angeles, 1986): 84.

38. Wechsler, 1985: 158.

39. Schafer, 1963: 102. Two ostriches came as tribute in the seventh century. Schafer maintained that no foreign animal was a greater marvel in the Tang.

40. The shendao of one of the sons of Gaozong, Li Hong, was recently studied. The 18 sculptures of the imperial son who died in 675, at the age of 24, were considered to be among the best preserved. (See Ruo Shi, "Tang Gongling Diaocha Jiyao," *Wenwu*, 1985.3: 43-45; a lion and column are illustrated.)

41. Weinstein, 1987: 28.

42. Zhongguo Shihui Kexueyuan Kaogu Yanjiusuo Xian Tangcheng Gongzuodui, "Tang Chang-an Ximingsi Yizhi Fajue Jianbao," *Kaogu*, 1990.1: 45-55. A section of the temple, 15 percent, was unearthed; its identity is certified by objects that bear its name. Over 150 Buddhist statues survived but are in poor condition; bricks, bowls, coins, and other objects were also found. According to the temple records, this temple was exempt from and thus survived the great proscription of 845; it is believed the sculptures were hidden at that time.

43. Arthur Wright, *Buddhism in Chinese History* (Stanford, 1959): 70.

44. Guisso, 1978: 36, cites Japanese scholarly evidence that this sutra existed in the Northern Liang period; several copies of it were found at Dunhuang. Kenneth Ch'en, *The Chinese Transformation of Buddhism* (Princeton, 1975), agrees.

45. Ch'en, 1975: 111.

46. Fitzgerald, 1968: 127.

47. Unfortunately the colossal image was repaired in the Qing dynasty. *Zhongguo Shiku: Dunhuang Mogaoku*, vol. V, 1987: 264.

48. Weinstein, 1973: 298.

49. Weinstein, 1987: 37. This relic is one of the most treasured among the cache of ritual objects found in the storerooms of the pagoda Famen Temple outside of Xian. (See chapter XVII.)

50. L. Carrington Goodrich, *A Short History of the Chinese People* (New York, 1963): 127. These loan words were chosen on the basis of phonetic similarity to the sounds as well as on meaning.

51. Fifty-six monks are listed and discussed. (See Yi Jing, translated by Lahiri, 1986.)

53. Weinstein, 1987: 299.

53. Guisso, 1978: 36.

54. Guisso, 1978: 301.

55. Guisso, 1978: 303.

56. The niche measures 38 meters in length and 33.5 meters in width; the main Buddha measure 17.14 meters high. (See also Amy Mcnair, "Early Tang Imperial Patronage at Longmen," *Ars Orientalis*, 1994, XXIV: 65-81, esp 74ff.)

57. The Wanfotong cave was built in commemoration of the pious deeds of Emperor Gaozong and Empress Wu Ze-tian and their sons by imperial edict in the first year of Yonglong (680) by eunuch Yao Shen-piao and monk Chi Yun, who was in charge of the rites at court.

58. The main Buddha is 4 meters high.

59. *Zhongguo Shiku: Gongxian Shikusi* (Wenwu and Heibonsha Presses, Japan, 1983), pls. 227-28, 231-32.

60. Henansheng Gudai Jianzhu Baohu Yanjiusuo, "Junxian Qianfodong Shiku Diaocha," *Wenwu*, 1992.1: 31-39. The authors divide the period of activity from 680 or before, 680-690, and 690-737. In the late period inscriptions employ the new writing style introduced under Empress Wu.

61. Gansusheng Wenwu Gongzuoyendui, *Qingyang Beikusi* (Beijing, 1985). There are several dated caves--one from 656 and another from 659. Cave 32 is dated 692. These caves are not far from Maijishan, which is to the southwest.

62. Gansusheng Wenwu, 1985: pls. LIV-LXIV. There is an extraordinary range of style in the carving of the sculptures of this cave; the main Buddha group appears to be in a much less skilled and later style than the innumerable smaller niches carved into the surrounding walls.

63. A. C. Soper, "A T'ang Parinirvana Stele," *Artibus Asiae*, 1959, vol. XXII: 159ff.

64. P. E. Karetzky, "A Scene of the Parinirvana on a Recently Excavated Stone Reliquary of the Tang Dynasty," *East and West* (Rome), 1988, vol. 38: 221ff. This reliquary is unique; it reflects the development of the death theme found at Dunhuang.

65. The main sculptures of this large cave have been repainted in Qing times.

CHAPTER IV

EMPEROR ZHONGZONG

In 684, Zhongzong was named emperor following the death of his father; he ruled for a mere 55 days before his mother usurped the throne. With the deposition of Empress Wu, in 705 he reascended the throne, and the Tang dynasty was restored. But Zhongzong (r. 705-710) did not enjoy a long reign; he died in an untimely fashion within five years. Moreover, his reign was marred by the ambitions of his wife, Empress Wei, granddaughter of Empress Wu. She used her influence for acts of self-enrichment, profiting greatly from the sale of ordination. Some suspect that her husband's growing alarm at her flagrant behavior led her to have him poisoned. The court was determined to prevent Empress Wei's usurpation of the throne and she was executed.[1] Following the death of the empress, Emperor Ruizong ascended the throne.

ARCHAEOLOGY

The short and relatively uneventful reign of Zhongzong is noteworthy because of the four imperial burials undertaken by him on behalf of the princely youths who were victims of Empress Wu. Historians may have exaggerated some of the horrible deeds of which the empress was suspected. Some claim she had her granddaughter executed, but according to the mortuary inscription in her tomb, Li Xian-hui (Yong Tai 684-701), granddaughter of Emperor Gaozong and Empress Wu, died of natural causes, although this account has been questioned.[2] The murals of the four tombs, a rich source of information on portraiture, architecture, and landscape painting, fill the void of firsthand knowledge of Tang painting, which was previously known only through copies of the ancient masters. Initially there was much debate over the question of whether the famous court artists of the time were employed in the decorations; but the current consensus is that the murals were the product of artisans whose major commissions were funereal. The paintings reflect the style of art at court because the illustrations draw upon aristocratic pastimes such as hunting, polo, and musical parties.[3]

All four imperial youths were reinterred in attendant tombs of the Qianling mausoleum of Emperor Gaozong and Empress Wu by order of Emperor Zhongzong. They are generally similar in plan to the earlier satellite tombs: A deeply sloping tomb path leads to a series of passageways with niches housing ceramic objects that alternate with air shafts. Next, on level ground, is an inner passageway leading to a chamber in which funereal articles were placed; a corridor connects it with the rear coffin chamber. Tomb articles fashioned of precious materials were stolen soon after the tombs were completed, but hundreds of pottery figurines and pottery horses, a stone coffin, and stone burial tablet still remain. Since the tombs share so many common characteristics, only two will be discussed.

LI XIAN'S TOMB

Li Xian (654-684), posthumously called Zhang Huai, was the second son of Emperor Gaozong and Empress Wu. In 675 Li Xian was designated crown prince. According to Chinese historians, the occupant was licentious and depraved, being inordinately fond of women and wine. Modern scholars have agreed with this assessment.[4] Complaints of his behavior led to a search of his domicile, where "illicit arms" were found; some maintain these had been placed there to incriminate him. For plotting to seize political power, in 680 he was stripped of all rank and position, made a commoner, and confined to Chang-an. Fearing a loyalist insurrection, in 684 Empress Wu ostensibly sent a general to protect the prince on his move to Sichuan. Whether under her direction or not, the general reputedly contrived Li's death; it appeared as if the prince took his own life. Although traditionally Li was thought to be Empress Wu's son, making her crime all the more heinous, Fitzgerald has convincingly argued that, in fact, Li was her nephew, the illicit child of her sister and the emperor. It seems possible that loyalist factions, seeking to restore the Tang, gathered around Li and thus threatened not only Empress

Wu's reign, but her hopes for her son and chosen heir.[5] Modern Chinese sources explain that Li was guilty of organizing a number of scholars to write an exegesis on the text--the *History of the Later Han Dynasty*--by Fan Ye; their aim was to attack Empress Wu as an illegal occupant of the throne by drawing analogies to an ill-fated Han empress and the disastrous results of her short reign.[6]

Li's tomb, dated 706, has 50 groups of murals totaling a painted area of around 121 square meters. The tomb was robbed but some silver vessels remain. (As testimony to their greed and hasty retreat, one of the raiders was found lying dead in the passageway.) A series of spectacular compositions was painted. Depictions on the east wall include a hunting party, the entertaining of foreign guests, honor guards, and the Green Dragon the symbolic representation of the east; on the west wall are scenes of a game of polo, the entertaining of foreign guests, honor guards, and the White Tiger, the symbolic representation of the west. Many of these paintings reflect Western influences on court life.[7] Most obvious is the presence of foreign officials, who were expected to take part in certain imperial ceremonies, notably weddings, funerals, and state rituals.[8] Several extant, late copies of Tang paintings of foreigners paying tribute at court are attributed to various artists, including to Yen Li-ben, who was an artist highly honored at the court of Empress Wu; these indicate the popularity of the theme.[9] Attempts have been made to identify the nationalities of these individuals by their carefully rendered articles of clothing.[10] (FIGURE 25) Special attention has obviously been given to the costumes' details: An envoy from Korea in a voluminous belted tunic over trousers and felt shoes wears a feathered cap; a Persian is recognizable by his large-lapelled tunic open at the throat, trousers, and boots. Bringing up the rear of the cortege is a figure in fur pants and fur hat, the winter garb of the tribes inhabiting the northern steppes. These figures are a contrast to the three Chinese officials in long court robes, upturned shoes, and tall starched silk caps who lead the procession. The painting on the west wall of the passage shows men of other nationalities of the northern steppes and three lesser-ranking Chinese officials (to judge by their low caps and less formal robes). These portrayals exactly conform to the Tang monumental figure painting style: They are shown against a blank background, in large scale, grouped in a variety of postures--frontal, profile, three-quarter frontal, three-quarter rear, and full rear. Each figure is individually rendered--details are meticulously observed in drawing the their postures, physique, facial features, and expressions.

Aristocratic sports are an important theme in these royal tombs. Hunting, held in high esteem during the Tang, was enjoyed daily by Li's father, Gaozong.[11] Here the hunting party is a spectacle, with over 50 horsemen in a landscape of sparsely placed trees and large boulders. All of the horsemen and their mounts are individually portrayed; not only has the artist rendered the hunters' racial characteristics, garments, physiognomy, and posture but also their psychological bearing as well. (FIGURE 26) The horses are shown in a wide variety of poses, many in full gallop. In the foreground, outriders carry banners and flags with the insignia of the prince. The composition extends across the walls in a figural arrangement that creates a horizontal movement common in long hand scrolls. Like later landscape painting, this organization of motifs may be compared to a musical composition. The introductory passage states the hunting theme: A few outriders are distributed across the picture plane; next, the opening theme is developed, and the composition grows in complexity and size, building to a climax near the center. The mounted hunters become more numerous; riding in full, flying gallop, they are in tightly packed formation. Gradually the theme subsides, and the group thins out to a small cluster of outriders. Finally, in the background, a small caravan of camels is seen through a screen of tall leafy trees. This funnellike distribution of figures--slowly building to a crescendo and winding down to a denouement of a few characters-- is common in Tang hand scrolls; the technique is seen in later Japanese scrolls.[12] Remarkable details of the horsemen and their paraphernalia reveal the particulars of the aristocratic pastime of hunting. On silk, tasseled pillows placed behind the saddles of some of the riders are seated cheetahs; some hunters hold falcons, others have dogs in their laps. Hunting animals, familiar in the West, were used by the nobility in China for a brief period during the Tang. As in the West, falcons and dogs accompany the hunt. According to documents, hunting hounds were sent to China from Samarkand in 713 and 721.[13] Hawking was an ancient sport in China, but although it continued to be popular in the Tang, it was considered frivolous and outlawed by Gaozong. From these illustrations it is clear that after the emperor's death the sport was resumed.

Polo, which is widely believed to have originated in Persia, was introduced in the early Tang and was promoted by Emperor Taizong as a sport and military exercise. A polo arena from the late Tang has been discovered as well as bronze mirrors decorated with representations of polo sticks.[14] Polo was a favorite sport enjoyed by both men and women as seen in the several ceramic figurines depicting the sport that were found, like those in the tomb of Wei Jiong (dated 692).[15] Polo's popularity reached its height during the reign of Xuanzong, whose court artists made several paintings of the imperial members at play.[16] But this mural is the earliest extant representation of the sport. Here the game, played by five contestants, takes place in a hilly, sparsely wooded landscape. Four of the horses are in full gallop, with all of their hooves in midair. (FIGURE 27) The riders are shown in a variety of active poses; the lead rider, turning backward in his saddle, hits the ball with his mallet, his horse rearing as he takes his shot. Three others close in on the ball. This is a portrait of strong competitors at play.

More conventional subjects like dancers and court attendants are painted on the walls of the passageway. The ideal of female beauty represented here is one of youthful delicacy; the girls wear slim dresses that fall gracefully, a short shawl covers their shoulders. Occasionally one wears a deeply cut garment that reveals cleavage, a rather unusual occurrence in Chinese art of other periods. These garments are probably based on the latest imported fashion.[17] The girls' tresses are gathered on top or at the back of their heads in a natural way; there is no exaggerated piling up of hair. Here, for the first time, narrative interest can be seen in the depiction of the palace attendants. In one extremely telling detail, the artist has rendered a woman reacting to a specific situation--she protects her face against a gust of wind. (FIGURE 28) In another, a young palace maid, holding a large colorful rooster, turns her head to rebuff the seemingly lewd comments of a male attendant. His head, with large bulbous nose, thick reddened lips, and buck teeth, is tilted upward; leaning forward, he eagerly anticipates her response. Other groups of figures include unusual characterizations and odd types: In one, a portly older woman with a high, piled chignon is attended by a female dressed as a Central Asian male and a dwarf in court dress.[18] The Tang artists delighted in depicting both a variety of figure types and individual moods. Dramatic contrasts among the figures are achieved. The artists carefully illustrate the physical type and psychological reaction through attention to physiognomy, pose, and expression.

LI ZHONG-REN'S TOMB

Li Zhong-ren (682-701), posthumously known as Yi De, was the son of Zhongzong and grandson of Gaozong and Empress Wu. At age 19, Li, his sister, Li Xian-hui, and her husband, as a result of being critical of the favor shown to the two youthful Chang brothers, met a sad fate. In one version of the story, Empress Wu ordered all three to end their lives; in another account, Wu Ze-tian had Li flogged to death.[19] His tomb, one of the largest, has the greatest expanse of murals.[20] Li's tomb is also unique because of the large-scale architectural renderings: Four enormous, paired "jue" towers with a hipped roof, painted red are seen against a blue and green mountainous landscape. (FIGURE 29) Supported by terraces on elevated bases, these towers commonly flanked the entrance to palaces and indicated high rank. In addition to an honor guard of 196 soldiers, infantry, cavalry, and chariot corps (who were probably the left and right wings of the palace guard) are 24 attendants with racks of halberds; imperial rank determined the number of halberds displayed in front of palaces, courts, and mansions. These military themes indicate that the rank of the deceased was of the highest.[21] The status, posture, and physical features of these military and official personnel are carefully delineated in the portrait style that characterizes the four imperial tombs.

Although there are no hunt scenes in this tomb, many related themes appear: Along the passageway is a series of attendants holding falcons and Afghan-like hunting dogs.(FIGURE 30) Next, one sees a series of men, each separated by small-scale trees and rocks; some hold a cheetah on a leash or have a falcon perched on a gloved hand. Both the hunting animals and their grooms are of Central Asian or Western origin. Dressed in wide-lapelled tunic and trousers, the trainers resemble the tribesmen of the northwest, who were celebrated for their animal training skills.   Lastly, on the east wall, rear chamber, are female palace attendants carrying offerings, dishes, and musical instruments.

CERAMICS

Polychrome glazed figurines and vessels did not appear until the eighth century. In the early phase there were kilns at sites in Chang-an, Luoyang, and Gongxian. By the middle of the century, production of the tricolor (*sancai*) glaze ceased, in favor of monochrome glazes. These imperial tombs supply important evidence for the reconstruction of the development of polychrome ceramics because they provide examples from several stages in the steady progression of experimentation and perfection of the tricolor glaze technique. Of the 777 unglazed and painted pottery figurines found in Li Xian's tomb, 60 are done in the three-color glaze style. Soldiers, servants, huntsmen, courtiers, horses, and camels are all represented.

The ceramic form was made of a fine, white kaolin clay; those from Chang-an had a light pink coloration that was covered with a fine slip, an innovation that helped the glaze to adhere smoothly to the clay. Wax grease was applied in areas to make them resistant to color; the glaze was occasionally painted on with a brush. Soon artists were able to control the drips by adjusting the viscosity of the glaze. Another aid in controlling the glaze was to engrave lines around areas to prevent the glazes from dripping.[22] One figurine of an official illustrates the basic problems of applying and controlling the movement of the colored glaze when heated. Although many maintain that dripping was part of the aesthetic effect, this figure, whose face is covered with brown and green glaze released from the tall cap above his head, is silent proof to the contrary. Other examples from the same tomb are more effective: On one of the heavenly guardians the glaze is so expertly applied as to appear to be brown and green stripes on the armor; the shin guards are pure green, the toes of the boots brown. The squatting monster beneath his feet is treated with a proficient mixture of the two colors.[23] (FIGURE 31) Moreover, an advance is made in the figure's ability to engage the area around it; now the guardian's right arm and drapery project boldly.

Although several figurines are done in the old style of partial glaze technique, astonishing advances in technological production have taken place. A very unusual effect is the rich swirling pattern on the coat of the horse of an equestrian figurine: Fully glazed a rich chestnut color, the animal's coat has a black linear pattern that resembles marbling.[24] (FIGURE 32) The effect is actually the result of a careful mixture of two different colored clays--one white *kaolin*, the other iron-rich clay. Such motifs are more frequently found on decorative plates and bowls, of which several excellent examples are in the Shanghai Museum.

Among the hand-painted figurines, mention should be made of the outstanding quality of several of the pieces, which successfully convey extraordinarily naturalistic depictions of men and animals. As in the murals, the figurines capture a specific character reacting to a special situation. One equestrian's horse stands patiently alert while he, his long sword at his side, shoots his bow and arrow (now lost) into the air. The figure of the rider was not glazed; his features and garment were hand-painted after firing, but unfortunately much of the decorative coloration has been lost. Another unglazed painted example is a horse ridden by a foreigner dressed in typical garb-- belted tunic with wide, pointed lapels, trousers, boots, and a low, tied cap. (FIGURE 33) His horse stands at attention, calm but alert, as he turns in his saddle to ward off the attack of a wild animal; the horse's composure despite the claws digging into its flanks is a remarkable testimony to the training and excellence of these mounts. At this time, Huren (barbarians to the Chinese) were a popular theme for the ceramic artist. A bearded, half-naked Huren sits astride his horse; both hands tensely grasp the reins; his head is thrown back and he is open-mouthed and yelling; his muscles are flexed. The horse seems as if it had just responded to the rider's command to stop--the head is drawn in by the tautly held reins. One indication of the richness of these finds can be seen in the gilding on the straps of the bridling of several equestrian figures from Li Xian's tomb.[25]

Although representations of women are not as numerous among the pottery figurines at this time as those of Chinese and foreign men, the existing female figures reflect changes in fashion and taste. The feminine ideal is slim and youthful, with a long, rectangular head; the face is modeled simply, and eyes, nose, and mouth are hand-painted after firing.[26] In the several tombs dated to this era unglazed pottery figurines dominate, like the great cache of beautifully executed unglazed figurines found in Li Si-ben's tomb, dated 709.[27] Thus the manufacture of hand-painted figures continued despite the new polychrome innovations.

In summary, the ceramic artists who produced these small-scale sculptures during the first decade of the eighth century show a remarkable ability to portray men and animals in a lifelike manner under a variety of circumstances. Like the mural painters, the ceramicists were not only interested in formal representation, but in expressing inner qualities of their models. In this early stage of polychrome glazing, it is mostly figures and horses that are treated with the three-color glaze; the majority of the objects are still unglazed and hand-painted after firing. Later, the number and diversity of glazed objects increases dramatically to include lions, camels, mythological creatures, and various vessels. Whereas early tomb murals have representations of the ox-drawn carriages that led the funeral procession, by the onset of the eighth century it is predominantly horses and cavalry that are in the lead; moreover, these mounts and riders appear in great numbers among mingqi. Some historians see this as a new dependence on the mounted warriors.[28] The prevalence of equestrian figures is no doubt due to the abundance of horses imported and trained by the Uighurs. Moreover, these Hu people, expert at mounted battle, played an important part in the Tang army.

ZHONGZONG'S TOMB

Similar in plan to the tomb of his father, Gaozong, Zhongzong's funeral monument was also enclosed by a wall with four gates, outside of which were sedent stone lions.[29] Set up along the tomb path were paired winged horses, ostriches, five pairs of saddled horses (each with a groom), and ten standing officials. These sculptures are not unlike those of the tombs of Zhongzong's predecessors. Although the general forms and articulation of the figures are stiff and unconvincing, these large-scale sculptures are naturalistic in detail, most notably in the faces. Of the five stone officials that remain, two are damaged; one is more than half buried.[30] One of the two extant sedent stone lions is undamaged.[31] It is a very strong, energetic form, but the body is not well defined, especially the musculature of the chest and stumplike forelegs. However, the naturalism lacking in bodily form is found in the treatment of the head. The glaring eyes, exaggerated in shape, are outlined with additional engraving; the force of the ferocious facial expression causes a mound of skin to fold between the eyes. True to life, the nares flare widely; the snout, muzzle, and teeth are carefully rendered. Moreover, there is a fine linear articulation of both the mane and the hair on the chin.

BUDDHISM UNDER ZHONGZONG

Although emperor of the reinstated Tang, which asserted the primacy of Taoism, Zhongzong was a devout Buddhist who went so far as to take the vows of the Bodhisattva during his reign.[32] To celebrate the restoration of the Tang, he ordered a Taoist and Buddhist temple established in each province. In many cases, this involved only changing the name of the existing temples; for example, the Tayun temples of Empress Wu's reign now became the Lungxingsi (temple of the rising dragon). As a pious Buddhist, Zhongzong continued to support Buddhism, executing a number of policies established by his mother. As she and his grandfather had personally welcomed home the renowned Xuan Zang, Zhongzong greeted the foreign monk Siksananda, who had returned from Khotan in 708. Like his mother, he had the famous finger-bone relic of the Buddha housed in Famensi brought to the imperial palace for worship. Translation of Buddhist sutras persisted under the imperial aegis, and Zhongzong, in the manner of his predecessors, wrote an imperial preface for the translation of a sutra by Yi Jing.[33]

NOTES

1. R. Guisso, "The Reigns of Wu, Chung-tsung and Jui-tsung," *Cambridge History of China*: 326. The plot against Empress Wei is often attributed to the power-seeking Tai Ping princess.

2. Fontein, 1976: 121.

3. Mary Fong, "Four Chinese Royal Tombs in the Early Eighth Century," *Artibus Asiae*, 1973, vol. XXXV: 307, and Fong "T'ang Tomb Murals Reviewed in the Light of T'ang Texts on Painting," *Artibus Asiae*, 1984, vol. XLV: 35ff.

4. Twitchett and Wechsler, 1979: 271.

5. Fitzgerald, 1968: 85. His death is discussed on p. 95.

6. *Murals of Li Xian* (Peking, 1974): 1.

7. Jane G. Mahler, *Westerners Among the Figurines of the T'ang Dynasty of China* (Rome, 1959); and Karetzky, "Foreigners in Tang and pre-Tang Painting," *Oriental Art* (London), 1984, vol. XXX: 160-166; and Virginia Bower, "Polo in Tang China: Sport and Art," *Asian Art*, Winter, 1991: 23-47.

8. At the Feng Shan sacrifices of the preceding reign, emissaries of the kingdoms of the Turks, Khotan, Persia, India, Japan, and the Korean states of Silla, Paekche, and Koguryo were in attendance. (See Wechsler, 1985: 168.)

9. Cahill, 1980: 20ff.

10. Fontein and Wu, 1976: 94.

11. *Murals of Li Xian*, 1974: 3.

12. The horizontal composition was a common compositional device in later Japanese picture scrolls. One well-known example is the *Heiji Monogatari* (ca. twelfth century), in the Boston Museum of Fine Arts.

13. Schafer, 1963: 77, 88.

14. *Murals of Li Xian,* 1974: 3.

15. *Shaanxi Taoyong Jinghua*, 1986: pls. 62-63. The horses are in similar positions to those in the murals, but the riders gesture wildly in playing the game.

16. LTMHJ, Acker, 1954: 260.

17. Schafer, 1963: 29.

18. Schafer, 1963: 47, points out that dwarfs were not unknown in ancient times, citing Confucius on the subject. Dwarfs, as court entertainers, were sent as tribute from Hunan; others are recorded as having come from Samarkand and Sumatra.

19. Fitzgerald, 1968: 170.

20. Measuring 8 meters long, the painted area is about 400 square meters.

21. Chin Wen, "Two Underground Galleries of Tang Dynasty Murals," *New Archaeological Finds in China*, Part II (Beijing, 1978): 99.

22. William Watson, "On Tang Soft-Glazed Pottery," *Pottery and Metalwork in Tang China, Colloquies on Art and Archaeology in Asia*, no. 1 (London, 1970): 35-42.

23. *Shaanxi Taoyong Jinghua*, 1986: pls. 52 and 53, respectively.

24. Another tomb recently found in Henan had a pillow treated with this marbled effect; also found were several three-color glaze figurines of horses and a camel. The tomb occupant was not identifiable. Linruxian Bowuguan, "Henan Linruxian Faxian Yizuo Tang mu," *Kaogu*, 1988.2: 186-87.

25. Medley, 1981: 46.

26. Medley, 1981: 46.

27. Zhongguo Shehui Kexueyuan Kaogu Yanjiusuo Henan dier Gongzuodui, "Henan Yanshi Xingyuancun de Liuzuo jinian Tangmu," *Kaogu*, 1986.5: 436-442.

28. Kuwayama, 1986: 85.

29. Dingling, the funeral mound of Zhongzong is on Mt. Feng Huangsha, 5 kilometers north of Fuping county in Shaanxi.

30. It measures 94 cm. wide and 162 cm. from the ground.

31. The undamaged one measures 240 cm. across, 125 cm. tall.

32. Weinstein, 1987: 49.

33. Weinstein, 1987: 49.

CHAPTER V

EMPEROR RUIZONG

Ruizong (r. 710-712) was not a strong emperor; his short rule of two years was rife with political turmoil. Two factions battled for total authority: the Tai Ping princess and the future Emperor Xuanzong. Immediately following the Emperor Zhongzong's death in 710, Xuanzong took the throne but the Tai Ping princess forced him to abdicate to his father, Ruizong, and accept the role of crown prince. During this time the Tai Ping princess continuously tried to assume control of the throne; to rid herself of the crown prince, she accused him of treachery. Her plot failed, and Ruizong abdicated to his son. Still hopeful of ruling, Princess Tai instigated an armed coup, but she was killed by supporters of the throne.

Ruizong had little time or power to enact many changes. To help resolve the financial problems left by his predecessors, he reduced the number of officials and those admitted to office through the exam system.[1] Immediately after gaining the throne, he issued an edict to reduce Buddhism to a secondary status, making it a co-religion with Taoism.[2] There were two apparent reasons for this action. The first was to restore Taoism, the dynastic religion of the Tang, after its eclipse during Empress Wu's reign. Secondly, a great deal of rancor was caused by the enormous wealth of the Buddhist church in this time of financial distress. Ministers wrote memorials to the throne criticizing Buddhist illegal land holdings and those who sought sanctuary in the church to avoid corvee and the burden of taxation. Measures were taken to examine the legitimacy of Buddhist establishments. Within the short reign of Ruizong, not much was accomplished; the task was left to his son and successor, Emperor Xuanzong.

ARCHAEOLOGY

One tomb dated to this short reign is that of Madame Xue, a magistrate's daughter who died in 710. The murals comprise a variety of figural types in different postures. One slim maiden has her hands wrapped in the folds of a scarf at her chest. Her head is turned sharply to the right; this tilting of the head adds an air of liveliness and enhances the gestural expression. Her hair, drawn into an elaborate knot at each side of her head, frames her face, with its thick brows and highly colored cheeks. Other, less youthful ladies wear similar garments, but have more modest hair styles. Some of the female figures are dressed as Central Asian men. There are contrasts among the figures' facial features; there is real individuality in the drawing of the eyes and nose, but the mouth is treated as a more generalized form, with small pursed lips.[3]

A second tomb belonging to Li Yu, dated 710, discovered in Shaanxi in 1980, has several high-quality ceramics treated with the three-color glaze method.[4] Although this tomb's contents are meager, it yielded a remarkable figurine of a seated young lady holding a duck. The face, neck, and hands of the figure are not glazed, but the mottled three-glaze style is applied to her garment and the duck she holds in her lap. A large, bulbous, blue-glazed pot with lid was also found here. Blue-glazed vessels are somewhat of a rarity, due to the scarcity and high cost of the blue color agent, cobalt, which was imported from Persia.

RUIZONG'S TOMB

Ruizong's tomb, which dates to 716, is laid out exactly like that of his predecessors: The shendao has two stone columns, a pair of winged horses, paired ostriches, five pairs of saddled horses with grooms, and ten pairs of officials.[5] Much of the sculpture has been preserved, including all four stone lions inside the gates; the columns, steeds, and winged horses also remain, but nearly all nine pairs of officials are damaged. Typical of the early stage of stone carving, these sculptures lack any true sense of three-dimensionality and have only random areas of naturalistically observed details. Two sets of paired lions differ slightly in posture; two turn their heads, the others look out in front of them.[6] Here the sculptors had enough confidence in their medium to cut away the area between the legs. But the large, tense bodily forms are treated abstractly; articulation of the parts is only occasionally detailed. In contrast, great attention is paid to the head: Linear patterning delineates the mane and hair; the teeth and fangs are visible in the snarling, open mouth; the eyes bulge out from somewhat distorted, fleshy eyelids; and the ears lie flat against the head. The four extant horses differ only in the treatment of the horse blanket, whether it is underneath or covering the saddle, and the ornaments of the bridal. The horse sculptures are also freed from the stone support between the legs, yet, here too, the animals are stocky with thick, poorly shaped legs and a small head. Engraved lines carved in delicate linear patterns indicate the manicured mane. A similar carving style is evident in the chimera, but the supporting stone between the legs was not removed. As in Gaozong's and Zhongzong's tomb path, there are similar relief sculptures of ostriches.[7] The artist's attempt at naturalism here is quite successful; the curious pose of the bird is well rendered--turning its head, it preens its feathers, which are carefully carved wavy lines. Moreover, the ostrich is placed in a natural setting; now it stands on a hilly landscape made up of irregularly shaped rocks. (FIGURE 34)

NOTES

1. Guisso, 1979: 327.
2. Weinstein, 1987: 49.
3. *Tang Mu Pi Hua Jijin*, 1988: 135-142. Discovered in 1953 in Zhangjiawan, Xianyang city, the tomb consists of a passage, air shaft, tunnel, and coffin chamber. The paintings in the rear chamber have fallen off the wall, but those in the front room are preserved. One of the attendants holds a hound, another a parrot. There are also a weapon stand and attendant officials.
4. Changzhishi Bowuguan, "Changzhishi Xijiao Tangdai Lidu, Songjiajin mu," *Wenwu*, 1989.6: 44-50. Unfortunately the reproduction of the pot is not in color.
5. The Qiaoling, Ruizong's tomb, is located on Mt. Jinzhi, 15 km. northwest of Pucheng county. Over 50 pieces are intact.
6. The lions measure roughly 270 cm. high and 120 cm. broad.
7. The bird measures 196 cm. tall.

PART TWO

MIDDLE TANG (712-805)

Although this era began with the most glorious of all reigns, by its end signs of an unstable imperial government, a weakness that was to characterize the later Tang, were already in evidence. During the middle of the eighth century, An Lu-shan's barbarian troops invaded and looted the capital, and forced the emperor to flee, thus threatening central authority with complete annihilation. However, this threat was relatively short-lived, and the last quarter of the eighth century saw the restoration of Tang imperial power.

Depictions of women were quite common by the middle Tang era. The prevalence of the female image was no doubt related to the role of women in society: For the first and nearly only time in China's history, women were important in politics. In the early Tang, not only had Empress Wu ruled in her own name for over 15 years, her daughter Empress Wei and the Tai Ping princess were extremely influential. The eighth-century court of Xuanzong was dominated by the concubine Yang Gui-fei (736-755). A popular poem exalted the new desire to bear female offspring to ensure social advancement. These women, however, were vilified by post-Tang historians for their pernicious influence; subsequent historians promoted the thesis that the role of women in politics was deleterious.[1] Women were prevalent in all areas of Tang art. Tang literature was filled with love poems and odes that celebrated women, including lonely harem ladies.[2] The number of female figurines, which increased in the last decades of the early Tang era, continued to grow in the middle Tang. Similarly, women were portrayed in nearly all of the tomb murals; the court lady became an independent theme. Such masters as Zhang

Xuan and his successor Zhou Fang were renowned for their portrayals of aristocratic ladies. In Buddhist art as well, the pervasive influence of women was seen in the growing feminization of deities, like Guanyin, whose male identity was lost; the divinity took the form of an androgynous creature who became increasingly feminine. Several regional female cults focused on incarnations of Guanyin.[3] Personifications of the rainbow, of water (in particular of rivers), and of the moon were also celebrated as feminine in contemporary myths and legends,[4] some of which were the subject of short stories.[5] The physical image of women in the middle Tang revealed a changing ideal of beauty: At the inception of the era, figures were corpulent and coquettish; then their size grew further, but at the end of the era figures assumed more slender proportions. It should be noted that corpulence is observable in much of middle Tang art, notably in the shendao sculptures of officials, Buddhist figures of heavenly Guardian Kings, and ceramic tomb figurines of guardians.

Stylistically the period began with a high point in naturalistic representation, observable in all forms of art. Whereas the earlier realism at the end of the seventh century led to the contrasting of individual characters within groups of court ladies, officials, or guardians, mid-Tang artists favored more varied depiction--old men, dwarfs, figures carrying a heavy load, and horrific supernatural creatures of intense ferocity. There was also a distinct infusion of narrative content in both the murals and in the ceramics. No longer content to capture merely a physical resemblance, artists suggested a story through the depictions of the figures' manner, movements, expression, and by the inclusion of a setting.

An innovative compositional format was introduced in middle Tang tombs: The tomb wall was divided into tall, rectangular units with painted borders that resembled the panels of a folding screen. Each panel featured an aspect a subject--animals in a garden, ladies in a garden, or scholars at leisure. That this format was a popular furnishing in palatial apartments is evident in several contemporary examples preserved in Japan's imperial repository, the Shosoin.

In ceramics, the tricolor glaze was brought to technical perfection. Experimentation with several modes of applying the colored glaze yielded the maximum polychromatic effects. But by the mid-eighth century, triglaze production was abandoned and figurines once again were hand-painted after firing. However, technical experimentation continued and improvements in glazing were achieved in utilitarian ware; in particular, white porcelain was perfected for the production of bowls, cups, boxes, and small dishes.

The abundance of gold and silver objects from the middle Tang demonstrates the growing acceptance of these precious materials. A variety of functional forms evolved: cups, vases, bowls, plates, medicine bowls, hairpins, and jewelry were created out of an expanding vocabulary of complicated and refined forms with a variety of decorative themes, some of which had narrative content. Although the ancestry of the production of gold and silver was undeniably Western, this stage in its development was characterized by a purely Chinese approach to manufacturing techniques and decor.

Esoteric Buddhism, with its gorgeous magical mandalas, magnificent ritual objects, and Tantric sculptures that attested to the superb artistry of Buddhist art at this time proliferated among the courtly classes. New iconographic forms reflected contemporary religious trends in India. Increasingly, independent icons prevailed, most especially those of Guanyin, who appeared in a new guise related to the esoteric teachings--the image was cast as six-armed, eleven-headed, or one thousand-armed. Deities expressing the Tantric concept of the universe, which encompassed all aspects of life, both good and evil, were drawn in awesome guises: Some displayed multiple heads and arms; others, seated in fiery grottoes, had flaming hair, fangs, angry grimaces, and weapons. The Guardian Kings (Tianwang) became extremely important.

Several of the older schools of Buddhism had continued support. The cult of Amitofu enjoyed widespread popularity. At Dunhuang, the theme was expanded to include representations of the four paradises of the Directional Buddhas that were painted on the walls of the cave-chapels. Portrayed holding a medicine bowl, the Buddha of Healing and of the East was added to the pantheon. After the An Lu-shan rebellion, both Chan Buddhism and the cult of Wenshu became prominent. One remarkable development in Buddhism at this time was the continuation and growth of popular sponsorship. Several large-scale projects were undertaken by public conscription under the leadership of a local, eminent monk. Formerly, projects of such grandeur were inaugurated under imperial patronage.

By the end of the middle period, the naturalism that epitomized the art of the opening decades of the eighth century gave way to a concern for the portrayal of details in all their complexity. First, these particularities were treated in an extremely realistic manner; their prominence detracted from the images themselves, which seem at times to be lost in a plethora of drapery and scarves. Second, in the articulation of the physiognomy, there was an observable hardening of the features; figures appear mannered and overly refined. This effect was in part due to the esoteric Buddhist aesthetic, for a similar development was seen in Japan where, by these artistic means, the familiar Buddhist icons were reimbued with power and mystery in the early Heian period. But manneristic hardening of forms is also understandable as stylistic change; new creative ideals emerged that were the inevitable consequence of the earlier eighth-century perfection of naturalism.[6] In Buddhist paintings, especially at Dunhuang, fresh compositional values were evident. There was a diminution of three-dimensional space and form in favor of a pictorial unity that was achieved through color harmony and a greater concern for the manner in which the paint was applied. This refinement of style was also at the expense of naturalism.

NOTES

1. See Fan-pen Chen, "Problems of Chinese Histography as Seen in the Official Records of Yang Kuei-Fei," *Tang Studies*, 1990-91, vols. 8-9: 83-96, for a study of the writing of her history.

2. Hans Frankel, *The Flowering Plum and the Palace Lady: Interpretations of Chinese Poetry* (New London, 1976), has two chapters dedicated to these major themes in Tang poetry. Li Bo's work is from the middle Tang. The trend continues with poets of the late Tang, like Li Ho and Li Shang-yin; women are the most frequent subject of their work.

3. Yu Chun-fang, "Feminine Images of Kuan-yin," *Journal of Chinese Religions*, 1990, no. 18: 62.

4. Edward Schafer, *The Divine Woman* (San Francisco, 1980), discussed the development of these divine manifestations of women in the Tang. (See p. 55ff.)

5. One such short story is "The Dragon King's Daughter," by Li Zhao-wei, ca. 800, in Yang Xian-yi and Gladys Yang, *The Dragon King's Daughter, Ten Tang Stories* (Beijing, 1954):16 ff.

6. A similar aesthetic development was observed in the aftermath of the Italian Renaissance. (See John Sherman, *Mannerism* [Great Britain, 1967].) The introduction offers a broad definition of mannerism (p. 18): In the sixteenth century "it was understood that *maniera*, whether in people or in works of art, entailed refinement of and abstraction from nature. . . ."

CHAPTER VI

EMPEROR XUANZONG

Ming Huang, also known as Emperor Xuanzong (r. 712-756), ruled over a period of time when some of the most extraordinary achievements in the fields of art and literature were realized. This era was later regarded as the apogee of lyrical verse and the poetry of social conscience. In the visual arts the heights of portraiture were realized, and polychrome glaze technique and porcelain manufacture were perfected. Among the remarkable inventions of the era was the mechanical clock created by a Buddhist master.[1] However, it was also a time when the Tang, having reached an apex of brilliance, fell into a sorry state. The Tang experienced its first low point after a series of political humiliations and military defeats at the hands of the subjugated forces the dynasty had for so long held in check. In 755, the capital was invaded by hostile troops and the emperor was forced to flee the court. Historians often describe Xuanzong as a model Confucian emperor during the first half of his rule, deeply concerned with affairs of state. But, in the middle of his reign, an era of relative calm, Xuanzong, having lost interest in political concerns, devoted his time to his harem and the study of the esoteric doctrines of mystical Buddhism and Taoism. His preoccupation with personal matters is often cited as the cause of the chaos that destroyed his reign and nearly ended the Tang dynasty.

When Xuanzong took the throne many severe problems existed that he resolved by administrative reform and military stratagem. The first decade of the eighth century had been marked by a catastrophic succession of events that threatened the empire's stability; this turmoil was the legacy of Empress Wu. The excellent reputation of the emperor was secured by the measures he undertook to reduce the

burdens on the state because of the prodigious donations to the
Buddhist church as well as the costs of maintaining a court, a standing
army, and the growing bureaucracy. He decreased the revenues of the
princes, reevaluated land distribution, and modified the taxation
system by stiffening penalties for infractions of the law.[2] In 714,
sumptuary laws were enacted that restricted the manufacture and use
of luxurious articles, and the emperor began to limit the number of
women in the harem.[3] Efforts were made to elevate the qualifications
of the candidates for civil service. It was the emperor's desire to
reestablish the capital at Chang-an, which he did, but frequent
difficulties in keeping the city supplied demanded the transfer of the
court to Luoyang. To remedy this, in 730 he ordered Pei Yao-qing,
vice-president of the Board of Finance, to study the problems of the
transportation of grain. The subsequent reforms resulted not only in
facilitating the transport of sufficient food supplies but in great
commercial success. By appointing special commissions to find
solutions to specific issues, Xuanzong inaugurated an efficient
problem-solving policy. Revision of the administrative legal code was
accomplished in 737.

However, not all of Xuanzong's measures met with success; some
had disastrous effects. Three major problems threatened the unity of
the Tang domain: the strength of the landed gentry, the independence
of the provincial areas, and the power of the eunuchs. The struggle
between the newly expanded civil bureaucracy and landed aristocracy
was eventually won by the latter, with a resultant decentralization of
power. Increasingly, dominion was assumed by large families, who
grew in wealth and independence.   Similarly, the allegiance of
northern border states, where the standing armies were maintained,
was strained. In these areas the troops were predominantly comprised
of minority peoples, particularly of the nomadic tribes of the steppes,
who were well-suited to the hardships of military life; many
vanquished Turks became valued generals in the Tang army.[4] The
decline in the number of Chinese soldiers is sometimes explained as
an indigenous distaste for career soldiering; but Arthur Waley has
suggested that a military career was economically disadvantageous.[5]
By 747, control over the heterogeneous population of the border
regions was given to local military governors, even though they were
not of Han--that is, Chinese--descent. When these military dominions
achieved near autonomy, loyalty to the central government was
undermined. In addition, the growth in the number and influence of
the eunuchs, which came about because of the unduly large number of
women in the harem (the sad fate of the lonely, ignored ladies was a

common theme in contemporary literature), led to an expansion of their power. Taking on responsibilities beyond the traditional management of the harem, the inner court, and overseeing of the supply of imperial provisions, eunuchs (such as Gao Li-shi) became eminent advisers to the throne. They functioned as unofficial political envoys, gained control over the emperor's personal treasury, and even exerted military authority.[6]

In the early part of Xuanzong's reign successful military campaigns brought prosperity. The Turks of Mongolia and Xinjiang were brought into submission by 727, and the Tibetans were subdued in 733. But the Khitan became a menace in 734. In addition, the Arabs threatened China's immediate neighbors, and the kingdoms of Central Asia requested help from China. One general in particular, An Lu-shan, was successful in these various military campaigns. His power steadily grew and by 733, An was a Military Governor; his ongoing battlefield triumphs made him increasingly valuable to the throne, so that by 750 he was, in an unprecedented manner, made a prince. His rise in court was sponsored by two benefactors. One was the aristocratic president of the Board of War, whose idea it was to employ non-Chinese as military governors in the frontier states; the other benefactor was the imperial favorite, the concubine Yang Gui-fei. A concubine of Xuanzong's son, once favored by the emperor, she was gradually promoted through the ranks of the harem to the highest status.[7] Her support of An led to an extraordinary event in 751--the ritual adoption of the general by the emperor; in a ceremony the obese and uncouth barbarian general was dressed as an infant and presented to the imperial parents, Xuanzong and Concubine Yang. When Yang Gui-fei's cousin ascended to the positions of President of the Board of War and of Chief Minister, relations between the central administration and An Lu-shan became acrimonious. Finally, An led an armed rebellion in 755: His frontier troops (with the allegiance of the province of Hebei) marched into Luoyang, captured the city, and inaugurated a new dynasty of which he was the first emperor.[8] In 756, he took the capital of Chang-an, causing the emperor and his consort to flee. On their way to Sichuan the imperial guards killed Prime Minister Yang Guo-chu, demanded that Yang Gui-fei be surrendered, and summarily strangled her. The emperor's son, the heir apparent, went to the northwest to organize resistance to the rebels and proclaimed himself emperor in his father's absence, ascending the throne as Suzong.[9]

Xuanzong's devotion to mysticism at the end of his life has often been cited as the cause of his downfall. But his devotion was not only the selfish practice of alchemical Taoism: He elevated the religion to the level of a state institution and successfully established the supremacy of the Taoist church. Taoist scholarship became a subject in the state civil exams; Xuanzong even wrote a commentary to the *Taotejing*. In 740, Taoist temples were established in all districts of Chang-an, and Taoist icons were installed. Taoist steles, like the one dated 740 now in the Shanghai Museum, most often present a trinity that closely resembles the Buddhist icons. The central deity is haloed and seated on a lotus base; specific differences are the bearded face of the central figure and the garments, although the drapery is treated much the same. (FIGURE 35) Other Taoist images, one in particular, dated 719, have been studied for their relationship to Buddhist icons.[10] In some cases the Taoist icon was accompanied by images of Xuanzong and his son and grandson.[11] It seems clear that the evolution of Buddhist images was of central importance both in the stimulus to create and the proliferation of Taoist icons.[12] Cave-chapels were excavated in the same manner as Buddhist ones. Several dated examples are in Sichuan, with outstanding examples at Renshou Niujiaozhai and Anyue Xuanmiaoguan.[13] (FIGURE 36) In 741, the temple at Laozu's birthplace was enlarged to mammoth proportions; and, setting a new precedent, Xuanzong himself repeatedly presided over the offerings. In 743, two great palaces were erected to the Taoist thearch in Chang-an and Luoyang.[14] Recent scholars view Xuanzong's actions as an attempt to create a stable and long-lasting cult in a time of political uncertainty. Thus he promulgated the celebration of his birthday, the Festival of a Thousand Autumns, as a national holiday and in 744 installed images of himself (as one of a trinity with Buddhist and Taoist icons) in the national temples.[15] His attempt to achieve immortality through a search for the magical elixir was not unrelated to these activities. It seems apparent that these efforts were directed toward the unification of the country. By merging Taoist cult worship and the cult of the emperor, Xuanzang followed the earlier example of rulers who, espousing Buddhism, modeled themselves as universal sovereigns in the image of Asoka.

COURT ARTS

At the beginning of his reign Xuanzong was heralded as a model emperor. Establishing the Hanlin Academy for poets and scholars was an important act in his career as patron of the arts. In 738, a small academy in the Hanlin was established for business matters. It became one of the most prestigious institutions for scholar-officials in future dynasties. Among the renowned poets who lived during Xuanzong's reign were Li Bo, Du Fu, Meng Hao-ran, and Wang Wei. Their topics were wide-ranging, from Li Bo's (d. 762) celebration of friendship, drinking, and the exotic life in the capital to the social criticism and heartfelt warmth of Du Fu (d. 770), to the meditative poems of Wang Wei (d. 761), and to the majestic beauty of landscape sung by Meng Hao-ran (d. 740).[16] Xuanzong was a refined aesthete, taking pleasure in all forms of the arts: He was a poet, calligrapher, and accomplished musician (he himself played in the court's Pear Garden Orchestra), and his love of music led to the creation of a music school. Lastly, some of the most celebrated painters, including horse, landscape, and figure specialists, were active at his court.

Like Taizong, Xuanzong was an admirer of the noble breeds brought from the West as tribute. His love of horses is reflected in the excellent equine paintings commissioned by the court. There were several such artists who specialized in horses. Among them were Wei Wu-tian, Chen Hong, and Han Gan.[17] Zhu Qing-xuan related:

> When the K'ai Yuan period brought peace to the world, blooded horses were sent hither in relays from foreign lands, though they crossed such wide stretches of desert that their hooves wore thin. Ming Huang used to select the best of these and have them portrayed along with his Chinese coursers. From then on the imperial stables possessed mounts of the "Flying Yellow," "Night-lighting," "Drifting Cloud," and "Five Blossom" types. They had unusual coats and their whole appearance was remarkable; their sinews and bones were rounded, and their hooves thick. . . . First they were depicted by Ch'en Hung and then by Han Kan.[18]

The rivalry among the horse painters is revealed in the following anecdote. Ordered by the emperor to study the work of Chen Hong, a favorite equine artist, Han Kan, a native of Chang-an who died around 781, responded:

> His majesty's servant has taken his own models, all the horses in His majesty's stables.[19]

In view of the overriding aesthetic of naturalistic portraiture during this era, this comment is particularly telling. Traditionally, artists copied masters' works for instruction and inspiration, and, in this context, Han's copying from nature is a radical departure. Horse painters were celebrated by Tang poets, whose poems recorded the experience of seeing the works; in this way, the poets have assured the longevity of the artists' reputation.[20] One work, assigned to Han Gan, an ink painting now in the Metropolitan Museum of Art,[21] captures the spirit and nobility of the breed in the facial expression and the posture; the mount struggles valiantly against being tethered.[22] Damage and repainting have confused what might have once been a more convincing anatomical rendering of the breast; also, the tail is missing.

The "blue-green" style of landscape flourished during this period. The artists Li Si-xun and his son Li Zhao-Tao are credited with being the "most excellent" practitioners of this highly decorative technique, which is distinguished by the use of brilliant colors that were additionally adorned with gold. Cousins of the imperial family, the Lis were well-placed in the government and received imperial commissions.[23] The Tang art historian, Zhu Qing-xuan, ranked them high in his hierarchy of artists in the "Inspired" category. According to him, the Lis' landscapes were

. . . supremely excellent. Birds and beasts, or plants and trees, he always characterized perfectly.[24]

The same source records:

(They were) . . . ordered to paint some screens in the Ta t'ung hall by Ming Huang in the 742-55 era. He congratulated the elder Li saying: "From the screen you painted, sir, I have heard the sound of water coming at night. Yours is a mastery that partakes of the divine, and your landscapes take first place in the dynasty.[25]

Unfortunately, nothing remains of their art, though many art historians have sought evidence of their work in other media, including maps and such decorative objects as musical instruments, silver vessels, and mirrors with landscape designs housed in the Shosoin Imperial Repository in Japan. This storehouse contains treasures that were dedicated to the Great Eastern Temple, Todaiji, at its opening in 756, ritual objects owned by the temple as well as the possessions of Japanese Emperor Shomu (r. 724-749). Many of the pieces are believed to be of Chinese manufacture or Korean or Japanese copies of Tang objects.[26] After the Emperor Shomu's death, the repository was closed, allowing all objects to be securely dated. Before the rich Chinese archaeological finds of the last decades, the treasures of the Shosoin were one of the few documented sources of Tang art. Recently excavated tomb objects--like the three-color glazed ceramic landscape sculpture of rocks and trees--also attest to the widespread popularity of the depiction of natural forms in the middle Tang.[27]

The best documented examples of Tang landscape are the murals that decorate imperial tombs, like that of Li Zhong-ren, dated 706. (FIGURE 30) Here the antiquated iron-wire line has given way to a more cursive brush whose contours change in width so as to suggest three-dimensionality more convincingly. Light tones of brown enhance the rocky appearance of the land forms and suggest solidity through modeling. Unlike Western-style modeling in light and shade, there is no uniform light source; the application of light and dark color tones only suggests random highlights and shadows. Other examples of Tang landscape may be found in details from the Buddhist murals at the site of Dunhuang in Gansu. In Cave 209 or Cave 321, for example, highly colored landscape passages are used as a background for narrative scenes; accordingly, the figures are still large in relation to the landscape elements. Although the demands of continuous narrative require independent episodes, the artist has set the events in a unified mountainous landscape, distributing the different scenes in distinct spatial areas. Since the Han dynasty (206 B.C.E to 220 C.E.), landscape provided a setting for figural action, but the landscape vocabulary of trees, grass, rolling hills, and decorative garden rocks did not convey a developed sense of foreground, mid-ground, and background or deep recession. In the Six Dynasties, space cells comprised of landscape elements (hill, trees, and rocks), arranged as a stage for figural activity, were loosely linked across the picture plane like pearls on a necklace. One example of this is found at Dunhuang, in the narrative *Ruru Jataka*, painted on the walls of Cave 428. One of the Tang achievements was to create a unified pictorial composition by adapting the archaic format, forging groups of space cells together into a realm of dramatic illusion. Moreover, for the first time, landscapes appear to be independent of figural activity, although figures in a landscape continue to be portrayed. Conversely, Tang monumental figure paintings are often devoid of elaborate landscape settings and utilize only a minimal number of props.

Two landscape techniques are identifiable at Dunhuang, both employing the blue-green palette: The first, seen in Cave 209, like the tomb mural, uses a fluid brush to create the contours for the landscape forms; variety in the width of the outline and interior drawing suggest three-dimensionality. (FIGURE 37) Color is applied decoratively. The second style, employed in Cave 321 (FIGURE 38), manipulates broad washes of brilliant blue-green and earth colors; outlines are entirely absent. Highlights and shadows are created with darker and lighter tones of these hues. At Dunhuang, there are even rare cases of isolated passages of landscape that appear to be free of figural activity, they were probably meant as space filler, as in the well-published Cave 217, painted in this second style. These examples are evidence of the growing autonomy of landscape as a pictorial subject, an independence the theme had long enjoyed in literature.[28]

One of the most famous painters active in Xuanzong's court was the artist Wu Dao-zu (Wu Tao-hsuan), who worked approximately from 710-796. Wu was celebrated in the art historical texts as the greatest genius of the brush,[29] especially in the field of landscape painting. Zhang Yan-yuan described his accomplishments:

> But as for Wu Tao-hsuan, he was endowed by Heaven with a vigorous brush (stroke), . . . and would occasionally paint (frescoes) on the walls of Buddhist temples, employing according to his fancy strange rocks that (looked as though) one might touch them, and rushing torrents from which (it seemed) one might dip (water). And furthermore while on the road to Shu (Sze ch'uan) he drew the landscape (along it) from nature, and as a result of this the development of landscape (painting) began with Wu. . .[30]

Zhu Qing-xuan adds that it was Xuanzong who required the sketch of the scenery of the Jialing River on the road to Sichuan. After apparently no preparatory work, Wu decorated Datong Hall with a "panorama of 300 li in a single day," which greatly pleased the emperor.[31] Unfortunately, nothing is left of Wu's art. Efforts have been made to examine extant art for traces of his mastery, but these works are of disappointing quality and are not only uninformative but misleading. Wu is remembered as a great painter of Buddhist, Taoist, and landscape themes, and one can only rue the awesome ravages of time that have left only a name and vivid anecdotes.

Wang Wei is probably the most famous Tang landscape painter, though once again nothing is securely attributed to his hand. Because of his many achievements in addition to his painting skills, his fame increased with each succeeding century. Contemporary art critics ranked his painting considerably below that of Wu and the Li family.[32] But as a high-ranking official--Junior Councillor to the Department of State--and as a major poet, Wu was the ideal master of the Three Jewels--poetry, calligraphy, and painting. One of the compositions that influenced later artists and is recorded in the art historical accounts is his painting of his villa and its surrounding landscape:

> He did a panorama of Wang Ch'uan, in which mountains and valleys, close crowded, turned this way and that, while clouds and water streamed by. His conceptions left the dusty, everyday world behind and marvels grew from his brush tip.[33]

It is only in the case of the eighth-century artist Wang Wei that accounts of the role of the artist seem elevated; however, this is misleading, as Wang was first and foremost a poet and high-level official who practiced landscape painting as a leisure activity. His importance grew with succeeding generations which saw in him the paradigm: official, scholar, poet, and painter.

Equally difficult to assess is the art of Zhang Xuan, active around the Kaiyuan era (713-742), who was one of the figure painters continuing in the tradition of the Yen brothers. One problematic work associated with him is a painting believed to be a copy of his *Palace Ladies Making Silk* by the Song emperor Huizong; it is now in the Boston Museum of Fine Arts.[34] Showing the palace ladies engaged in the laborious activities of making silk is analogous to Marie Antoinette and her attendants performing the menial chore of milking cows. Court ladies, dressed in their elegant finery, attend to such humble tasks as pounding silk threads or ironing the woven silk with a charcoal brazier. One subtext of the painting, however, may be found in the traditional Han poems that celebrate spring's arrival and its concomitant activities, which would include the sensuous, lightly dressed young peasant girls at work rhythmically pounding the silk, their sleeves rolled up, beads of sweat glistening on their temples. Analyzing this copy of the master yields little certain information of the artist's style. The most that can be said is that it preserves the formal composition of the monumental figure style: The women occupy the entire area of the composition, their substantial girth swathed in luxurious garments; their hair bejeweled with adornments, fastidiously piled on their heads.

ARCHAEOLOGY

Despite the lack of works by Tang masters, several tombs dated in the reign of Xuanzong provide concrete examples of the contemporary style of figure painting. Exhibiting a range of figure types, portrayals are not limited to the portly beauties frequently associated with the period. In addition to the distinctions between race, station, age, and character, there is a very earnest attempt to show people engaged in various daily activities, with appropriate expressions and gestures. The fragment consisting of a woman's head, a mural remnant from the tomb of Xue Mo, dated 728, conforms to the widely noted fashions of the day.[35] The large, corpulent face does not have delicate features: Thick brows top a pronounced nose and pursed lips. She wears a tall, crown-shape cloth hat. For the most part a rather portly beauty dominates, as seen in a fragment of a painting found in Astana, Turpan, dated to the Tianbao era (742-756). This court lady plays a board game: Head bent in concentration, she, bejeweled with adornments, moves the pieces with her left hand. (FIGURE 39) Her garments mirror the height of fashion: Brilliant hues of orange and green render the intricate brocade patterns that comprise her gown, jacket, and transparent shawl.[36] Her face, with bright cherry cheeks, has a decorative tattoo between the eyes; her voluminous tresses, piled on top of her head, are held in place by delicate hairpins. Among the murals of this era, there is also an interest in rendering unattractive characters, not just those of ideal beauty. One fragment, a sketchlike portrait of a middle-aged male servant, is a telling vision of age: A low, cloth cap is tied on his head, his brow is furrowed, and there are deep wrinkles around his mouth.[37] (FIGURE 40) These renderings may be attributed to Western influences, perhaps transmitted through Buddhist art from the West or through the works of the highly regarded Western artist, Wei Chi Yi Seng, active in Empress Wu's court. Numerous male portraits, like those of the Huren entertainers are found in the tomb of Su Si-xu, dated 745.[38] Accompanied by a nine-piece band and two singers, the dancing central figure widely spreads his long-sleeved arms. (FIGURE 41) Exaggerated features, such as the hook nose, not a Chinese characteristic, are rendered with a sketchy brush; the figure sports foreign garb--cloth cap, tunic, trousers, and red boots. Similarly clad, the singers call out, their faces expressive of the lively mood of the tune, their arms reaching out in emphasis. Another mural from this tomb is an attempt to represent the strenuous effort of two men carrying a trunk; the depiction is marred, as are several others of this tomb's murals, by poor draftsmanship.[39]

A standard Tang painting format--a series of panels, each with a single tree and figure--makes its appearance in Su's tomb. This example features gentlemen, probably hermits: Some are seated, while others stand with their hands folded in their voluminous garments or gesticulate as if in conversation. The trees, for the most part, are repetitive, sketchily drawn, leafless forms.[40] A far better example of this format was found in Astana, Turpan, in Xinjiang Province, dated 715.[41] Three of eight segments of a screen with horses and grooms were discovered. Only one is fully intact; the others are but fragments. (FIGURE 42) True to this era, the drawings of the grooms and horses are not only naturalistically rendered but appear to be individualized portraits. The background is done in the vivid blue-green style. There are midground trees and in the foreground are scattered grasses and plants. In another such mural there is an interesting variation; among tall weeds and rocks aquatic birds are drawn in delicate colors.[42] This compositional format of a series of panels with figures beneath trees, is also observable on contemporary Japanese screens.[43] Little need be said about the tomb mural portrait of an official (possibly the tomb occupant, Gao Yuan-gui), holder of a high-ranking post in court who died in 756.[44] Frontally seated on a high-backed chair and looking out, the official has a meditative expression. But what is noteworthy in this tomb is the delicately drawn Dragon of the East, in flight among a multitude of cloud swirls. Lightly applied lines convincingly convey the contrasting textures of the beast--snake body with scales, feather, and fur--and suggests the mastery of the drawing of supernatural images by Wu Dao-zu. Although this dragon belongs to a set of the spirit creatures of the Four Directions, it recalls the stories told of Feng Shao-zheng, the great expert at bird and dragon pictures whom Xuanzong summoned (from 712 to 742) to draw dragons on the walls of the new hall raised near Dragon Lake.

> Shao Cheng began by drawing his dragons in outline, giving them an undulating look as if they were on the verge of launching themselves upward. . . . the Supreme Lord and his courtiers . . . watched as the scales all grew wet. . . .[45]

Before completion of the painting, a storm cloud arose. The dragon materialized and dove into the lake.

CERAMICS

The many high-quality ceramic figurines datable to this reign are informative as to the high level of portraiture. By this time the overproduction of Tang figurines was such that there were imperial orders to constrain consumption. Sumptuary laws of 742 sought to limit both the size and the number of figures for the various official ranks.[46] One of the highlights of this era is the perfection of the three-color glaze technique, which had its first stage in the opening decades of the eighth century. The style spread through the empire, with important kilns in Chang-an, Luoyang, Gongxian, at other sites in Henan, and in provincial locations in Yangzhou.[47] Both the number and variety of ceramics found in recently excavated tombs are extraordinary. In general, a large increase is seen in the production of female figurines. Some are even equestrian figures dressed as foreign males.[48] A tomb in Zhongbao, Xian, dated by the presence of coins of the Kaiyuan era (713-742), yielded over 70 objects, a large percentage of which were female representations.[49] These corpulent women are fashionably dressed in high-waisted gowns, with a scarf drawn over the left shoulder.[50] Only their garments are treated with the three-color glazes. (FIGURE 43) That there was experimentation with glaze application techniques is evident in the diversity of effects--several kinds of splash patterns or mottling of the polychrome appears, often in contrast to other parts of the garment that are monochrome. Fleshy, columnar shapes that narrow at the base, the figures stand with their feet together, their skirts covering their shoes. Their heads support voluminous coiffures: The hair is brought forward in a large loop at the center of the forehead; at the sides, framing the face, the hair is draped like a thick cap.[51] Pear-shape, dimpled, and delicately featured, the faces have a distinctly fleshy appeal enhanced by the application of exotic makeup: Black dots accentuate either side of the mouth, and there is a red dot in the middle of the forehead. The heads are upturned in a variety of poses that accentuate the figures' individuality and express their mood.[52]

The emphatic naturalism characteristic of high Tang art is also seen in the ceramic figurines. For example, a dramatic figure of a Guardian King is shown in a posture of violent torsion. Twisting his upper body to the right, his hips swivel left; the right knee is bent and his right arm is raised in a fist. (FIGURE 44) The head is turned, bulging eyes glare fiercely, and the snarling, open mouth reveals fangs. By now, the ceramic artists' expertise in the application of polychrome glaze is evident. The various parts of the armor--monster-head sleeves, shoulder pads, breastplate, skirt, and shin guards--are each treated with a different glaze technique, including stripes, mottling, and dotting that contrast with monochrome areas. Energy pervades the piece: The belt strings stand up in a starched fashion; the skirt flares out behind the figure, and the spiked hair provides a corona for the tall bird perched on top of the guardian's head. The naked demon he tramples is no less fierce: The disfigured monster, with contorted features and curly red hair and beard, displays his large, naked torso, huge, swollen belly, and nipples dotted with blue glaze.

Figurines of animals reflect the high level of animal painting at court. One of the most splendid examples is a camel carrying six musicians on its back; the camel rears its head as if bellowing; even the tongue and teeth in the mouth are rendered. Roughly textured clay is used for the three-dimensional tufts of hair on its head, throat, and front legs. (FIGURE 45). The musicians are seated in decorous postures playing their instruments--horizontal and vertical pipes and a stringed lute. Standing at the center of the players is a figure performing the sleeve dance. A variety of gestures and expressions are articulated: The camel rears its head, the band gaily plays, and the dancer twirls. Parts of the group are treated with colored glaze: The camel is a light tan color, the garments of the musicians and the saddle blanket are rendered in tones of green and brown. But the faces of the figures show traces of hand-painting after firing. The theme of musicians on a camel or on an elephant is a familiar one in the Tang; it is a romantic evocation of the exotic concerts led by Central Asian entertainers. Several such themes are found on objects in the Shosoin collection, and most noteworthy are those that adorn musical instruments.[53]

Toward the later part of this reign, there are several noticeable changes in the figurines. First, nonglazed figurines replace the tricolor style. The reasons for abandoning the tricolor glaze are unknown. It has been speculated that the manufacture of tricolor glazed objects ended with the invasion of the capital by foreign forces in 755. Others have determined it was the extraordinary expense involved in their production, and one explanation attributes its demise to the poisonous character of the lead glaze. The second development is that the female figures are less naturalistically represented--they become ideal beauties rather than individual personalities. For example, the female figurines in the tomb of a military official, dated 748, have a more swollen form and an exaggerated stance: The belly projects forward in a pronounced way, then the shape of the figure curves downward, tapering at the feet.[54] (FIGURE 46) The garment is an untailored gown with sleeves of exaggerated width; the extremely long skirt extends beyond the shoes in poollike eddies. There is a distinct feeling of soft rolls of flesh beneath the gown. The hair is loosely drawn up in a topknot, leaving thick loops to frame the face. The topknot is precariously balanced to the side of the crown of the head; sometimes it is placed at the center of the head. The faces are pear-shape with delicate, hand-painted features--the face of one figurine differs little from another. A third development is the distinct presence of narrative content in the ceramic sculptures. One remarkable group of figurines from an undated tomb found in Hongqing village, Shaanxi, and ascribed to the Tang recreates the mood of the storyteller with his attendant musicians.[55] The small-size sculpture is of a seated musician. He claps his hands, turning his upper body to the right. His head is uplifted, his face bears an expression of interest in, if not communion with, the other players. The storyteller, seated on a stool, raises his arms in a conversational gesture; his head is uplifted as if he is speaking. (FIGURE 47) These are a natural complement to Su's mural of the male entertainers dated 745.

Continuous experimentation in and refinement of ceramic production resulted in a great variety of utilitarian vessels in this era.[56] Many are employed for the relatively new social custom of drinking tea. The tomb of a Taoist, dated 745, had several such pieces, among which were white porcellaneous wine cups and teacups.[57] The tomb also had a tall, handled ewer with a spout. Slightly wider in general and with a much larger neck and lip, this "hu" still recalls the silver wine jugs that proliferated in the early Tang.

GOLD AND SILVER

Gold and silver objects were extremely popular during Xuanzong's reign. The opulent group of silver and gold objects found in a hidden cache in Hejia village outside of Xian has been attributed to this reign in the belief that it was interred at the time the court fled An Lu-shan's invasion of the capital.[58] Recently the curators at Shaanxi Provincial Historical Museum have divided the material into two chronological groups, one from the beginning of the Tang to 684 and another from 684 to 755. The range of articles is great: There are three solid-gold bowls, 45 small silver bowls, 51 plain silver plates; of the 27 drinking vessels, five are gold, 12 silver, and five are jade. Fifty-one utensils were for the preparation of medicine. Clear evidence of foreign influence is established by both the presence of Persian coins and the use of Western technology and design in the production of the precious objects. In fact, the appearance of so many silver objects--plates, ewers, and small bowls--is relatively new to China; previously, silver articles were little appreciated. The technique of silverworking seems to have derived from the Sasanians; the new fashion was introduced into China at the end of the seventh or early eighth century. That Persian silversmiths lived in Chang-an is well known. Certain vessels, in particular faceted cups, lobed bowls, and lobed cups with flat handles, are of Western inspiration, though by this date much of the decoration is Chinese.[59] Among the most dramatic pieces from Hejia is the small, octagonal, footed, gilt silver wine cup with round handle. Each of its eight facets shows a vividly projecting musician against a background of granulation design with scattered landscape motifs, birds, and plants.[60] (FIGURE 48) This cup has been ascribed to the earlier period of manufacture, perhaps because of its clear reliance on Western prototypes. The punched-out decor of a gold pedestal bowl, made in the repousse technique imported from the West, is shaped into lotus petals that are engraved with ornamental deer, birds, and flowers. The extraordinary opulence of this piece is evident not only in the remarkably delicate engraving of the floral patterns and background design on the body of the bowl, but in the decoration of the bottom of the vessel as well, an area not usually visible. On the basis of the delicate floral background, this bowl has been attributed to the later period of production. Many silver objects show an admixture of decorative techniques; some vessels, like the covered silver jar, are inlaid with gold designs. Li Jin-guo's recently discovered tomb, datable to 738, has several exquisite silver boxes and bowls whose style is extremely similar to the Hejia village material. Two gold boxes with inlaid silver merit attention. Both the six-lobed box design and hinged clamshell box (FIGURE 49) have a delicate gold floral and bird design set against a ring pattern. A gilt bronze mirror from a tomb dated 738 and a silver mirror are also noteworthy for their high level of execution.[61]

Since the Zhou dynasty, bronze mirrors were cast for auspicious reasons; their decorative vocabulary comprised images with magical powers for the prolongation of life,[62] protection from evil, or rebirth in a Taoist paradise.[63] Most frequently, mirrors were associated with the performance of alchemy and Taoist ritual. The lore of the mirror and its usage related more to its magical properties than aboveground cosmetic function, although the famous Gu Kai-zhi painting in the British Museum attests to its use as a toiletry article, as do the poems of the late Tang poets Li He and Tu Mu.[64] Mirrors were also worn by officials, who hung them from their belts. The greatest variety in shape and decorative themes of mirrors was achieved at this time. Once restricted to square or round shapes, mirrors were now formed like radiating petals or were multilobed, resembling the gold and silver dishes. No longer made solely of bronze, they were now inlaid with silver, gold, or mother-of-pearl or covered with lacquer. Their designs are both decorative and symbolic. Among the popular motifs of this era are the emblems of time and space--the animals of the four directions who have spiritual and apotropaic powers, and the zodiac animals. Other mirrors have Taoist imagery, particularly the beings associated with the preparation of the elixir of immortality, such as the Xian, or winged immortals, deer, and hare pounding the mortar. Mirrors decorated solely with landscape motifs, mountains, and rivers, or with sages seated in a garden setting, are also found. (FIGURE 50) Although mirrors are rarely associated with Buddhism, one exception has an auspicious ancient Buddhist emblem of a reversed *swastika*, a symbol of universal directionality and timelessness, at its center. Few Tang mirrors are dated, so most attributions are based on style.[65] The symbolic content of other themes is less clear, for example, the lion and grapevine motif is surely of Persian derivation and may have some relation, ultimately, to the Greek cult of Dionysius.[66]

XUANZONG'S TOMB

Xuanzong's shendao was laid out in the typical manner, with the addition of eight standing figures.[67] Much of the sculpture is still in situ: Six of the eight lions placed at the four gates, one broken column, two flying horses, and two peacocks have survived, in addition to nine pairs of men, and 11 of the 16 horses. Two examples best demonstrate a remarkable stylistic change, an unprecedented degree of naturalism in the carving of large-scale sculptures. The marvelous quality of horse painting practiced at court is mirrored in the form of the winged flying horse. (FIGURE 51) Although the figure is still predominantly a squarish block of stone, and the area between the legs is once again retained for structural purposes (disguised as cloud swirls), the head is a portrait of a noble, gentle steed. The mane falls naturally. Unlike the earlier treatments, the wings are thick bands of feathers terminating in swirls. An even more dramatic change has taken place in the depiction of the officials. (FIGURE 52) The modeling of the facial features is truly subtle: A fleshy, pear-shape face has gentle, rounded cheeks; the bony structure supporting the thick flesh is indicated in areas like the brow. Deeply carved eyes are delicately rendered, with the skin of the eyelid stretched over the protruding eyeball. The slightly raised eyebrow and the faintly turned-down mouth convey a stern, discerning expression.

Like its counterparts in the tomb murals and figurines, this is a true portrait of an individual character.

BUDDHISM UNDER XUANZONG

Xuanzong's attraction to the Taoist arts made him amenable to the practice of esoteric Buddhism, which flourished during his reign. But problems with the Buddhist church persisted and he directed himself to the reform of its abuses of privilege, efforts that were initiated by his father. The extreme wealth of the Buddhist church and the growing number of clergy were a constant concern. To this end, several measures were enacted to bring the church under state control. Wealthy landowners were no longer allowed to build the Buddhist or Taoist monasteries on their estates that made them eligible for tax easements. Construction of new monasteries was prohibited and the repair of extant ones restricted. Now, the monastery alone was the focus of all religious activities: Making images and copying the sutras were only to be performed there; lay individuals could no longer assume such undertakings. Clergy were no longer free to proselytize in the villages; their activities were restricted to preaching in the monasteries. With local shrines and temples closed, their icons were redistributed among the major monasteries in the area. In 722, investigations into the holdings of the Buddhist and Taoist churches led to a reassessment of the amount of land each monk was entitled to own in perpetuity.[68] The second major area of reform concerned the clergy, especially the reported abuses in the practice of ordination. It was difficult to distinguish the true clergy from those who had bought their station through the purchase of ordination from local monasteries, government officials, and even members of the imperial family. Such monks were often not even instructed in the doctrine but merely acquired their ordination to avoid the duties and responsibilities of lay citizens. To allay this problem, in 729 a register of monks was ordered to be compiled triennially.

Although Xuanzong did not establish any new temples, he ordered that each prefecture and both capitals have two state-supported temples, one Buddhist and one Taoist, both bearing the reign title *Kaiyuan*. At these temples prayers for the well being of the emperor, for his longevity, and for the celebration of his birthday were offered. The emperor welcomed and sponsored several Buddhist masters who arrived from the West. Two famous monks of the esoteric school made a considerable impression; they introduced him to the mystical aspects of Buddhism by demonstrating their magical powers. The

Indian Tantric master Subhakarasimpha (637-735), who arrived in 716, and Vajrabodhi, who arrived in 719, both appeared to have the ability to make it rain. Vajrabodhi, honored as National Teacher, was a companion of the emperor; not only did he possess the magical powers of rainmaking but on one memorable occasion he cured the emperor's daughter. Xuanzong imperially supported efforts to translate the scriptures into Chinese: Vajrabodhi worked in tandem with Yi Jing, an eminent monk called to court in 717, who was equally versed in the Taoist arts.[69] The esoteric doctrine depended on secret sacred words, or mantras, magic formulas, prayers, images, and rituals to impart the difficult teaching. Art was of paramount importance in the explication of the doctrine. The esoteric sects, with their penchant for secrecy, utilization of opulent diagrams and ritual objects, and the building of temples in remote and beautiful hideaways, had a natural attraction for the aristocracy.

BUDDHIST ART

As in the Tang imperial style art of Xuanzong's court, naturalism is demonstrable in Buddhist works: The progress made in secular pictorial expression is reflected in religious art. In depicting Buddhist deities, there is an interest in realistically rendering posture, body parts (that are now revealed to an unprecedented degree), and decorative details. At the caves of Tianlongshan, notably Cave XXI, the seated Buddhas have lost the commanding and awesome appearance of Longmen; they sit comfortably on lotus seats.[70] Their anatomy, bared by the artful draping of their garments, is now clearly and well defined; the torso, breast, nipples, and the swelling flesh of the belly, including its navel, are all deftly delineated. Naturalism is also apparent in the gentle folds of the garments that cling, in Western fashion, to the forms beneath; the cloth even catches on the edges of the petals of the lotus base. Although the site has suffered much destruction in the last quarter of this century, the remaining works still express the new achievements in figural portrayal. For example, a Bodhisattva figure from Tianlongshan sits in a most extraordinary posture, one that breaks the central axis of the body and destroys the formality of the figure: The head is sharply inclined to one side; the shoulders are relaxed; the legs are casually bent in the posture of "royal ease," one leg pendant, the other bent at the knee. (FIGURE 53) The multiple scarves are simplified and manipulated to expose the protruding belly that is further accentuated by a tight belt, constricting the flesh just below the waist. Although this figure's face has not survived, others are aristocratic and have fine features that are also sensuous--high, arching brow, almond-shape eyes, and pursed, curvaceous lips. Inspired by Indian art made available by the flourishing traffic with the West, a new cosmopolitan ideal of beauty was formed; the result is that Bodhisattvas were cast as androgynous beauties, an ideal that was based, according to rumors, on local singing girls.[71]

Several developments in Buddhist art reflect the dynamic changes in Tang Buddhist thought. Increasingly independent images of Guanyin, the Bodhisattva of Compassion, appear. Freed from the traditional triad composition flanking Amitofu, Guanyin becomes a colossal icon of devotion in both sculptural and painted media. Singled out for particular attention by the leading Tang poets, Guanyin had a special appeal for the intelligentsia of the middle Tang era.[72] But this deity of compassion also won favor on a popular level as well: Several forms of Guanyin are forged with myths of local women.[73] It was during this era that esoteric forms of Guanyin appear; the multiheaded icon, in particular, proliferates. Several sculptures of this type were found at Chibaotai, the Terrace of Seven Treasures, at the Kuangzhai Temple in Chang-an. One stele, now in the Freer, has 11 heads. However, the figure appears in a much earlier style; the body is uncharacteristically stiff and in an archaic stance--standing firmly on two feet, the axis of the body is rigidly maintained. In typical middle Tang fashion, the face is fleshy, with mature facial features and rings of fat beneath the chin, and the swelling forms of the body are clearly articulated.[74] Like a crown, the ten extra heads of the deity are arranged in three diminishing tiers. The multiple heads and numerous appendages are symbolic of awesome divine power; with these extra sensory organs, the Bodhisattva is better able to aid humanity. The elongated proportions of the arms, also found in India, demonstrate that the dimensions of the figure are based on sacred canons of proportion rather than current ideals of beauty. Here paramount importance is afforded to the efficacy of the image assured by strict observation of the rules for the creation of the icon; aesthetic considerations are secondary.

Most Tang caves at Dunhuang are ascribed to this period; Caves 328 and 45 are excellent representatives. Although the image of the Buddha at Dunhuang shares the characteristic exposure of the torso and swelling flesh, the nipples and navel are not indicated. (FIGURES 54 and 55) As at Tianlongshan, the legs are in lotus position, the drapery cascades over the lotus seat; catching on the petals, the folds of cloth create a rhythmic, linear design. The slim, elongated figures of the Bodhisattvas are also sympathetically carved; their heads incline slightly (like those on secular ceramic figurines and in mural portraits). Usually they are brilliantly white-skinned and have fine facial features. Realistic representation is particularly apparent in the sculptures of the disciples Ananda and Kasyapa. No longer abstract representations of age and youth, these are individual personalities with unique head shapes and features. Like the official's head from Xuanzong's shendao, they have deeply cut, narrow eyes; the taut eyelid reveals the eyeball structure beneath. Even the monks' shaven pates are painted in a lifelike manner: The dark stubble contrasts with their rosy pink complexions. Ananda, wearing a tailored robe, sways slightly; his head is inclined and he looks out with a benign expression. Kasyapa, on the other hand, stands erect; his head leans forward with a stern countenance and raised, thick eyebrows; the dark stubble of his beard is painstakingly delineated with minute brushstrokes. The drapery of his traditional untailored garment is treated as real material, falling in thick folds along the shoulder and lower skirt. Both of their robes are made of rich brocade patterns accentuated with painted gold. Resembling the excavated tricolor ceramic figurines, the guardian figures flanking the pentad stand with one leg bent, one arm raised, their heads tilted; they look down with a martial grimace of furrowed brows and snarling mouths.

Paintings at Dunhuang also provide pictorial evidence of the independence and the increasing feminization of Guanyin. On the side wall of Cave 45 is an extremely beautiful, oversize painting of this God of Compassion standing beneath a heavily jeweled canopy. (FIGURE 56) The pale-faced deity looks out with eyes that are rendered in a new way--the eyeballs are painted black and the iris is a pale color, creating a most striking and mesmerizing effect. The body is slim but fleshy and totally obscured by an elaborate arrangement of aqua and terra-cotta scarves, jeweled pendants, necklaces, and bracelets. Flanking the oversize figures are small-scale narratives set in a unified landscape dominated by water; these scenes illustrate the many perils the devout may escape if they invoke the assistance of the deity.[75] An exemplary icon is the Bodhisattva in Cave 33: The entire figure is painted black; white lines define the facial features, and green and gray tones are used for the opulent jewels and scarfs. (FIGURE 57)

Comparing the depictions of the Vimalakirti Manjusri debate of earlier reigns with that painted on the door wall of Cave 103, dramatic strides in portraiture are readily appreciated. (FIGURE 58) The image of Vimalakirti is one of an elderly, discerning gentleman, with thick, expressive eyebrows, a deeply furrowed forehead, and wrinkles between his brows, around his eyes, and on his cheeks. His long nose projects boldly over an open mouth in which the teeth are drawn; scraggly whiskers are painted with a fine line. Sitting in a posture of ease, legs crossed, and leaning on an armrest, he listens to his opponent's arguments, a fan relaxed in his left hand. Carefully drawn toes peek out from the drapery of his long gown. A similar style of delineation is used for his retinue, foreigners from throughout the world.

Popular espousal of Buddhism is evident in several large-scale projects sponsored by the local populace under the direction of a guiding monk. For example, the colossal sculpture of the Buddha of the Future, Milo, in Leshan in Sichuan, was undertaken by a local monk in 713. The location of the sculpture is dramatic: It resides at the point of confluence of three tributaries of the Yangze, an area plagued by frequent flooding. Thus the huge 71-meter seated Buddha was built to protect the area by spiritually calming the waters. The project took nearly one hundred years to complete.[76] Similarly, at Dunhuang a colossal Buddha of the Future was created under the leadership of a monk and local residents.[77]

Sichuan was a particularly important site for both the imperial government and Buddhism. Located on tributaries of the Yangze River, Sichuan was in a prime position for trade with the West. During the Tang it was a fertile, prosperous land, with a rich culture. As a Buddhist area, it was well endowed. It maintained a production of rich and important art from the fifth century throughout the Tang. Sites like Wanfosi are well known for the excellent execution of art as well as innovative Buddhist iconography. Esoteric forms of Guanyin, such as the Thousand-eyed, Thousand-armed, or a combination of both begin, to appear in this period; these images were heralded in the scriptures translated at the opening of the eighth century.[78] Several examples are found in Sichuan's rock-cut cave-chapels, such as the one in Qiongxia, Shisunshan: The main icon is a Thousand-armed image of Guanyin; twenty arms radiating from the figure are carved in the round, the remaining 980 arms are carved in low relief on the halo. Supported on lotus flowers are the members of the entourage.[79] (FIGURE 59) Other figures in this group evince innovative treatment: the *Tianwang*, or Guardian King, appears in a new-fashioned garment, a long skirt that reaches to the floor. Here the muscular, seminude guardian by the niche frame also has six arms and, like the familiar esoteric images of Tibet, wears a necklace of what appears to be skulls with a halo of flames. (FIGURE 60) Carved into the cave niches in Renshou Niujiaozhai, Sichuan, are scenes of both the Paradise of Amitofu and the Vimalakirti debate.[80]

The site of Wutaishan in Shanxi, with its five majestic mountain terraces from which its name derived, was important during Xuanzong's reign, especially in the latter part of the era. The Foguansi Temple has yielded several stone sculptures--a large, central Buddha dated by inscription to 752, and two standing monks.[81] Like the Dunhuang material, the monks are shown as individuals, with extremely different appearances: The smooth-faced compassionate Ananda looks out of semiclosed eyes, while the elder monk has a furrowed brow and a sterner expression on his wrinkled face. Their garments are simply articulated; the only drapery folds are those that gather around the elder monk's outer robe and those on the long sleeves of the younger monk. The Buddha is of majestic girth and formality; this sculpture, with its triangular folds of drapery cascading over the base, is an important monument in the dating of Tang sculpture.

In summation, the reign of Xuanzong has been heralded as the climax of artistic expression in the Tang. The opulent and luxurious style is attributed to this emperor's refined taste and love of artistic expression in all its forms--literature, calligraphy, poetry, painting, music, sports, and horsemanship. The Buddhist arts flourished with a new vividness and literalness in the portrayal of the divine aspects of heavenly beauty. But much of the splendor and extravagance of the imperial court was the subject of rebuke by poets of the day who saw the disparity between the extravagance of imperial pleasures and the hunger and want of the common people. The most famous of these protest poems is represented here by the mourning plaints of the great poet Du Fu (712-770), writing at the time of the rebellion led by An Lu-shan:

> Behind the red painted doors wine and meat are stinking,
> On the roads lie corpses of people frozen to death.
> A hairbreath divides wealth and poverty.
> This strange contrast fills me with unappeasable
> anguish.[82]

Du Fu also wrote of the Huaqin spa where the emperor and Concubine Yang retreated for relaxation:

> Yet warm vapours swirl above the jade-green pool,
> Round which imperial guards jostle one another;

There our prince and his court take their pleasure,
The whole vast sky rings to the sound of music,
Only the highest in the land may bathe here,
The low and wretched have no part in their feast;
But the silk shared out in the Vermilion Hall
Was woven by the hands of poor women,
Women whose men were whipped in their own homes,
By tax collectors who took the silk to court.[83]

Up until the recent archaeological discoveries, the grandeur of Xuanzong's court was remembered best by the literary descriptions of its achievements. The new finds certainly live up to their reputation. But in the end, the tomb materials and Buddhist art are still only a reflection of the art of the court.

NOTES

1. One such clock was built by the Buddhist master Yi Jing. See Robert
Temple, *The Genius of China* (New York, 1985): 106.
2. Dawson, 1972: 80ff.
3. Twitchett, "Hsuan-tsung," *Cambridge History*, vol. III: 360.
4. Pulleyblank, 1976: 36ff.
5. Waley, 1949: 71.
6. Dawson, 1972: 85.
7. Fan, 1990-91: 83-96, pointed out that Concubine Yang was in fact married
to Xuanzong's son; he analyzed the historical accounts of Yang Gui-fei that
were written after the rebellion.
8. Edwin Pulleyblank, *The Background of the Rebellion of An Lu shan*
(London, 1966).
9. The story of the escape and execution is the subject of a long poem by the
ninth-century poet Bai Ju-yi, in *Poetry and Prose of the Tang and Song*, eds.
Yang Xian-yi and Gladys Yang (Beijing, 1983): 109ff. There is a new
translation by Paul Kroll, "Po Chu-i's 'Song of Lasting Regret' a New
Translation," *Tang Studies*, 1990-91, vols. 8-9: 97-105. The story was also
the subject of a poem by the ninth-century poet Chen Hong.
10. Hou Yi, "Tangdai Laojiao Shizaoxiang Changyangtian zun," *Wenwu*,
1991.12: 42-47.
11. The subject of Xuanzong and Taoism is treated by Edward Schafer, "The
Dance of the Purple Culmen," *T'ang Studies*, 1987, no. 5: 45-69.
12. The stimulus to anthropomorphize the Taoist principles has also been
attributed to the prominence of Buddhism and its art in the Six Dynasties
period. (See Welch, 1966: 135.)
13. *Zhongguo Meishu Quanji: Diaosubian*, vol. 12, *Sichuan Shiku Diaosu*,
ed. Li Ji-sheng (Beijing, 1988), pls. 97-98, p. 32, for niche 40 at Renshou
Niujiaozhai; the niche is dated in the Tianbao era (742-756). Anyue
Xuemiaoguan niche number 11, ascribed to the Kaiyuan-Tianbao era (713-
756), features a Taoist trinity and surrounding figures. (See pls. 103-104, p.
34ff.)
14. Schafer, 1987: 50.
15. Much of the material is drawn from Charles Benn, "Religious Aspects of
Hsuan Tsung's Taoist Ideology," *Buddhist and Taoist Practice in Medieval
Chinese Society* (Hawaii, 1987): 127-145. (See also Welch, 1967: 153 and
159.)
16. Arthur Cooper, *Li Po And Tu Fu* (New York, 1973) and Arthur Waley,
Li Po (New York, 1969); G. W. Robinson, *Poems of Wang Wei*, (Great

Britain, 1973); and H. C. Chang, *Chinese Literature 2: Nature Poetry* (New York, 1977): 82, for Meng Hao-ran.

17. TCMHL, Soper, 1958: 217.

18. TCMHL, Soper, 1958: 215.

19. TCMHL, Soper, 1958: 221; Chen Hung is described as an expert portraitist and painter of secular figures and gentlewomen. He was rated "Excellent grade" but Han Gan was two grades higher in the "Inspired class." Han Gan was also known as a painter of Buddhist subjects. (See TCMHL, Soper, 1958: 214-215.)

20. Du Fu, however, was not an admirer of Han Gan, as is evident from a poem dedicated to the painter Zao Zhi:

> *Han Kan, your follower, has grown proficient*
> *At representing horses in all their attitudes;*
> *But picturing the flesh, he fails to draw the bone--*
> *So that even the finest are deprived of their spirit.*

In Witter Bynner, *The Jade Mountain* (New York, 1959): 164. Also Suzanne Cahill, "Reflections, Disputes, and Warnings: Three Medieval Chinese Poems about the Eight Horses of King Mu," *T'ang Studies*, 1987, no. 5: 87-94; Yen Li-ben painted the imperial mounts, and Yuan Zhen and Bo Ju-yi, both celebrated poets of the later part of the eighth century, wrote about such paintings.

21. Cahill, 1980: 11, designated this an important early painting, but the attribution to Han Gan is questionable. The earliest inscription on the scroll is that of Emperor Li Hou-zhu (937-978) of the Five Dynasties.

22. Suzanne Cahill, "Night Shining White: Traces of a T'ang Dynasty Horse in Two Media," *T'ang Studies*, 1986, vol. 4: 88-92, asserts that a poem by Lu Guei-meng is a description of the painting by Han now in the Metropolitan Museum of Art. An interesting thesis presented here is that this poem was intended as a remonstrance with the emperor for his indifference to affairs of state. Cahill sees this painting as a depiction of the extraordinary feat that the charger Night Shining White could perform--dancing while holding a cup. (See p. 90.) A short story written in 850 by Zheng Qu-hui, poignantly described the misuse of the dancing horses after Ming Huang's downfall, in Waley, 1952: 181-183.

23. According to TCMHL, Soper, 1958: 214: The elder Li was appointed general of the Bodyguard in the 713-742 era. His son was vice-president of the crown prince's Grand Secretariat.

24. TCMHL, Soper, 1958: 214.

25. TCMHL, Soper, 1958: 214.

26. One example might be the Shosoin silver jar dedicated in 765. However, master copyists that the Japanese were, the origin of many of these objects is questionable.

27. Some were found in Xian tombs. (See Shaanxisheng Wenwu Guanliweiyuanhui, "Xian Xijiao Zhongbaocun Tangmu Qingli Jianbao," *Kaogu,* 1960.3: 34-38.)

28. One of the most revered landscape poets was Xie Ling-yun (385-433); see J. D. Frodsham, *The Murmuring Stream* 2 vols., (Malaya, 1967).

29. For example, TCMHL, Soper, 1958: p. 208, ranks him in the highest class with the single entry: "Inspired class, top grade, one man."

30. LTMHJ, Acker, 1954: 156.

31. TCMHL, Soper, 1958: 209. The landscape artist Li Si-xun did the same subject but took several months; the emperor judged both works as "the extreme of excellence."

32. TCMHL, Soper, 1958: 218, note 74.

33. TCMHL, Soper, 1958: 218-219.

34. According to Cahill, 1981: 4, the attribution to the Song emperor Huizong's copying a work by Zhang Xuan is based on a colophon written by the Jin dynasty emperor Zangzong (d. 1209). None of the entries listed in Cahill's catalogue are ascribed to Zhang; all are rated as later copies.

35. *Tang Mu Pi Hua Jijin,* 1988: 144-146. Little is published about the occupant of this tomb, found in 1955 in the eastern suburbs of Xian. The tomb consists of a passage, tunnel, and coffin chamber; the chamber is roughly square in shape, measuring less than 4 meters a side. This would be considered typical of the time. (See Fong, 1991: 147-199.)

36. *Han Tang:* pl. 198, p. 148. The tomb in which this painting was found is dated to the Tianbao era (742-756). It was discovered in 1972 in tomb number 187 at Astana, Turpan, in Xinjiang Province.

37. Dated 710, from the tomb of Lady Xue, Dizhangwan, Xianyang, Shensi. Also in Mary Tregear, *Arts of China* (Tokyo, 1968), fig. 197, pp. 224 and 228 and *Wenwu,* 1959.8.

38. *Tangmu Pihua Jijin,* 1988: 147-152. Also in Tregear, 1968: figs. 194-196, p. 224. The tomb, in western Xian, has a passageway with four niches, tunnel, and coffin chamber. There are over 20 paintings; its occupant was an adopted son of a eunuch who held an official post and had a reputation for being a ruthless general.

39. *Tang Mu Pi Hua Jijin,* 1988: fig. 185, p. 148. This mural fragment is in the Shaanxi Provincial Historical Museum; it appears as if several painters of varying ability worked in this tomb.

40. Tregear, 1968: fig. 229, p. 228; also *Kaogu,* 1960, no. 1. A similar composition, without the landscape elements, was found in Astana, Cave 216. (See Wang, 1990: fig. 9, p. 99.) This is ascribed to the "mature" Tang, which is Xuanzong's era.

41. *Han Tang Sichou zhi Lu,* 1990: fig. 194, p. 165. This is from Cave 188, Astana, Turpan. It is now in the Xinjiang Museum.

42. Wang, 1990: fig. 10, p. 85. Also from Astana, tomb no. 215.

43. As in the Feathered Lady and Tree scenes housed in the Shosoin; see Nara Kokoritsu Hakubutsukan, *Shosoin-ten* (Nara, 1988): 16-23. These ladies standing or seated under trees have always been viewed as the archetypal Tang, eighth-century beauty; they strongly resemble the ladies of Xuanzong's reign in their physical stature and fashions. One remarkable aspect of the Shosoin screens is that only the faces are polychromed, since feathers were attached to decorate the garments. So, too, the trees were only done with ink; no color was applied to the leaves or trunk. A similar figure and landscape screen owned by Toji, the Japanese temple, is based on a Tang original. See T. Akiyama, *Japanese Painting* (Geneva, 1977): pls. 31 and 71, respectively.

44. *Tang Mu Pi Hua Jijin*, 1988: 148 and 153. Gao was the younger brother of a palace eunuch. His tomb was found in Gaoloucun village in the eastern suburbs of Xian. It is the usual construction. Among the painted themes are the directional creatures, the dragon and tiger, a bodyguard on horseback, waiting maidens, a dancing girl, and flowers.

45. TCMHL, Soper, 1958: 224.

46. Mahler, 1959: 130.

47. The tricolor glaze style spread as far as Yangzhou, as recent excavations testify. Yangzhou Bowuguan, "Yangzhou Situmiaozhen Qingli Yizuo Tang Muzang," *Kaogu*, 1985.9: 859-860. Sites in Henan have also been found. Yichuanxian Wenwuguan, "Henan Yichuan Faxian Yizuo Tangmu," *Kaogu*, 1985.5: 459. Here glazed horses, camels, foreign trainers, double-handled long-necked jars, and a silver mirror with the four directional animals have been found.

48. One fashion of the era was for women to dress as foreign men; they are so portrayed in tomb murals as well as in figurines. Women also played polo. One richly polychromed female equestrian, dressed as a foreigner, was among the ceramic figurines in the tomb of Lizhen, Prince of Yue (eighth son of Gaozong), who committed suicide in defiance of Empress Wu in 683 and was reburied with honor in 718 in the Zhaoling. His tomb, 46.1 meters long, contained 130 funerary objects. (See "Tang Yuewang Li Zhenmu Fajue Jianbao," *Wenwu*, 1977.10: 41-49, and also *Quest for Eternity*: figs. 82-83, p. 139.)

49. Shaanxisheng Wenwu Guanliweiyuanhui, *Kaogu*, 1960.3: 34-38; also in Kuwayama, 1986: 138. The ceramic objects found included small-scale arrangements of rocks and trees, pigs, camels, horses, ladies, and grooms. The tomb guardian, with spiked, flaming hair raised from its head, has triglaze stripes on the body and on the feathers, an open mouth, and exaggerated, trapezoidal, bulging eyes; it sits on its haunches on a rocky base naturalistically treated in the sancai glaze technique. Similar figures and

a camel, oxen, and smaller barnyard animals were excavated from Xianyu Tingha in Xian; this tomb is dated 723. (See *Wenwu*, 1958, no. 1: 42-52.)

50. Fashions in the Tang were as ever-changing as in modern times. (See Sunji, "Tangdai Funu de Fuzhuang yu Huazhuang," *Wenwu*, 1984.4: 57-69.)

51. For Tang hairstyles represented in murals and figurines, see He Jian-guo, Zhang Yan-ying, and Guo You-ming *Hair Fashions of Tang Dynasty Women* (Hong Kong, 1987).

52. *Shaanxi Taoyong Jinghua, 1986*: 28, figs. 67-70. Even the camels found in this tomb are modeled in evocative postures, with neck up-stretched, mouth agape, calling out.

53. Hayashi, 1975: for the famous painted lute guard, see p. 112, fig. 121, for the mother-of-pearl inlaid lute, see p. 52, figs. 45 and 28.

54. Hang Dezhou et al. "Xia Gaokoucun Tangdaimuzang Qingli Jianbao," *Wenwu cankzo ziliao*, 1955. 7: 103-109; Tomb 131 of Wu Shouzhong in Gaolou village, Xian, is dated 748.

55. They were discovered in Xian in 1959 and are now in the Shaanxi Historical Museum, which attributes them to the Tang dynasty. (See Wang, 1990: 255, fig. 14.)

56. For example, one kiln excavated in the capital in 1959 was reexamined in 1984. The tomb contained mostly utilitarian objects and a few tricolor glazed pieces, among which was a dragon's head. (See Shaanxisheng Kaogu Yanjiusuo Tongchuan Gongzuozhan, "Tongchuan Huangbao Faxian Tangsancai Zuofang he Yaolu," *Wenwu*, 1987. 3: 23-31 and 37.)

57. Beijingshi Wenwu Gongzuodui, "Beijingshi Faxiande Bazuo Tangmu," *Kaogu*, 1980.6: 498-505.

58. Shaanxisheng Bowuguan, "Xian Nanjiao Hejiacun Faxian Tangmu," *Wenwu*, 1972.1: 30-42. Jessica Rawson, *The Silver Ornament on Chinese Silver of the Tang Dynasty*, British Museum Occasional Paper, no. 40, 1982: 4, proposes an attribution to Li Shou-li, Prince of Bin, who died in 741. His son may have sought refuge with Xuanzong on his flight to Sichuan. The earliest evaluation of the date of the cache was late eighth century, but more recently it has been ascribed to the mid-eighth century, perhaps on the basis of similarity with the Shosoin objects. Over two dozen coins were found; a Japanese coin had a date of 715, but these merely provide a terminus post quem.

59. Rawson, 1982: 21-22.

60. The cup is only 6.5 cm. tall; the pedestal bowl, discussed next, measures 5.5 cm. tall and 13.5 cm. in diameter.

61. Zhongguo Shehui Kexueyuan Kaogu Yanjiusuo Henan Dier Gongzuodui, "Henan Yanshi Xingyuancun de Liuzuo Jinan Tang mu," *Kaogu*, 1986.5: 442-448.

62. These are the so-called Renshou mirrors popular since the Sui. (See A. C. Soper,"Addendum, The Jen Shou Mirrors," *Artibus Asiae*, 1967, vol. XXIX: 55-66.)

63. Michael Loewe, *Ways to Paradise* (London, 1979), has studied a set of mirrors inscribed with prayers for immortality addressed to the goddess Xiwangmu. For funeral uses of mirrors, see Karetzky, "A Scene of the Taoist Afterlife on a Sixth Century Sarcophagus Discovered in Loyang," *Artibus Asiae*, 1983, vol. XLIV: 5-20.

64. The scroll of the *Admonitions to the Palace Ladies*, in the British Museum, is believed to be a Tang copy near to the fifth century original. For the poetry, see A. C. Graham, *Poems of the Late Tang* (Great Britain, 1965). For "A Girl Combs her Hair," by Li He, see p. 115; for "On the Road," by Tu Mu, which begins "Sadness at the silver hairs in the mirror is new no longer. . . ., " see p. 129.

65. Wang, 1990; for mirrors with directional animals and zodiac creatures, see p. 177, fig. 21; often it is one or more of the spirit animals that is the theme (see p. 179, fig. 24 and 25); for rabbit and deer, see p. 165, fig 25; an exceptional Buddhist mirror, with a date of 693, has the Buddhist symbol of the swastika as its only design (see p. 165, fig. 27). There is also one marked with the trigrams of the *YiJing* (see p. 165, fig. 26); for an example of a landscape with a sage, see p. 180, fig. 27; for a pure landscape, see p. 180, fig. 29.

66. Li Zhen-qi, Shi Yun-zheng, and Li Lan-ke, "Hebei Lincheng Chizuomu," *Wenwu*, 1990.6: 21. (See also Nancy Thompson, "The Evolution of the Lion and Grapevine Mirror," *Artibus Asiae*, 1967, vol. XXIX: 24-54; as well as S. Camman, "Significant Patterns on Bronze Chinese Mirrors," *Archives of Asian Art,* 1955, vol. IX: 25ff; and his "Lion and Grapevine Patterns on Chinese Bronze Mirrors," *Artibus Asiae*, 1952, vol. XVI: 266ff.)

67. The Tailing funeral mound is located on Mt. Jinsu, 15 km. northeast of Pucheng county.

68. Most of this account is based on Weinstein, 1987: 51-57.

69. Weinstein, 1987: 51-57.

70. Visiting the site is extremely disappointing, for little remains of the beautifully executed sculptures. One needs to refer to much older photographs of the images. See H. Vanderstappen and M. Rhie, "The Sculpture of T'ien-lung Shan: Reconstruction and Dating," *Artibus Asiae*, 1965, vol. XXVII: 208ff, which offers a detailed description of the caves based on the records of other historians. Rhie more recently concluded that the Cave XXI images are datable to 703-711 based on stylistic evidence; see her "A T'ang Period Stele Inscription and Cave XXI at T'ien-Lung Shan," *Archives of Asian Art*, 1974-5, vol. XXVIII: 6ff. See also, *Zhongguo Meishu*

Quanji Diaosubian, Gongxian, Tianlongshan, Anyang, vol. 13, ed. Ding Ming-yi (Beijing, 1989): 22, pls. 98-103.

71. This story is associated with the figure painter Han Gan, who painted some murals at Baoyingsi, with the celestial maidens modeled on the donor's singsong girls. LTMHJ, Soper, 1958: 215, note 64.

72. Such as Du Fu. C. N. Tay, "Kuan Yin: The Cult of Half Asia," *History of Religions*, 1976, vol. 16, no. 2: 160.

73. Yu, 1990: 62.

74. The Freer Gallery has two such 11-headed Guanyin steles from that same set ascribed to the first two decades of the eighth century; inv. no. 09.98.

75. Aspects of the cult of Guanyin have been studied by Miyeko Murase in "Kuan-yin As Savior of Men," *Artibus Asiae*, 1971, vol. XXXIII: 39-73.

76. Begun under the leadership of the monk Haitong in 713, who died before it was half completed, the colossal Milo was completed under the aegis of the local magistrates.

77. This colossus, nearly 25 meters high, is also a Milo icon in pendent leg position. Undertaken by priest Qu Yan and local residents like Ma Si-zhong, it is dated to ca. 713-741.

78. Like "The Thousand-Hand-and-Thousand-Eye Kuan-yin Great-Compassionate-Heart Dharani Sutra," translated by Bhagavaddharma ca. 700. (See Tay, 1976: 171.)

79. *Zhongguo Meishu Quanji: Diaosubian*, vol. 12: pls. 76-79, p. 26. This is the third niche; it has 114 images.

80. *Zhongguo Meishu Quanji: Diaosubian*, vol. 12, pls. 92 and 93, p. 30. These are ascribed to the middle Tang.

81. Akiyama, 1962: pls. 185-86, p. 239, these were from the Wugou Jingguang Pagoda.

82. Robert Payne, *The White Pony* (New York, 1947): 183.

83. Yang Xian-yi, *Poetry and Prose of the Tang and Song* (Beijing, 1990): 43, from the poem "A Lament after Travelling from the Capital to Fenxian."

CHAPTER VII

EMPEROR SUZONG

With his father's forced abdication, Suzong (r. 756-762) assumed the throne. He reigned but a short time, seven years, and his was an unfortunate legacy; the empire was under siege by the rebellious troops of An Lu-shan, and the gradual dissolution of the authority of the central government in the provincial states had begun. Even after An was assassinated by his son trouble continued; the latter ruled in his stead until defeat in 763. Although the rebellion was temporarily quelled, the Uighurs, whose support was essential in the subjugation of the insurgent factions, became ungovernable and looted Luoyang.[1] Later, their demand that amnesty be given to the provincial rebels had the ironic result in some provinces of the rebels remaining as governors still in possession of their armies. The two areas of greatest independence were Hebei and Shandong.[2] Another of the difficulties of Su's reign was the continued popularity of his father. Some admonished him for his unfilial usurpation of the throne; when he began to fear a restoration of Xuanzong, he had his father sequestered.[3]

COURT ART

Not much innovative art was produced under this short reign. Zhang Yan-yuan records that as a consequence of An Lu-shan's looting, a great many works were lost, and that since Suzong himself did not care about maintaining a collection, he distributed the artworks among the imperial clan, who sold them.[4] But the great artists of the previous era were still alive and continued to practice their skills. Although nothing remains of the works commissioned by the court, literary records preserve the names and specialties of painters who were active at this time: Both Wang Wei and Wu Dao-zu were remembered for landscape paintings; Zhou Fang, who lived until 800, was still painting his favorite subject, palace women, as well as religious murals; and Zheng Hung, a renowned portraitist, painted Emperor Suzong as well as Taoist adepts.[5]

SUZONG'S TOMB

Suzong's shendao conforms to the standard imperial set of monumental animals (lacking Xuanzong's additional eight standing sculptures).[6] The four lions that were placed outside the four gates, one of the two ornamental columns, one ostrich, all ten pairs of officials, and six single stone horses of the five pairs have all survived.[7] In general, these shendao sculptures are still relatively well carved, but the details are treated less naturalistically. Like the horses of Xuanzong's reign, these are beautifully executed in the articulation of the body, but here the faces lack strength and nobility. Looking at the flying horse, some details still recall the earlier period of workmanship, like the careful delineation of the mane. However, the three-dimensional forms, such as the wings, are shallowly carved. The sculpture of the official has a large, thick body and aristocratic facial features.[8] Holding his head aloft, his fleshy face has an imperious expression. Unlike Xuanzong's guardians, the bony structure of this face is overwhelmed by the bloated flesh of the cheeks. (FIGURE 61) Falling naturalistically over the body, the garment's details are somewhat fussy in their treatment, especially along the edges of the sleeves. A decrease in artistic craftsmanship is clearly seen in the ostrich, whose body is now covered with an unchanging triangular pattern that feebly renders the plumage of the exotic bird. There is a lack of three-dimensionality due to shallow undercutting, especially evident in parts like the neck and head, which, being barely modeled, appear flat.

BUDDHISM UNDER SUZONG

Suzong and his court turned to the Buddhist church for financial aid in regaining the empire. A tempting source of income for the impoverished central government, whose resources were depleted by the cost of the ongoing war, was the collection of monies from the sale of ordination. Although the practice did not originate with this reign, its growth as a profitable source of income was unprecedented. The Buddhist church was also sought out for its spiritual aid. A Tantric master, Bu Kong (Amoghavajra), who had been a student of Vajrabodhi, was raised to great eminence. He had been active at the end of Xuanzong's reign; in the ensuing turmoil, he sought refuge from the war-torn capital with the rebels in Hoxi.   After An's rebellion, Bu Kong was summoned back to the capital, where Suzong had a special chapel built in which to conduct rituals to purify the newly recaptured palace.   For the third time during the Tang the famous Famen bone relic was brought to the capital for daily worship. A chapel built in the Linde Hall of the Daming Palace was the site for an unusual ceremony.   For this rite, palace attendants and army officers were dressed as Buddhist deities to whom the ministers addressed their prayers for aid.   It is also reported that the empress copied the sutras in her own blood to aid her sick husband.[9]

BUDDHIST ART

It is easy to imagine the headless Bodhisattva figure discovered among the ruins of the Daming Palace in Chang-an as belonging to the newly refurbished Linde Hall, although the piece is only ascribed to the Tang.[10] (FIGURE 61) It is a most graceful image, ironically named by the modern Chinese as the Venus of the East.   Classical restraint is exercised in the slight hip-slung pose and limited amount of adornment consisting of a simple necklace, a single scarf that crosses the chest and is looped in a very natural way, and a neatly tied belt. Not only are the protruding belly, navel, and nipple indicated, but beneath the thin drapery of the skirt, the bony structure of the knees is visible.[11] Yet compared to the art of the previous reign, there appears to be a slight hardening of the forms of the body, and a crispness and greater linearity in the carving of the drapery and jewels.

NOTES

1. Michael T. Dally, "Court Politics in Late T'ang Times," *Cambridge History*: 567.
2. Twitchett and Wright, 1973: 9.
3. Twitchett, 1992: 184.
4. LTMHJ, Acker, 1954: 129.
5. TCMHL, Soper, 1958: 222.
6. Located in the Wujiang Mountains, 15 km. northeast of Liquan county, is the Jianling tomb mound. Due to its relatively isolated location, the shendao is in unusually good condition.
7. Cheng, 1988: pls. 42-43, for the ostrich; pls. 66-69, for the officials; and pls. 103-104, for lions.
8. Wang, 1990: for the official, see fig. 22, p. 74; for the flying horse, fig. 16, p. 77.
9. Weinstein, 1987: 57ff, is the primary source for this account of Buddhism under Suzong.
10. Several writers ascribe this piece to Xuanzong's reign, like Rhie, 1975: 17, who gives it a date of 703.
11. A very similar, also headless, Bodhisattva is in the Freer Gallery, inv. no. 16.365.

CHAPTER VIII

EMPEROR DAIZONG

Daizong (r. 763-779) inherited a weakened and chaotic empire. Tibetans invaded Chang-an in 763 chasing the emperor and his court out of the capital. Next, Pu-gu Huai-en, a general of Turkish stock, plotted against the emperor and threatened the capital. However, this threat ended with his sudden death in 765. Both the local and central governments were in disarray, the financial structure was collapsing, and rebellion continued in the provinces.[1] The emperor proved weak and ineffectual. Because of the recent adversities with rebellious generals and recalcitrant provinces, the court was particularly wary of the army. For this reason, eunuchs were appointed to supervise the military and to keep the court informed. Designated to hold the official hierarchy and military establishments in check, the eunuchs challenged provincial and military authority. In this way Daizong's reign was dominated by the eunuchs, who, during the periods of anarchy, became even more powerful. Daizong, fearful of provoking more military insurrections, accepted the status quo of rebellious provinces, especially Hebei. The goal was to maintain a balance of power among the provinces by playing them off against each other at times of contention, thereby achieving some stability.[2] By the end of Daizong's reign, central authority was reestablished in south and central China.[3]

ARCHAEOLOGY

Beginning with the reign of Ming Huang, gold and silver were collected by local officials, who sent them to the emperor as gifts.

The practice, which began with the Kaiyuan era, broke off during the An rebellion and resumed with Daizong's reign. Typically, such precious gifts were offered on four occasions: Chinese New Year's Day, the winter solstice, the Dragon Boat festival, and the birthday of the emperor.[4] The hoard of golden objects found in Dantu county, Jiangsu, may reflect such practices. The 950 objects, 760 of which were hairpins, are ascribed to the later part of the middle Tang on the basis of their construction and decoration. Many of the pieces are inscribed with a single character, Fang, which has led some to believe all of these objects were made for the same Tang official.[5] Most of the hundred or so larger scale articles are plates, but there are also silver bowls, covered boxes, and ewers. Smaller objects, like spoons and bracelets, are engraved with fine floral and naturalistic bird designs. In addition, there is a gold incense burner and an inlaid silver and gold drinking-game candle.[6] Several multilobed boxes have intricately worked designs of a decidedly greater three-dimensionality than the Hejia material. Often it is a raised design of flying, paired birds against a fine, punched ring background. New forms appear in the middle Tang replacing the Western prototypes of the last century. Foremost among them are replicas of natural objects, such as the clamshell from the Hejia finds or the Dantu covered dish made to resemble exactly a lotus leaf, curling at its edges, with its stem upright at the center. (FIGURE 63) Controversy surrounds the question of the dating of these and other gold objects. One Chinese scholar noted that the production of golden objects actually increased after the An Lu-shan revolt;[7] this is in accord with the recent archaeological finds that have yielded numerous golden objects of great beauty dated after the An rebellion. Previously it was thought that the late-eighth-century hostilities with Tibet resulted in a shortage of gold because Tibet was an important source. Thus works of extraordinary craftsmanship in precious materials were ascribed to the earlier reign of Xuanzong.[8] Such erroneous attributions were prevalent in China and elsewhere.[9] But Tibet was not only the source of gold in the Tang, it was also mined in the south, particularly in Sichuan.[10]

DAIZONG'S TOMB

Not much remains of this emperor's tomb. The general layout of the shendao was not different from that of his predecessors. But now all that remains is one toppled column.[11]

BUDDHISM UNDER DAIZONG

Daizong has been called one of the most devout of all the Tang rulers. Perhaps his espousal of Buddhism was in part the result of the efficacious way the religion appeared to have saved the state during the period of military instability. The eminent Tantric master Bu Kong had a prominent role in the practice of state Buddhism. Active under the two previous emperors, he again took on the role of intermediary between the Tang state and the Buddhist esoteric deities, forging a strong link through a number of acts. First was his gift of a white sandalwood image, he himself made, of the esoteric goddess Marici ("remover of all obstacles") and a copy of the sutra that expounded her powers.[12] A special altar was set up in Daxingshansi for prayers for the benefit of the empire.[13] Esoteric scriptures were translated. One scripture, the *Sutra of the Humane King*, believed to have the power to protect against calamity and rebellion, had a foreword written by Daizong in the manner of his predecessors.[14] Great fanfare attended its completion: leaving the Daming Palace, the sutra was ceremoniously carried through the streets. The subsequent failure of both the rebellious troops and the Tibetan threat was attributed to the efficacy of the scripture, and the Tantric master who introduced it was amply rewarded. A chapel was built in the Daming Palace and staffed with 100 monks. There, the emperors of the past, Taizong and Gaozong, were memorialized with Buddhist services.

As usual, Buddhism was not only supported by the emperor but also by high-ranking officials at court; however, at this time the scale of some of their undertakings was quite extraordinary. Mention should be made of Wang Jin, brother of the official-literati-artist Wang Wei, who had the Baoyingsi converted into a monastery in 769. But the most extravagant project was the erection in 768 of a magnificent temple consisting of 48 buildings of more than 4,130 bays. A high-ranking eunuch undertook the project, dedicating it to the emperor's mother. When construction materials proved inadequate, several government buildings were taken apart to supply the necessary materials. Tang officials expressed their impotent outrage in memorials. Daizong was severely criticized for depleting the imperial treasury to finance these lavish structures and for having thousands of monks ordained.[15]

A stupendous amount was spent for the construction of the Jinkossu, a temple in the Wutaishan religious complex, which was completed in 767. Although there were followers of many schools at the site, the main deity was the Bodhisattva of Wisdom, Wenshu (Manjusri in

Sanskrit). Although this Bodhisattva originated in India, Chinese myths claimed that he was born in China; this is the first occurrence of a native birth attributed to a Buddhist deity. Wutaishan, believed to be the place of his birth, became the most important center of his cult.[16] Myths propounding that the deity of wisdom now resided in China led to a parade of Korean, Japanese, Indian, and Central Asian monks making their way to Wutaishan to worship him and hoping for a manifestation of his divine person.[17] After the An Lu-shan rebellion, the cult of Wenshu became more important and widespread. Pu Kong's success in propounding the worship of Wenshu on Wutaishan was in part due to the deity's apparent ability to protect the state. Thus, by the 770s, shrines of Wenshu were ordered by imperial edict to be set up in every temple.[18] Branching out from the religious center at Wutaishan, the worship of Tantric Buddhism also spread to nearby Taiyuan, at Zhidesi, and at Taijingsi.[19]

It has been asserted that the cult of Amitofu did not receive substantial court patronage nor did it gain great popularity until after the An Lu-shan rebellion.[20] The monk Fa Zhao was especially dedicated to spreading Amidism throughout the country. Living at Wutaishan in 770, he moved to Taiyuan in 774, and at the end of the decade, he reached the capital and was invited to court. Later, Daizong made him National Teacher.

BUDDHIST ART

Recently, two small twin pagodas in Anyang, Henan were studied; one was found to have an inscription of 771.[21] The pagodas have square bases and are crowned with nine square tiers. The front face is marked by a door with ornamental arch and flanking divine guardians, one in full armor, the other naked to the waist. (FIGURE 64) Above the arch are celestial creatures. The Guardian Kings, typical of the middle Tang, are corpulent. Their fleshy bodies are a striking contrast to the tense muscularity of the earlier Tang. In the guardian from the western pagoda the body is expansive: The muscular chest and flabby belly bulge beneath the scaled armor.[22] The important role of the esoteric Buddhist sects described in the historical accounts is illustrated by a number of archaeological finds within the capital of Chang-an. Ten such sculptures were unearthed in 1959, at what is believed to have been Anguosi, a temple adjoining the palace precincts.[23] Anguosi was prominent in the Tang; the historical records of this reign mention it several times. The most momentous event held there was the convocation called by Daizong to settle questions of the *Vinaya*, or monastic rules.[24] Descriptions of Anguosi's decor are also found in Duan Zheng-shi's travelogue description of the temples in Chang-an.[25] The Anguosi sculptures represent Tantric deities whose protective powers were invoked in this troubled era, but there are no inscriptions providing definite data.[26] The sculpture of Acala Vidyaraja is most impressive: stiffly seated in lotus position, Acala's left arm holds a sword, the right has a noose.[27] (FIGURE 65) Drawn into a topknot, a hank of hair falls over the shoulder. This deity has a fiercely grimacing face. Characteristic of the art of the post-An Lu-shan period, the adornments are rather minimal: The fleshy torso is bare but for a necklace and diagonal swath of drapery, and a scarf swirls behind the figure in a halolike configuration. The fierce wind that once enlivened the divine scarfs seems to have subsided, and the ribbons flow with less vitality than in previous pieces. Viewing the Acala image in conjunction with the other icons at the site suggests that these are the remnants of a sculptural mandala, or cosmic diagram of the divine forces of the universe, perhaps the eight-syllable mandala espoused by Pu Kong.[28] Such sculptural mandalas survive in Japan; for example, the one dated 829 at the Eastern Temple, Toji, in Kyoto.[29] Among the other Tantric figures that appear at this time is an exquisite head of an Eleven-headed Guanyin that was found in Xian in 1963. The head is undated, but the fleshy forms of the cheeks and thick chin and the elegant coldness of the carving style are hallmarks of the late middle Tang style. (FIGURE 66) Crisply carved, the face has a distant look, appropriate perhaps to its esoteric character. The pursed lips are not smiling, and the highly arched brows create an unyielding expression.[30] Rising above the wavy hair are a series of heads arranged like a crown; at the front is a standing figure of Amitofu.

The early standard representation of Wenshu in the great debate with Vimalakirti appearing in the Six Dynasties period continued to be popular through the Tang. In this guise, the Bodhisattva of Wisdom appealed to scholars and monks.[31] However, in the middle Tang, Wenshu also appears as an independent icon: Dressed as a Bodhisattva, holding his attribute a sutra scroll, he is seated on a lotus base. The Bodhisattva Wenshu found at Anguosi is carved in the later middle Tang style with a corpulent face, fleshy jowls, and an aloof expression. The torso is elongated, and the constriction of the belt causes the belly to protrude. Few jewels adorn the neck and arms, and the ribbon that ties around the torso as well as the drapery that falls over the forearms hangs straight down. As is common in icons of the esoteric sects, the hands are delicately poised in one of the secret mudras. Sumptuous treatment is afforded the lotus flower in the upper section of the hourglass-shape base: Each petal is carved in relief with a brocade pattern. Another increasingly popular icon is Wenshu seated on a lion.[32] Deities mounted on animals are an ancient Indian iconographic tradition.[33] One such exquisitely carved, white marble sculpture was found at Foguansi. Unfortunately, the head and an arm are missing, but one can still determine the posture of royal ease; the shoulders are turned to the left, the hips to the right. (FIGURE 67) Luxuriantly carved details convey the texture of the lion's mane, his rippling muscles, snarling head, large clawed feet, saddle rug, and fringed adornments of the halter.

As a result of the An rebellion, many eminent monks sought refuge in Sichuan, which partly explains the extraordinary richness of its sculpted mountain caves. At Qiongxia Shisunshan, in a niche dated 768, there are the three icons sacred to the Huayan school: Buddha, flanked by Wenshu on his lion, and Samantabhadra on his elephant.[34] Nearly always, Wenshu on his lion is paired with the Bodhisattva Samantabhadra seated on an elephant, an important Tang iconographic convention. One explanation of the images has been traced to a story told in the *Huayan Sutra (Avatamsaka Sutra)* of a precocious child, Sudhana, seeking counsel from Wenshu; he is sent on a pilgrimage in search of spiritual wisdom that culminates in his studying with Samantabhadra, at Wenshu's instruction.[35] The child is often included in Wenshu's retinue, in addition to a dark-skinned attendant holding the reins of the lion; Samantabhadra, on his elephant, often has similar accompanying figures. On the side walls framing the niche at Qiongxia, ferocious athletic guardians strike dynamic poses; with fierce grimaces, they wield their thunderbolts, or *vajras*. (FIGURE 68) The musculature of their chest, arms, and calves bulges in a dramatic, though anatomically incorrect, manner.

Once again the art of Dunhuang reflects the metropolitan style and its sculptures display many of the stylistic and iconographic characteristics of the post-An Lu-shan era. With a hardening in the articulation of the anatomical and decorative forms, it is clear that the era of naturalistic representation has passed. Perhaps this is best seen in the sculptures from Cave 194. The proportions of the body of the Bodhisattva have been altered: There is an elongation of the torso and arms, and the shape of the head is a protracted oval. The delicate restraint and sensuality of Tianbao-era sculptures have given way to a harshness in the modeling of the facial features: The now ovoid face has fleshy jowls, a somewhat larger nose, and a mouth that seems to be artificially pursed. The brows are stiffly arched in an exaggerated manner and extend across the forehead. In compensation, there is an emphatic delicacy to the hands in complicated hand gestures, or mudras, common to esoteric icons. Although the particulars of the inclined head and smiling face of the Bodhisattvas and the teeth-baring grimace of the Guardian King, or benevolent expression of the young monk Ananda seem naturalistic, the overall effect is stilted. There is a disparity between the figural definition and the attention to details and their overly dramatic effect. This is also visible in the rendering of the garments, with their multiple scarves and jeweled adornments. Thus the images that once gave the naturalistic impression of being individual portraits now, through slight exaggeration of details and stiffening of the forms, take on more of a generalized appearance, nearly approaching caricature.

It is singularly fortunate to have one of the caves at Dunhuang, Cave 148, dated 775 by inscription, for it provides a standard of style and iconography. Paradise scenes dominate the room with Maitreya, the Buddha of the Future (south wall), the Buddha of Healing (east wall, north side), and Amitofu, Buddha of the West (east wall, south side). (FIGURE 69)   The Buddha of Healing was the most recently introduced: Sutras devoted to him were translated by two important Buddhists at the Tang court, Xuan Zang and Yi Jing.[36] The theme of the Buddhas of the Four Directions became standard in the middle Tang period.[37] Despite the presence of the depiction of the paradises of the four Buddhas, the mural of the Western Land of Amitofu is still preeminent; it is the largest of all such compositions at Dunhuang. Some changes in its delineation are evident: The architectural forms are now drawn with tight symmetry and are strictly organized. The Buddha at center is seated in front of a hall with a double tiered roof; the lateral halls extend behind him and project forward at right angles. Punctuating both the terminals of the halls in the foreground, and the places where they intersect with the lateral halls in the mid-ground, are two-story pavilions. In the background are additional adjacent pavilions and two independent circular-columned pavilions. Each of these units is filled with celestial occupants strolling through its halls. In the lotus pond that reaches from the foreground to the mid-ground is a very complicated arrangement of jeweled terraces connected by a series of bridges. Arranged on each terrace are groups of figures: Two flanking Buddhas with their retinues are in the foreground; a multisectional orchestra and dancers supported on five terraces are in the middle ground. One can only marvel at the complexity of these architectural forms and imagine how they may reflect some of the grandiose constructions, with their numerous accessory buildings, undertaken at the time.

Despite the extraordinary care the artist has taken in drawing the individual details of the divinities (multitudinous deities bedecked with halos, jewels, and flowing scarves) in their celestial environment (with jeweled and tiled architectural forms and furniture, intricate lamps, incense burners), the painting is dominated by its architectonic elements. The symmetrical character of the composition is further emphasized by the distribution of the pigments, which creates an overall two-dimensional pattern. The areas of aqua-blue that describe the celestial waters of the foreground and mid-ground create a field upon which earth tones are applied to define the figures and the palatial constructions. Individual celestials no longer have any singular importance; now one sees large groups arranged in matching configurations. The earlier style of painting, which employed strong outlines to create the illusion of three-dimensional figures and highlighting and shading to enhance volumetric delineation, has become flattened by a monochrome wash technique. Broad strokes of color represent the figures. Attention is drawn more to the rhythmic way the chromatic pigments are applied in flowing strokes rather than to the forms they depict.

There is a noticeable increase in the genre details in the paintings. For example, in the lateral halls of the mid-ground of the Paradise of Yakushi, figures stroll and chat. Newly born beings emerge from lotus buds in the foreground pool of water; they seem to be at play, splashing or swimming freely. Now narrow vertical strips of narrative flank the major Paradise compositions becoming a significant part of the decor. Often these vertical areas have painted illustrations from the sutras that describe ten meditation techniques for visualizing Amitofu that were practiced by Queen Vaidehi.[38] Narratives of famous men may also be used to fill this vertical area.

NOTES

1. C. A. Peterson, "Court and Province in the mid- and late T'ang," *Cambridge History*: 485 ff.

2. Pulleyblank, 1976: 58-59.

3. Twitchett, 1976: 106.

4. Lu Zhao-yin, "Cong Kaogu Faxiankan Tangdai de Jinyin 'Jinfeng' zhi Jing," *Kaogu*, 1983.2: 175ff.

5. Dantu Xianwenjiaoju Zhengjiang Bowuguan, "Jiangsu Dantu Dingmaoqiao Chuti Tangdai Ginto Jiaocang," *Wenwu*, 1982.11: 15-28. The authors believe the contents to be from the late part of the middle Tang (see p. 24). (See also Lo Jiu-gao, Liujianguo, "Dantu Dingmaoqiao Chuti Tangdai Jinto shixi," *Wenwu*, 1982.11: 28-33, for an analysis of the designs.) The presumption is that the objects were buried soon after they were made because of the chaos in the capital during An's rebellion, but there was sufficient turmoil, owing to the Tibetan invasion of 763 and Pu Gu's threats of the following year, to ascribe the burying of the treasure to a slightly later date.

6. Donald Harper, "The Analects Jade Candle: A Classic of T'ang Drinking Custom," *T'ang Studies*, 1986, no. 4: 60-91, explains the use of this object.

7. Wang, 1990: 152.

8. Medley, 1970: 16.

9. One exception is the study by Duan Peng-qi, "Xian Nanjiao Hejiacun Tangdai Jinyin Qixiaoyi," *Kaogu*, 1980.6: 536-541 and 543. Duan has analyzed some of the decorative motifs on dated vessels and drawn comparisons to the usage of floral and bird motifs in different reigns.

10. Schafer, 1963: 254.

11. Cheng, 1988: 131.

12. Much of this discussion is based on Weinstein's account, 1987: 77ff.

13. Duan Zheng-shi, touring the capital in the mid-ninth century, made a record of his experiences visiting its temples. He wrote that the temple, remembered since the Sui period, was famous for a sandalwood image that was destroyed in a seventh-century fire and a jade image from Khotan. (See Soper, 1960: 22).

14. Dalby, 1979: 579.

15. Dalby, 1979: 579.

16. Reischauer, 1966: 195.

17. Raoul Birnbaum, *Studies on the Mysteries of Manjusri, Journal of Chinese Religions,* 1983: 10-12, writes of a story about an old Indian monk who came to China to visit Wenshu. In the mid-ninth century Ennin arrived and recorded meeting a multitude of monks of various nationalities at the sacred mountain. (See Reischauer, 1966: 195).

18. Birnbaum, 1983: 30ff, discusses Pu Kong's relationship with the Bodhisattva of Wisdom and the spread of his worship at Wutaishan.

19. Weinstein, 1987: 83.

20. Weinstein, 1987: 59-74.

21. Henansheng Gudai Jianzhu Baohu Yanjiusuo, "Henan Anyang Lingguansi Tangdai Shuang Shitai," *Wenwu*, 1986.3: 70-79. The temple was established in 546. These pagodas function as large-scale, free-standing sculptures measuring around 5.2 meters tall.

22. Paula Swart and Barry Till, "The Xiudingsi Pagoda," *Orientations*, May 1990: 64-76. This pagoda has been recently restored; it is covered with ceramic tiles of extraordinary richness. The subjects depicted on the tiles include foreigners, musicians, angels, and auspicious emblems. In addition, there is a four-armed guardian similar to the one in the pagoda in Henan.

23. Cheng Xue-hua, "Tang Tiejin Huacai Shike Zaoxiang," *Wenwu*, 1961.7: 61-31. These are now in the Shaanxi Provincial Museum.

24. Weinstein, 1987: 87 and 132, relates that this monastery was described as one of the major ones in Chang-an and that it had been turned into an imperial garden; it was still important during the reign of Emperor Yizong who visited the monastery. (See p. 146).

25. Duan records that the temple had five black and white panels done by the famous Wu Daozu. See Soper, 1960: 20ff.

26. Cheng, 1961: 63.

27. This figure is commonly known in Japanese as Fudo Myoo.

28. Birnbaum, 1983: 68, discusses at length the eight-syllable mandala and its use in the worship of Wenshu.

29. Toji Homotsuden, *Toji no Myo Ohzo* (Toji, 1988): 16, diagram on p. 17.

30. The esoteric sculptures of the first half of the ninth century in early Heian Japan have a similar unapproachable quality, particularly the sculptures from Todaiji and Muroji. See Yutaka Mino, *The Great Eastern Temple* (Todaiji) (Chicago, 1986): 54 and 80.

31. See Soper, *Literary Evidence*, 1959: 220, for Wenshu's association with the *Avatamsaka Sutra*, or *Huayan Sutra*.

32. The mid-ninth-century Japanese traveler Ennin, visiting Tahuayansi on Wutaishan, was told by an elderly monk the story of an artist who failed to correctly sculpt the image of Wenshu. Then the artist had a vision of the deity after which he completed his icon perfectly. The vision showed Wenshu on a golden lion. Reichauer, 1955: 200ff.

33. The close association of deities with animal mounts is of ancient Indian derivation: Deities stood on animal "vehicles" on the pillars of the stupa railing from Bharhut, ca. second century B.C.E. See Ananda Coomaraswamy, *History of India and Indonesian Art* (New York, reprinted 1965): pl. XI, fig. 39; pl. 40, for example, shows the thunder god Indra. A more contemporary

image from the Guptan era is the goddess Ganges standing on a sea monster. One from Besnagar, ca. 500 c.e., is in the Boston Museum of Fine Arts. (See pl. XLVII, fig. 177 or 175.)

34. *Zhongguo Meishu Quanji: Diaosubian,* vol. 12: pl. 88, p. 29.

35. Soper, *Literary Evidence,* 1959: 221. Samantabhadra is important in the later chapters of the *Lotus Sutra* and elsewhere. (See pp. 224-225.)

36. Raoul Birnbaum, *The Healing Buddha* (Boulder, 1979), has translated these and two earlier scriptures devoted to the healing Buddha.

37. Soper, *Literary Evidence*: 183.

38. Soper, 1959: 144ff. These sutras are a type of *Guan* or text for visual meditation often associated with Amitofu.

CHAPTER IX

EMPEROR DEZONG

Tang historians laud Dezong (r. 779-805) for his determination to regain imperial control of the empire. Building on the relative stability established under his predecessor, he attempted to restructure central authority. But the rampant militarism of the previous five years created serious difficulties. The gravest problem was that the majority of military personnel were stationed along the frontiers of the empire, but none were at its center. To remedy this, Dezong instituted a palace army that shifted the military emphasis back to the center. It was this palace army, under the direction of the central government, that would challenge the provincial military forces. To rectify the problems of collecting taxes, the two-tax system of 780 was instituted.[1] New taxes were levied on buildings, commercial transactions, tea, and salt; and taxation based on paper money was set up. Other fiscal reforms were enacted; the state issued a decree that called for the confiscation of the property of deceased members of the Buddhist church.[2] There was partial success in regaining control of some of the provincial areas of the empire and in the collection of monies. However, collection of these new taxes was still fraught with difficulties and frequently led to a confrontation with the provincial powers. Among the problematic legacies of the previous reign was the growing power of the eunuchs, who now not only oversaw the palace army but functioned as overseers of the provincial administrations. In addition, inequity in the distribution of official power persisted. Despite the growing prosperity of the south, court officials tended to be chosen from among the large and important aristocratic clans of the north, though there were some exceptions to this.[3]

Dezong's rule was rife with martial confrontations. Contesting the authority of the provincial governors had disastrous effects in the northeast: A series of uprisings in Hopei and Shandong, which began in 781, lasted for five years. In the end, the central government's army was not sufficient to quell rebellion within the empire or along its borders. For the third time a Tang emperor was forced to flee the capital when, in 783, rebels revolted. Foreign threats continued: The Tibetans attacked and took Chang-an, but before long they were expelled. Tibet, though no longer an invasion threat, retained control of Dunhuang until the middle of the next century. By the end of the century relative peace was established in the empire. In the aftermath of the rebellious confrontations, Dezong refrained from challenging the provincial governors, establishing an uneasy peace in the northeast. The southern part of the empire remained loyal, and the central government was able to maintain control over most of the country.[4]

In contrast to the auspicious beginning of Dezong's commitment to government affairs, he apparently spent the last ten years in retirement. In his absence from court politics, rival factions jockeyed for power. The importance of selecting an heir was crucial and the choice problematic, for Dezong's candidate was sick and severely impaired; indeed, his successor did not live through the year. Dezong was especially devoted to Taoism. Before his ascension, as a young man, he sought retreat at the Isles of the Blest Academy outside of Chang-an.[5] This interest in the alchemical side of the search for immortality did not wane after his ascension to the throne. It is said that Dezong spent the last decade of his reign practicing the esoteric arts.

COURT ART

Dezong's success in restoring comparative stability to his regime and maintaining the throne for over two decades is reflected in the flowering of court arts. Among the literary lights of this era were the poets Du Fu, Bai Ju-yi, Han Yu, and Yuan Zhen. One unusual group of literati was the five sisters of the Song family; their natural abilities and excellent education provided by their father won them influence at court that began with this reign but extended well beyond, through the reigns of three subsequent emperors. Their affiliation at court was literary; Song Ruo-xin, for example, who died in 791, was in charge of records.[6]

The pictorial arts also flourished: After relative silence concerning art produced under the previous emperor, historical records abound with reports of artists in Dezong's court. The emperor's commitment to the Confucian imperial ideal is reflected in his appreciation of the didactic function of portraiture. Thus his desire to restore imperial authority encompassed a recognition of the lost glories of the Tang and of the flowering of the arts under the patronage of his august predecessors. His support of artistic projects may be a conscious attempt to regain that lost imperial splendor. A proclamation of 789 transcribed by the eleventh-century art historian Guo Ruo-xu reveals Dezong's enjoyment of portraiture and its Confucian function:

> Cheng-yuan era, chi-ssu year, ninth month of autumn: in going through the Western Palace, We have observed the impressive construction of its vast pavilions and have looked upon the portraits left to us of venerable ministers, so full of dignity and majesty, with a harmonious respectfulness in their (very) colors. (They have) called to Our mind thoughts of the harmonious correspondences of cloud and dragon, and (have made Us) feel the pains and difficulties of their achievements. Gazing thus at the past, (We) have thought of the present, (in which) the type (of man We) have obtained is not very different.[7]

In Zhu Qing-xuan's record of a portrait of a government official painted by Zhou Fang, the new ideals of figure painting are expressed. No longer content to merely represent the outward appearance of the person, now the artist strove to express his inner character. Both Zhou Fang and the elder Han Gan painted a likeness of a high-ranking official. Asked which work was superior, the wife of the subject answered in admiration of Zhou's achievement:

> . . . The first painting has merely mastered my husband's features. The other has also conveyed his expression; it has caught his personality, and the way he looks when he is speaking with a smile.[8]

When the eminent Zhou Fang painted on command for Dezong, the request was couched in the most polite terms. Through the intermediary of his brother, the artist was approached:

Your brother Fang, sir, is an excellent painter. It is Our desire
that he paint a deity for Chang ching ssu; notify him in a special
fashion of Our wish.

The author further related that after a summons was issued Fang did
the painting:

When he brought down his brush, the populace of the capital
came jostling each other to see, pushing their way to the garden
gate of the temple. Among them were both wise men and
simpletons; some talked of the excellence of the work while
others pointed out its flaws. The artist made revisions to suit
their ideas, and in little more than a month all criticism ceased.
There was no one who was not delighted with the exquisiteness
of the final product; and he was judged foremost in his time.[9]

This is a remarkable anecdote regarding the role of the artist in
society. Apparently, by the end of the eighth century, court artists
were summoned tactfully, a marked contrast to the regrettable garden
incident of Taizong's alleged slighting of Yen Li-ben. Yet Zhou's
response to satisfy the populace by correcting faults in his work
indicates the relative sensitivity of the artist to the evaluation of
others. The subjugation of one's personal aesthetic judgment to the
expectations of the viewer was the source of much dismay for later
aesthetes in the Song era, foremost among whom were Mi Fei and Su
Dung-po. Thus, by the end of the eighth century, the status of the
artist stood midway between court attendant and the emerging ideal of
the independent artist.[10] That the rank of the artist in middle Tang
society was elevated is evident in the discussion of one who advanced
in the social hierarchy solely on artistic merit, judging by Zhu Jing-
xuan's account of the artist Zhen Xiu-ji:

From the (785-805) era on, he was the only individual in the
capital who owed his advancement solely to his artistry as a
painter and was continually graced by imperial favor. He was
finest in landscapes, bamboo, and rocks, flowers and birds,
secular figures, worthies of old, votive icons, and strange
beasts, and in those subjects led his generation.[11]

There were a number of recorded painters at court. Han Huang, a
member of the Council of State, was described as a calligrapher and

painter of figures and scenes.[12] Although Han Huang as well as the aforementioned Zhen Xiu-ji portrayed a variety of subjects, some artists worked in a particular genre. One such Tang specialist of birds and flowers was Bian Luan:

> During the 785-805 era the kingdom of Silla sent some dancing peacocks as tribute. Te Tsung summoned Pien to depict them in the Hsuan wu Hall. One was shown from the front, the other from the rear. Their kingfisher-green hues stirred with life, their golden plumage shimmered and flashed; it was as if clear voices were linked in perfect time to the complicated measures of the dance.[13]

This kind of specialization, whether figures, landscape, religious subjects, feathers and fur (birds and animals), or bird and flower paintings, anticipates the Song dynasty, when artists were often expert in one kind of painting. The Song attitude is apparent in an art historical text of the period: Unlike the Tang essays on art, which were arranged according to the evaluation of the artist's achievements, Guo Ruo-xu arranged his discussion according to the type of painting.[14]

The high esteem for landscape painting, often spoken of as reaching its climax in the Song, likewise originated in the Tang. Historical accounts document the growing appreciation and prominence of the subject, like the poetic description of the work of Zhu Shen by Zhu Qing-xuan:

> His renderings of precipitous ridges, and the subtlety of his successive distances; the limpidness of his lake tones, and the splintered look of his rock markings; the peaks that towered upwards under his brush, and the clouds that mounted from its tip; the ravines and somber depths that he set within an inch or two; his intermingling of pines and bamboo groves, and the gloom or pallor of clouds and rain: all these, though they were invented by predecessors, were made by Chu into models for later generations.[15]

Moreover, landscape painters were the subject of poems like Du Fu's ode to the landscape artist Wang Zai:

> Ten days to paint a rock
> Five days to paint a stone

An expert is not to be hurried
Only so will Wang Zai leave you one of his authentic works.[16]

Artists were now free to represent nature without having to include
narrative figures, an independence that was burgeoning in Xuanzong's
academy of painters. Thus Wang Zai is credited with the painting of
a screen with just two trees. Several such landscapes have been
preserved; one popular theme of this era was the depiction of the four
seasons.[17] Just as officials in distant provinces were requested to
compose poems on their respective regions, so too, a governor of
Lianzhou was asked by the emperor to regularly submit paintings of
the scenery of that area.[18]

ARCHAEOLOGY

In comparison to the numerous archaeological finds from earlier
reigns, not much has been found belonging to this era. Only four
tombs are dated to Dezong's reign. Princess Tangan, buried in
Wangjiafen in Xian in 784, has the usual subterranean tomb, preceded
by a sloping path and offering room, with a domed ceiling in the
coffin chamber.[19] The decor is also consistent with earlier Tang
tombs: The walls are covered with paintings of serving maids and
men; the domed ceiling has a painting of the sun, moon, and
constellations. Several clay figurines, both human and animal, were
unearthed as well as a stone coffin with finely engraved designs of
guardian figures and dragons. The figure style of the murals does not
depart radically from that of Xuanzong's reign of the mid-eighth
century. Portly women and male officials are drawn with a line that
grows thick and thin for emphatic description of the drapery. The
ladies, though still large-bodied, are wearing a new style of high-
waisted dress with deep decollete, their hands wrapped in capacious
sleeves. (FIGURE 70) The drapery of their voluminous skirts
suggests the considerable girth of the forms beneath them. Looped at
the top of the head into a tall, slanted topknot, the hair forms a thick
corona around the face. One pear-shape figure with a split topknot
haircomb has wrapped a scarf around her upper body. Among the
male figures are officials, entertainers, and equestrians. Though these
sculpted ceramics exhibit an interest in capturing the essence of the
character, they fall short of portraiture, like the energetic rider astride
a now-lost mount or the several musicians modeled with animated
body gestures and facial expressions. Also found were some ceramic
heads of ladies (their bodies were not preserved); perhaps these heads

had wooden bodies, as this technique was practiced in the middle Tang era. These heads, in their three-dimensional form, resemble the plump beauties shown in the murals. As for the animal figurines, they represent, in a relatively clumsy way, a camel, horse, ox, and deer. (FIGURE 71) Another Shaanxi tomb deserves mention, though it is not nearly as rich. Among the ruins of its murals (dated 787) is a rather badly effaced figure of a serving woman.[20] Not withstanding its poor state of preservation, the fresco is a reliable example of the feminine ideal at the end of the eighth century. A large-bodied beauty stands in an exaggerated stance that emphasizes her swollen form--her shoulders lean back and her belly protrudes forward, much like the middle Tang Buddhist guardian figures. Her full face, with ample double chin, is topped by a voluminous amount of piled up "cloud hair." Few Tang burials were found in the area of Beijing, so the discovery of eight tombs, several of which are dated in Dezong's reign, is an interesting source of information.[21] Some are identifiable by inscription, like the one of 789 of a high official of Yinzhou. However, the wall paintings are no longer extant, and only a few pieces of pottery are left. The tomb of an army general, dated 792, in Shanxi, yielded several large, blue ceramic ewers with handles and spouts, four lugged jars, and two white porcelain bowls.[22]

The practice of giving gold and silver to the emperor reached its peak in the reign of Dezong; officials reputedly competed in the giving of opulent gifts.[23] Four dishes dated in Dezong's reign have a similar composition and design--large plates with a raised central motif of an animal in profile. This style did not originate at this time; many examples were found in the Hejia horde, but apparently this type of dish was quite popular at the end of the eighth century. A silver plate, found in Liaoning, dated 796, has a central design of a reclining stag; another, fashioned from gold, dated 780-802, found in the Daming Palace, has a double phoenix; and a third, made of silver with a standing deer modeled of raised gold, was found in Guanzheng, Hebei, in 1984.[24] Often the perimeter of these plates is treated as a six-petaled, open lotus flower; each lobe is filled with a vegetal or floral spray. Some, like the Hebei plate, have three feet; a similar one is found in the Japanese Shosoin.[25] This typical middle Tang style, with the main design of an animal at the center, is also adapted for other materials. A large copper plate found in northern Xian at Jengdizhai, dated to this reign, has a raised double phoenix as its central theme and peony clusters modeled on the six peripheral lobes.[26] (FIGURE 72) Also found in the Hebei tomb was a tall, silver Hu-shape jar with tall foot, narrow neck, and wide lip; its handle has been broken off. A common shape based on a Sasanian prototype that appeared before the Tang,[27] this type of vessel had great longevity in both its metallic form and its ceramic adaptation, which continued well into the Song dynasty.

DEZONG'S TOMB

Dezong's shendao has the same number and arrangement of figures as that of Xuanzong.[28] All of the lions are extant, as are the columns, ostriches, flying horses, and one standing figure; the official and horse sculptures are severely damaged. Although not substantially reduced in size, these sculptures demonstrate a decrease in monumentality: One of the winged horses stands nobly, but his head is disproportionately small.[29] Here, too, sculptural delineation of the details is decidedly flatter: The wings are so shallowly carved that they barely project beyond the surface definition of the horse's musculature. The carving of the ostrich, though resembling earlier examples in posture and setting, is much simpler in execution: Still raising a wing as it fluffs its feathers, the bird and its features are unconvincingly modeled. Additionally, in relation to the size of the stele on which it is carved, the bird is considerably reduced. Standing imperiously, his hands resting on the staff of office, the bearded official is a far simpler figure than his predecessors.[30] Still corpulent, this statue is not nearly as porcine as Suzong's sculptures of officials: The face is less plump and the fleshy jowls no longer obscure the bony structure beneath them. The garment is treated broadly, with less detail; this is especially noticeable in the carving of the drapery folds along the sleeves.

BUDDHISM UNDER DEZONG

Dezong made an effort to restrict the outrageous growth of the Buddhist church achieved under his predecessors. A number of acts ascribed to the early years of his reign make clear his desire to contain the far-reaching influence of Buddhism. For one, he had the palace chapel dismantled, and he abolished the services held at court for deceased emperors.[31] Government-sponsored ordination of monks ended. No new temples were undertaken with imperial support.[32] By rejecting the Taoist thaumaturges, Dezong displayed his displeasure with magicians and spiritualists at court. Dezong's early measures stand in contrast to his behavior later in the 780s, when he became a devotee of Buddhism; he even took the Bodhisattva vow in 786 from the scholar Dao Cheng. This espousal of Buddhism has been interpreted as a spiritual search for divine aid in response to his failure to subdue the military governors.[33] Among the belated acts of sponsorship of Buddhism were the reinstitution of masses for his father and the summoning of the renowned monk Fa Zhao to instruct officials in the recitation of Amitofu's name.[34] In 790, he had the Famensi bone relic brought to the capital; it was housed in the newly rebuilt palace chapel so that he could personally worship it. Translation activities continued under imperial patronage; in Chang-an an institute for translating sutras was established. Despite the chaotic times, foreign monks, such as Prana from northern India, who arrived in 781 with sutras of the Tantric school, continued to come to China. Not only was he welcomed at court, he was awarded the high honor of the purple robe and title of Master by the court.[35] In his later years, Dezong, like Xuanzong, espoused both esoteric Buddhism and the Taoist alchemical arts.

BUDDHIST ART

Although esoteric Buddhism had been honored at court since the reign of Xuanzong, not much of the art of that era is extant. Recently excavated material encompassing several media--sculpture, painting, drawing, and metal ritual objects--provide some of the earliest evidence available. Some of these ritual objects are dated to this reign; though not all of these finds are so dated, it seems prudent to discuss them as a body of work rather than individually. Each object was used in this time of turmoil in rituals that appealed to the gods of esoteric Buddhism for peace and stability.

Several small plaques have been found, some of clay, others of more permanent materials. This new format reflects developments in Buddhist art and iconography in India; small-size surfaces were also appropriated for mandalas, or religious diagrams of the cosmic deities. Such small-size icons, obviously meant for private rather than communal worship, were now independent of the architectural sites of which they were once an inextricable part.[36] One round, bronze mandala plaque, dated 796, has the major and minor deities of the cosmos in their hierarchical relationships arranged in a gridlike pattern around the Cosmic Buddha.[37] (FIGURE 73) Another particularly popular theme of Indian derivation shows several Buddhas and Bodhisattvas on bases whose stems connect with that of the central Buddha's lotus base. A clay plaque from Xian has eight Buddhas; their bases, and those of the two Bodhisattvas that flank the central Buddha, are similarly connected.[38] Directly based on Indian Guptan prototypes produced by the Sarnath school in northeast India,[39] similar examples of clay votive plaques from eastern India are still extant; this type of object was adopted in Central Asia, China, and Southeast Asia.[40] Prevalent in many different media in China, this Buddhist motif of linked vines is found in a simpler presentation on a clay plaque from Xian,[41] in a mural from Dunhuang's Cave 332 from the early Tang,[42] and carved in the rock of the cave of Jaijiang in Sichuan, to mention only a few examples.[43] Several of the Chinese clay plaques ascribed to the eighth or ninth century have inscriptions that identify them as "Shanye," or "excellent karma": As a final devotional act, the ashes of devout monks were mixed with the clay that was used to make the plaque.

A third theme found on a pottery plaque is an unusual depiction of 18 Lohans, or enlightened ones, who are placed in a gridlike formation surrounding the central, large, seated Buddha.[44] (FIGURE 74) Some of the Lohans hold special attributes; one is depicted covered with children. Originally, it was the ten disciples of the Buddha that formed the group but the number steadily increased to include patriarchs and other spiritual adepts. Most common are sets of the 16 Lohans like those that survive in Japan; one was brought back from China in 987 by the priest Chonen, but these were individual paintings.[45] More often, the Lohan theme appears in the temples on the side walls adjacent to the rear altar where, in the middle Tang, the number of depictions of "enlightened ones" can reach one hundred.[46] This clay plaque with 18 Lohans also has two monks carrying staffs with rings flanking the Buddha; on the sides are two vertical rows of four stupas with elongated crowning elements. At the bottom are four Guardian Kings, seated in rocky grottoes, with large, flaming aureoles; the guardians figure importantly as iconographical symbols of esoteric Buddhism.

Most rare are the several silk paintings of Tantric mandalas recently found in Tang tombs in Xian. Although each presents a different iconographical theme, all share a square format and a central deity surrounded by writing. One square of silk, measuring 26.5 centimeters a side, has at the center a fairly common image of a seated, eight-armed Bodhisattva, with each hand holding an attribute, such as a scroll, wheel, vajra, or thunderbolt. An additional unusual detail is the small, male devotee kneeling in prayer position on the left.[47] (FIGURE 75) Drawn in the iron-wire line technique, the Bodhisattva's figure is full-bodied; shading has been applied to the cloth draped over the seated legs. Most of the mandala is composed of incantations written around the central figure in a square formation; the periphery of the drawing, in ruinous condition, has auspicious emblems, like vajras. On the basis of the Sanskrit calligraphy this silk mandala has been ascribed to the late part of the middle Tang period. This ink drawing is particularly interesting because of an accompanying inscription that says that learning, and even wearing, the sacred writings will afford the believer the protection of the gods and the ability to achieve what he wishes.[48] At least four such mandalas were interred with the dead, making it clear that these paintings had a specific funereal function. The second silk mandala, from a tomb in Luoyang, similarly shows Sanskrit characters and a multiarmed deity at the center in addition to the four Guardian Kings prominently placed in their respective corners. Although this painting is dated, there is some question as to the interpretation of the *nianhao*, or reign date.[49] The third mandala, *a* square-shape silk measuring 35 centimeters a side, differs in the Chinese characters written around the central square and in the main theme--an image of a woman attended by a kneeling figure.[50] A series of hands drawn in various mudras form a square border.[51] These small paintings are related both to the large pictorial mandalas, which were described by the Japanese monk Ennin in the diary on his travels in China, and to the cosmic diagrams based on Tang prototypes, that are still used for worship.[52] Ritual use of these mandalas was transcribed by Kobo Daishi, a Japanese monk initiated in the esoteric religion in China, in 804.[53] A flower was thrown at the holy diagrams and the deity on which it fell was the patron deity of the novitiate.

Portraits of eminent Buddhist masters emerge as icons of devotion and instruction in this era. One of these, housed in the Toji Temple in Kyoto, is a portrait of the eminent esoteric master Amoghavajra, or Bu Kong; unfortunately, it is badly damaged.[54] The Indian teacher is seated on a simple dais against a plain background; highlighting and shading accent the drapery folds of his robes. The painting, part of a set of portraits of the five patriarchs of the Zhenyan sect painted by Li Zhen, a late-eighth-century artist (active from 780 to 804), was brought home from China in 807 by the Japanese patriarch Kobo Daishi.[55]

Bronze objects associated with Buddhist cults have also frequently been found in later Tang tombs. Among these ritual pieces are temple jars, ewers, and dippers. Of the several tombs that have yielded such articles, one is dated somewhat earlier, to 765: Here a long-handled bronze dipper, a tall, narrow-necked, bulbous bronze jar with fitted cap, and a bulbous bronze jar with pagoda-shape top were found together.[56] A second group of very similar contemporary objects was reported in 1988,[57] and temples in Nara, also dated to the eighth century, have matching bronze long-handled dippers and tall-necked ewers (water jars).[58] Some of these forms were made out of pottery, like the bulbous jar with fitted cap found in the tomb with the silk mandala from Xian.[59]

Extant temples provide evidence of Dezong's espousal of Buddhism. At the important site of Wutaishan is Nanchansi, a temple whose main hall and many of its statues are dated 782. Dominating the three groups of icons on the altar at the rear of the temple is a central, oversize seated Buddha. One-third-size attendant figures consist of pairs of monks, Bodhisattvas, and kneeling devas. (FIGURE 76) On the left of the platform altar is the most important patron deity of Wutaishan, Wenshu, the god of wisdom, seated on his lion. His counterpart, Samantabhadra, mounted on his elephant, is on the right.[60] Consonant with the late middle-Tang figure style, the body is treated less naturalistically; the articulation of anatomical details is no longer of primary importance. Their bodies have lost the quality of *prana*, or inspiration, of the earlier Tang; that is, the figures no longer seem to have taken a breath, but it is rather as if they have just exhaled it. There is a relaxation in the shoulders; the old sense of tension and animation is gone. Conversely, there is an increasingly realistic treatment of the details of the drapery, jewels, crowns, and attributes. At times the garments are extremely fussy; for example, the scarf across the chest of the attendant Bodhisattva winds in and out several times before it falls in an unnecessarily complicated arrangement of folds. This is also apparent in the scarf tied around the waist. This exaggerated realism in the details contrasts with the loss of particularities of character, so that these seem to be generic portraits with superrealistic details.

Following this stylistic transition is the later Tang emphasis on the emotional or expressive qualities of the icons. The first image to evince this change is the guardian figure. One headless sculpture of a guardian from Wanfosi in Sichuan is noteworthy for the extreme torsion of the body and the expressionistic portrayal of the muscles of the figure. (FIGURE 77) In this example, the naked torso identifies the guardian as a Dvarapala and not a Tianwang, who is always shown dressed as a Chinese general.[61] In its extreme emotionalism this sculpture from Sichuan demonstrates that this site once again heralds a new style that is even more dramatically stated at the end of the late Tang. Also from Sichuan, the central image of niche 64 at Sanlizhoushan is a Thousand-armed, seated Guanyin.[62] Like earlier sculptures of the image in Sichuan, its 20 extended arms, all now broken, are shown as if radiating out from the figure; each one held an attribute. The remaining hands are carved in low relief within the circumference of the halo.[63] Now flanking the central image are four additional small-scale, multiarmed Bodhisattvas, also incarnations of Guanyin. Descending on clouds on either side are several dozen attendant and worshiping figures; the full effect is one of an incredibly exuberant, heavenly vision. (FIGURE 78)

NOTES

1. See Peterson, 1979: 499, for an extended discussion of the tax system.
2. Weinstein, 1987: 93.
3. John Lee, "The Dragons and Tigers of 792: The Examination in T'ang History," *T'ang Studies*, 1988, no. 6: 25-47, points out that this year was exceptional because the examiner was a Southerner and, as a result, a high proportion of the successful candidates were from the south; most notable was Han Yu.
4. See Twitchett and Wright, 1973: 10; also Pulleyblank, 1976: 59, for a description of the An Lu-shan rebellion. See also Twitchett, "Varied Patterns of Provincial Autonomy in the T'ang Dynasty," ed. Perry, *Essays on the T'ang* (Leiden, 1976): 107.
5. Dalby, 1979: 592.
6. The nature of these records kept by Ruo-xin are not clear; Twitchett suggests they were part of the Inner Palace Diary. The Song sisters were influential under the succeeding reigns leading up to that of Qingzong, when one of the last surviving of the five sisters was implicated, albeit innocently, in the Sweetdew plot. (See Twitchett, 1992: 49ff.)
7. Guo Ruo-xu, Soper, 1951: 9.
8. TCMHL, Soper, 1958: 211.
9. TCMHL, Soper, 1958: 211.
10. This is a bit of an oversimplification. The artists who achieved aesthetic independence in the Song were few; such men were court officials or high-ranking members of the literati, like Mi Fu and Guo Xi, who painted only to satisfy themselves. Although court artists never achieved that kind of freedom, they were held in increasing esteem.
11. TCMHL, Soper, 1958: 223.
12. TCMHL, Soper, 1958: 220; Cahill, 1980: p. 9.
13. TCMHL, Soper, 1958: 224: "Bian Luan, a native of the capital, won success in the pictorial arts while still a youth, his forte being flowers and birds. The subtleties of his cut branches from plants or trees have never been equalled. One will find his brush-work light and keen, and his use of colors fresh and clear; he explored all the changing poses of feathered creatures, and caught the scent and charm of flowers."
14. See Soper's translation, 1951; Chapter II treats contemporary Song artists according to their speciality. Chapter I, dealing with the Tang painters, and so based on earlier texts, is still arranged according to an evaluation of the artists.
15. TCMHL, Soper, 1958: 218.
16. TCMHL, Soper, 1958: 220.

17. TCMHL, Soper, 1958: 219. This theme of the four seasons was usually expressed by a landscape scene with appropriate foliage, flowers, and animals.

18. TCMHL, Soper, 1958: 226: "Ch'en T'an worked in the field of landscape. In the reign of Dezong [780-804] when he was governor of Lien-chou Kwangtung, he was ordered to depict the scenery of that region and submit his work annually to the court. Rising above the herd both in his rough independence and in the loftiness of his emotions, he stands next to Chang Tsao."

19. Zhen An-li and Ma Ying-zhong, "Xian Wangjiafen Tangdai Tangan Gongzhu mu," *Wenwu*, 1991.9: 16-26.

20. The tomb of Duke Da Chang-gong in Huoyangdi Zhang Wan Tanguo (see Wang, 1990: 86, fig. 11).

21. The grave goods were not illustrated in the report, but two of the tomb records were. (See Beijingshi Wenwu Gongzuodui, "Beijingshi Faxiande Bazuo Tangmu," *Kaogu*, 1980.6: 498-505.) A second tomb is dated 808.

22. Changzhishi Bowuguan, "Changzhishi Xijiao Tangdai Lidu Song Jiajinmu," *Wenwu*, 1989.6: 47-50.

23. Lu, 1983: 176.

24. Kuanchengxian Wenwu Baohuguan Lisuo, "Hebei Guanzheng Chudi Liangjian Tangdai Yinqi," *Kaogu*, 1985.9: 857-858.

25. Hayashi, 1975: 16, figs. 4 and 12. This is a really large plate: The diameter is 61.5 cm.

26. In the Shaanxi Provincial Historical Museum.

27. According to the report, a similar one was found in 1975. (See *Kaogu*, 1978.2.)

28. The Chongling is located in the Cuo'e Mountains, 10 km. north of Yunyang in Shaanxi province.

29. Cheng, 1988, pl. 35, has the winged horse; pl. 43, top, has the ostrich.

30. Wang, 1990: 69, fig. 20, now preserved in the Shaanxi Jingyangzhenling Lingyuan.

31. Most of the information regarding Dezong's attitudes on Buddhism is based on Weinstein, 1986: 90-98.

32. Dalby, 1979: 580.

33. Weinstein, 1987: 95.

34. Weinstein, 1987: 74.

35. Weinstein, 1987: 98.

36. Karetzky, "Scenes of the Life of the Buddha and the Rites of Pilgrimage," *Oriental Art* London 1987, vol. XXXIII: 268-274.

37. *Han Tang Sichou zhi Lu*, 1990: fig. 182, pp. 135 and 164; it is now in the Shaanxi Museum. It has an inscription relating to the five Buddhas on its front face.

38. Wang, 1990: fig. 9, p. 278. Found in 1985, it is made of clay and measures 17.4 cm. high; it is now in the Shaanxi Xian Cultural Research Center; see also *Tangdai Yishu* (Xian, 1991), pl. 85.

39. Joanna Williams, "Sarnath Scenes of the Buddha's Life," *Ars Orientalis*, 1975, vol. X: 171ff.

40. W. Zwalf, *Buddhism* (Britain, 1985): 5, figs. 144-146; (for Southeast Asian examples, see: pl. 224, p. 164).

41. *Han Tang Sichou zhi Lu*, 1990: fig. 183, and pp. 136 and 164; it measures 50 cm. tall.

42. *Chugoku Sekkutsu Tonko Bakkokutsu*, 5 vols. (Heibonsha, 1980-82), vol. III: pl. 94; ascribed to the early Tang.

43. This theme persists until 845, for example, at Danlichigongshan (see *Zhongguo Meishu Quanji*, vol. 12: pl. 71).

44. *Tangdai Yishu*, fig. 79, pp. 87 and 102; the piece measures 13.7 cm meters and is made of clay.

45. Roderick Whitfield, "The Lohan in China," *Mahayanist Art after A. D. 900*, Colloquies on Art and Archaeology in Asia, no. 2 (London 1972): 97.

46. Most extant examples of the sets of Lohans painted or sculpted on the side walls of Chinese temples have been extensively restored. Charles Eliot, *Japanese Buddhism* (London, 1935): 137, notes the parallel development of the worship of Lohans in Japan.

47. Li Yu-zheng and Guan Shuang-xi (Shaanxi Bowuguan), "Xian Xijiao Chutu Tang dai Shouxie Jingzhou Juanhua," *Wenwu*, 1984.7: 50-52. This tomb also contained several pottery figures, and a tall, bulbous jar with fitted cap; its extant mural is fragmentary. Although there is no identifying record by which the contents can be dated, experts have decided that the tomb dates to the later middle Tang; that is, sometime after the Kaiyuan period. A very similar mandala was unearthed in Chengdu in 1944; it is now in the Sichuan Provincial Museum; a later mandala, dated to 980, was found at Dunhuang.

48. Li Yu-zheng, *Wenwu*, 1984.7: 52.

49. The question is whether it belongs to the later Tang (757-759) or Five Dynasties (926-930); in general, it is believed to be Tang. (See Luoyangshi Wenwu Gongzuodui, "Luoyang Chudi Houtang Diaoyinjingzhou," *Wenwu*, 1992.3: 96.

50. Wang, 1990: 226, fig. 4; this mandala was also found in a tomb in Xian. A fourth example, from the western suburbs of Xian, has only Sanskrit writing, and oddly, the center area is blank; (see p. 226, fig. 5).

51. It is interesting to note that a scroll of just the hand postures, found at Dunhuang in Cave 17, is ascribed to the late ninth century. See R. Whitfield, *Caves of a Thousand Buddhas* (New York, 1990): fig. 73, p. 94. A second scroll of just the hand postures is preserved in Japan in the Toji Temple. (See *Toji no Myo Ohzo*, fig. 35, p. 65.) In the Toji scroll the hand gestures are

afforded sole importance. Each is mounted on a lotus base with a flame aureole and an identifying title written in Chinese in the upper left.

52. Reischauer, 1955: 150.

53. Donald Keene, *An Anthology of Japanese Literature* (New York, 1960): 63-66; the monk is also known as Kukai.

54. Sickman, 1974: 182.

55. Cahill, 1980; 14. It is interesting to note that Li Zhen is not mentioned in the Chinese texts as a secular painter, but only as a professional Buddhist artist.

56. Luoyangshi Wenwu Gongzuodui, "Luoyang Tang Shen Hui he Shangsheng Tataji Qingli," *Wen Wu*, 1992.3: 64-67 and 75.

57. Zhang Yihua, "Xijiang Xiruichang Faxian de Tangdai Foju," *Wenwu*, 1992.3: 68-70.

58. Horyuji, a seventh-century temple has a set in its storehouse. (See *Horyuji Tojirukuroodo Bukkyobunka* (Tokyo, 1988): 189-193.)

59. Li Yu-zheng, *Wenwu*, 1984.7: 52.

60. *Wutaishan* (Wenwu Press, 1984): pls. 7-10.

61. Akiyama, 1972: pl. 167.

62. *Zhongguo Meishu Quanji: Diaosubian* vol. 12: pls. 59-61, p. 20. This site has 17 niches; this one is ascribed to the Mature Tang era.

63. Once again, images derived from Tang prototypes survive in Japan, in this case the Toshodaiji Senjukannon, a famous standing figure of the Thousand-armed Guanyin (see *Toshodaiji* Nara, 1985: 12ff). This temple was founded by a Chinese monk, Ganjin, in 754.

PART THREE

LATE TANG (805-905)

The quality of life in the late Tang was greatly changed. Political intrigue and upheaval, sporadic chaos, and military insurrections intermittently threatened daily existence. Some emperors' reigns were short-lived, lasting less than a year. The 300 years that comprise the Tang are fairly equally divided among the three periods--early, middle, and late, but the early period had five emperors (including Empress Wu); the middle period, four; and the late Tang, eleven. Imperial power was further compromised by political circumstances and the severely strained interaction among officials, eunuchs, and emperors. Communication among the ruling parties had so degenerated that at times decisions were made in private.[1] Because of political disruption, several institutional practices ceased. The updating of the official histories ended and there was no attempt to regularly renew the law code. The cessation of these activities was seen as the court's inability to maintain the activities of an earlier time.[2] Consequently the court suffered a loss of prestige. By the late Tang the exam system was of great importance for the recruitment of officials. Unlike previous eras, it was the main means of getting into office.[3] The Hanlin Academy, filled with literati, achieved its greatest prestige at this time.[4] Because this stage of development of the Hanlin Academy was an important model for the Confucian government of the Song, some historians see this era as the beginning of the modern period in China.

Trade with the West did not end when the overland route through Central Asia, having fallen under Arab control, became hazardous.

Sea routes from Canton and Guangzhou provided access to the West; the flow of commerce and the influx of foreigners were constant. As a result the south became extremely prosperous. It was not until the end of the Tang, when rebels looted these port cities and executed 100,000 foreign merchants, that trade with the West was seriously compromised.[5]

Late-Tang pictorial art is characterized by several artistic trends that foreshadow the well-known achievements of the Song dynasty. Song art is characterized by its variety of painting themes; however, several of these pictorial subjects were already important in the late Tang. Evidence gleaned from both art historical records and extant remains demonstrates that there were several Tang practitioners of genre narrative who portrayed scenes of daily life, such as tending children, banquets, and scholars in their gardens, in addition to painters who specialized in the depiction of "feathers and fur," "birds and flowers," and landscapes themes.

In the area of ceramic development as well, several of the hallmarks of Song style appear in the Tang. Archaeological evidence provides numerous examples of monochrome porcelain objects; vessels associated with tea and wine drinking, such as small plates, cups, and bowls, are particularly abundant. Technological advances in underglazing assured better adhesion of the glaze to the vessel's surface, resulting in a more even application of the glaze and a greater purity of color. Moreover, attention was given to perfecting relatively simple forms rather than to elaborate decor. Thus the white porcelains of Henan-Hebei and the celadon-glazed Yue area vessels are pre-dominantly small, refined, delicate shapes with a minimum of adornment. For the first time the so-called "secret celadon" porcelain appears. Thought to have evolved during the later Song era, the recent finds of the Famen Temple establish its presence in the last quarter of the ninth century.

Although the late Tang suffered a severe scarcity of metals, numerous gold and silver objects have been found. Despite this problematic shortage of metals, historical annals record new practices: Officials bestowed silver and gold gifts on the emperor, and scholars involved in compiling the annals were paid with silver vessels. Dated objects wrought from precious metals from the Famen Temple and elsewhere counter the long-held argument that after the An Lu-shan rebellion few skilled works were made, for these objects are of unsurpassed finesse, delicacy, and beauty.

Great literary achievements occur in the late Tang. The literati-official Han Yu forged new styles of poetry and prose that stimulated

artists in subsequent eras.[6]   Han Yu's style of writing was called
guwen, or ancient style; one of his goals was to return to the clarity of
thought and simplicity of expression of earlier times. It was also
during this late period that narrative prose evolved. New genres, such
as the short story, detective story, and narrative *quanqi*, or strange
tales, are cast in literary form. Like Han Yu's *guwen* ideal, much of
this narrative prose is distinctly nostalgic. Stories are often romantic
tales set in the earlier Tang; their main characters are heroes with
remarkable abilities.[7] Narratives that treat heroic themes unique to the
Tang are exemplified by "The Kunlun Slave"--the exploits of a
fearless black character with magical capabilities--or "The Curly
Bearded Hero," the story of an extraordinary soldier of fortune at the
time of the founding of the Tang.[8] A nostalgic mood also pervades
the courts of Muzong, Wenzong, and Wuzong, which were all
involved in the restoration of ancient monuments--a Han era palace
and buildings from Xuanzong's reign, among others. Similarly,
Buddhist art after the 845 religious persecution was marked by
imperial and popular efforts directed toward reconstructing the
temples and monasteries of the past.

Trends in literature parallel developments in the pictorial arts. As
interest in naturalism declined, narrative content and the portrayal of
mood became of paramount importance in court, tomb, and Buddhist
art. In a similar way the poets of the late Tang, notably Li He and Li
Shang-yin, were intentionally ambiguous in their literal meaning, but
their language was rich and strikingly evocative.[9]

Buddhism was not extirpated with the ninth-century persecutions.
To the contrary, immediately after the short-lived proscription of the
840s, the weakened central government sought strength and
confirmation of its authority in Buddhist institutions. Sponsorship of
the ordination of monks and the building and the repair of temples are
testimony of the faith that was still placed in the religion. For people
in the late Tang, life was fraught with hardships that only made them
more receptive to Buddhism. The Chinese were ruled by an unstable
central government, unable to maintain peace or assure prosperity;
burdened by taxes and unjust governors, they also endured
widespread banditry and frequent rebellions. Prominent among the
forms of Buddhism most revered were the esoteric cults that boasted
deities of extraordinary powers and divine attributes (the Thousand-
armed and/or 11-headed Guanyin, the Eight Classes of Beings, and
horrific guardians of the realm). By the end of the period, the paradise
cult of the West, which had promised otherworldly rewards,
continued to offer solace to the decimated population. In addition,

Chan, the school of personal cultivation that espoused rejection of society, was also extremely popular.[10] One of the great Chan poets, Han Shan, whose dates are unknown, is believed to have lived in the ninth century.[11] It is interesting to note the particular appeal of Chan in both the late Tang and the Southern Song era, for both periods were characterized by constant political danger and widespread destruction.

Innovations in the depictions of celestials and new iconographic patterns emerge in late-Tang Buddhist art. Heavenly Guardians, more prevalent than ever, loom as huge martial figures. Sometimes standing, they now also sit on demonic personifications of evil and ignorance. The six-armed Guanyin also assumes a new posture, a variant of royal ease; this pose is more frequently associated with Song icons. New decorative formats for painting appear at Dunhuang: There are vertical narrative panels behind the main icons on the rear wall, and the sloping sides of the tentlike ceiling were newly appropriated for the depiction of large-scale icons of the esoteric forms of the Bodhisattvas of Wisdom and Compassion as well as those of the Buddhas of the Four Directions.

In summary, because of the brilliance of the earlier Tang eras and late-ninth-century political chaos and unbridled militarism, the true accomplishments of the late Tang have gone uncatalogued. Moreover, many late-Tang achievements have been attributed to the subsequent Song dynasty. Despite the uncertain times, the late-Tang era produced innovations in several areas, including the civil service system, new narrative and prose movements in literature, the perfection of porcelain monochrome-glazed vessels, stylistic and thematic developments in the pictorial arts, and iconographic advances in Buddhist art.

NOTES

1. Twitchett, 1992: 37
2. Twitchett, 1992: 161.
3. Twitchett, 1992: 90.
4. Twitchett, 1992: 94.
5. Wang Zhen-ping, "Tang Maritime Trade," *Asia Major*, 1991, vol. IV: 7-38. (See also Edwin Reichauer, "Notes on T'ang Dynasty Sea Routes," *Harvard Journal of Asian Studies*, 1940: 142-164.)
6. Han Yu, for one, is credited with founding the neo-Confucian movement. (See Charles Hartman, *Han Yu and the T'ang Search for Unity* (Princeton, 1986): 217.)
7. Ch'en Shou-yi, *Chinese Literature* (New York, 1961): 277, says "these tales beguiled the tedium of existence."
8. Yang Xian-yi and Gladys Yang, *The Dragon King's Daughter* (Beijing, 1954): vi. Pei Xing, ca. second half of the ninth century, wrote the "KunLun Slave," which takes place in Daizong's era, 766-779, (see p. 82); Du Guangting, 850-933, wrote the "Man with the Curly Beard," which described the founding of the Tang;(see p. 87).
9. James Liu, "Ambiguities in Li Shang-yin's Poetry," *WenLin* (ed. Chow Tse-tsung, Wisconsin, 1968): 65-85; also, A. C. Graham, *Poems of the Late Tang* (Britain, 1970): 89-119.
10. Chan Buddhism, or Zen was introduced into court during the early Tang; Wu Ze-tian had invited two masters to court. It was not until the middle Tang and the so-called second patriarch that Chan became popular; it reached its first florescence before the An rebellion. See S. Dumoulin, *A History of Zen Buddhism* (Boston, 1963): 88, and 96ff. According to Dumoulin, Zen was one of the few sects to survive the persecution. (See p. 106.) However, recent evidence has shown the continued popularity of the esoteric and Amida cults as well.
11. Burton Watson, *Cold Mountain* (New York, 1970): 7ff; little is known of this mysterious poet who lived in the Tiantai Mountains and was immortalized in later Chan painting as a scruffy scullery character.

CHAPTER X

EMPEROR XUNZONG

Xunzong who ascended the throne in 805 was psychologically and physically incapable of ruling.[1] Sometime before his ascension, he had a stroke, lost the power of speech, and was unable to make decisions; yet, he was made emperor.[2] Not surprisingly, Xunzong's reign was short, lasting but seven months. During this period, two low ranking commoners assumed authority and attempted to take power away from the eunuchs. A coalition of usually antagonistic parties, high ranking officials and eunuchs, succeeded in a coup which set Xianzong on the throne.

Xunzong was a follower of Chan Buddhism, which he espoused long before his assumption of the throne.

NOTES

1. Twitchett and Wright, 1979: 11.
2. Waley, 1948: 36.

CHAPTER XI

EMPEROR XIANZONG

Xianzong (r.805-820), who became emperor at the age of 27, was one of the stronger rulers of the late Tang. Building on the achievements of Dezong, he was able to further consolidate the central government's authority and to establish a stability that lasted for 50 years. He has been called the last reformist emperor of the Tang.[1] His was a relatively long and stable rule. Under Xianzong, the empire was strengthened, militarily and economically. Rebellions in Sichuan and in the Yangze region were suppressed.[2] Between 810 and 820 the Henan region also was brought within the central government's sphere of control, but the campaign against the region of Hebei did not succeed. In an effort to demilitarize hostile provinces, when uprisings were successfully quelled, an attempt was made to destroy the political fabric of rebellious territories. [3] Xianzong also attempted to reconcile the differences among the various political factions. To assuage members of the slighted official class, the emperor bestowed on them honors and privileges for meritorious service. Despite Xianzong's successes, problems persisted in the provinces. The armies stationed along the borders of the empire were a financial burden to the people. A number of measures were undertaken to improve financial and political organization by limiting the power of the provincial governors to the prefecture of the provincial seat of government, leaving provincial matters and the collection of tax monies to be dealt with by the provinces directly. But taxes were difficult to collect, and succession to the military governorships was also a source of contention.

An effort was made at court to limit expenditures. Confucian scholars held up the extravagance of past emperors as a practice to be avoided. A series of memorials by literary figures, such as Yuan Zhen, early in the era called upon the emperor to lessen the size of his harem, to be more available to ministers, and to spend less time and money hunting. The court acquiesced.[4] In line with these financial restraints, histories record Xianzong's reluctance to make extensive repairs to older structures in the capital.[5] One solution to the perpetual shortage of metals and to the problem of inflation was to print paper money.[6] Books, games (playing cards), Buddhist scriptures, and art were also reproduced using the relatively new technique of woodblock printing.

Like emperors of the past, Xianzong collected art. His unbridled acquisitiveness is revealed in his requisitioning art treasures collected over the centuries by the family of Zhang Yen-yuan in 818. Zhang rued the loss; writing in 850, he reported that the objects demanded by Xianzong had long since been lost.[7]

When Xianzong died unexpectedly at the early age of 42, foul play was suspected.[8] Rumors persisted that he was killed by Buddhist eunuchs. The eunuchs claimed that he died from a preparation of the "Elixir of Immortality" prepared by the Taoists, since Xianzong was known for his interest in Taoist alchemy. In either case, the fierce political competition among the powerful cliques ended in turmoil.

Some of the greatest writers and poets were active during Xianzong's reign. Prose writers and poets like Liu Zong-yuan (d. 819),[9] Han Yu (d. 824), Yuan Zhen (d. 831), and Bai Ju-yi (d. 846), all served as officials; while the preeminent poets Li He (d. 817), Li Shang-yin (d. 858), and Du Mu (d. 852), did not participate in the government.

ARCHAEOLOGICAL EVIDENCE

Although much has been written about the lack of tomb figurines after the 750s, excavated tombs still contain such objects in addition to the more popular porcelain ware. In comparison to the sumptuary laws of Xuanzong's reign, the historical records testify to an increase in the number of figurines permissible in the tombs of the different ranks of officials; figurines of divinities and the 12 symbols of the hours were mentioned prominently.[12] The tomb of Zheng Shao-fang, dated 810, in Henan, produced 38 burial objects of which seven were pottery figurines. Although they are not illustrated in the archaeological report, the figurines are described as half-figures of three men and four women; the latter have tall topknots that lean to one side. Other tomb articles include a small silver box, reproduced only by a line drawing: Against a background pattern of ring-punched marks, the main design is comprised of two birds facing each other surrounded by leaves. There were also three porcelain pieces: a tall, bulbous jar with fitted lid, a funnel-topped spittoon, and a small, squat, covered water jar. This is the first dated appearance of a porcelain spittoon; another, excavated in Xian in 1955, was ascribed to the mid-ninth century. These spittoons are an adaptation of a middle Tang form first worked in silver and gold.[10] Also found in Zheng's tomb were a gilt bronze incense burner, two bronze mirrors, a set of stone buttons from a game, and other objects.[11]

One of the few dated pieces of Yue ware produced in Zhekiang comes from a tomb dated 810.[12] It is a short-spouted ewer with handle done in the characteristic yellow-green glaze of the area. The ceramics of the Yue region were well known and widely traded: Excavations at Samarra, not far from Baghdad, yielded several pieces attesting to Chinese commerce with the Near East.[13] As early as the famous *Classic of Tea*, ascribed to the poet Lu Yu, ca. later half of the eighth century, Yue ware is mentioned as exceptionally fine for drinking tea, as it casts a jadelike color on the liquid.[14] Early dated Yue bowls are rare, but later Tang examples are flower-shaped, decorated with delicate line engraving, and occasionally gold rimmed.[15] The other ware celebrated for tea drinking by Lu Yu was Xing ware--pure, creamy-white porcelain vessels described as silver or snow colored. Recent evidence, like the material from Zheng's tomb dated 810, suggests that Tang kilns producing the white ware were located in Henan.[16] Excavations at the Dingzhou kilns in Hebei as early as 1941, proved that white ware was already in production there in the ninth century, though evidence for antecedents is as yet lacking.[17] Typical Tang shapes include bowls with wide lips and narrow feet and ewers, often with funnel tops, short spouts and flat handles. Previously only the Song Xing ware produced in Xingzhou, Hebei, was celebrated.

XIANZONG'S TOMB

Laid out like the typical Tang imperial *shendao*, Xianzong's tomb path is reportedly in a good state of preservation.[18] All of the lions at the gates are extant; one of the columns is broken, the other is no longer standing; two flying horses, two ostriches, five stone officials, and eight stone horses remain. The standing guardian official is a tall, stiff figure, the jowls of his corpulent face hang well beyond the jaw. In striking contrast to the stiff appearance of the figure, are the delicately carved hands which rest on the ceremonial staff, and the rhythmic design of the long-sleeved drapery and the ribbons of the official standard.[19] Poor-quality craftsmanship is characteristic of the other sculptures. The horse is short and stocky and the details of its anatomy are not carefully articulated.[20] (FIGURE 79) The legs are squat, and the shape of the head has lost any resemblance to the physiognomy of a real horse. So, too, the naturalistic prototypes for the ostrich are long forgotten: Its neck is craned in an exaggerated loop, in ignorance of the bird's attributes; the wings are treated as a flat plane, and the landscape setting is no longer discernible.

BUDDHISM UNDER XIANZONG

Xianzong, like his father and predecessor, was an avowed Buddhist; his affiliation with the Chan sect antedated his ascension to the throne. The emperor had a close relationship with Duan Fu, a monk active earlier in Dezong's court. Despite his support of Buddhism, Xianzong was desirous of limiting the number of individuals who avoided civic obligations by taking on the role of a monk. In line with his policy to restrain extravagant expenditures, he attempted to limit the building of new, luxurious temples. One exception was the extensive rebuilding of Anguosi in Chang-an.[21] Xianzong also effected the most important change made in institutional control, placing the church under the supervision of the Commissioner of Good Works, a post managed by the eunuch generals.[22] One result of the new supervisory board was the enormous wealth eunuchs were able to amass.[23] In the last years of his reign, Xianzong performed many acts of devotion: In 817, he had a monastery constructed to commemorate his reign. The famous Famen relic was brought to the imperial palace so that he could worship it personally. When the writer Han Yu wrote a letter to the throne in 819, decrying the practice, he was banished.[24] The streets were thronged during the procession bringing the relic to the capital; frenzied worshipers from all levels of society jostled one another and competed in performing extreme acts of devotion to the relic, not the least of which were displays of self-mutilation. In addition devotees gave vast sums of money to the Buddhists.

NOTES

1. Dalby, 1979: 537.
2. Twitchett and Wright, 1979: 11ff; Pulleyblank, 1976: 59 ff, also Dalby, 1979: 525ff. The rebellions, in general, were the result of the problems of succession to the governorship in these quasi-loyal provincial governments.
3. Twitchett, 1976: 106.
4. Waley, 1949: 42.
5. Edward Schafer, "The Last Years of Ch'ang-an," *Oriens Extremis*, 1963, vol. 10, 159.
6. Temple, 1985: 117.
7. LTMHJ, Acker, 1954: 138-143.
8. Waley, 1949: 132; and Dalby 1979: 537, call it outright murder.
9. Y. W. Ma and J. Lau, *Traditional Chinese Stories* (New York, 1978).
10. For similar porcelain vessels, see Watson, 1973: 142, fig. 288; for silver and gold vessel of the same design found in Hejia village, see Wang, 1990: 155, fig. 5.
11. Zhongguo Shehui Kexueyuan Kaogu Yanjiusuo Henan dier Gongzuodui, "Henan Yanshi Xingyuancun de Liuzuo Jinian Tangmu," *Kaogu*, 1986.5: 448-451.
12. Medley, 1981: 103, fig. 94. This piece is from the tomb of Lady Wang Xu-wen in Xiaoxing.
13. Medley, 1981: 101. The shards were found in 1910, but it was the excavation undertaken by Sarre in 1910 and 1912 that identified them as Yue pieces.
14. Michael Sullivan, *The Arts of China* (Berkeley, 1982): 138.
15. Medley, 1981: 101-119.
16. Excavations were reported by Li Huibing, "Tangdai Xingyao Yaozhi Kaocha yu Chubu Tantao," *Wenwu*, 1981.9: 44-48; and Hebei Lincheng Xingci Yan Zhixiaozu, "Tangdai Xingyao Yi Diaocha baogao," *Wenwu*, 1981. 9: 37-43, but dates were not attributed to the finds.
17. Medley, 1981: 80 (see also Li, *Wenwu*, 1972.3: 34-48).
18. Cheng, 1988: 130-131.
19. Cheng, 1988: 64, right; horse: 57, bottom; ostrich: 43, bottom. Wang, 1990: 68, fig. 19, shows the whole figure of another official, which is simplified and not at all refined in any of the details.
20. Wang, 1990: 77, fig. 18.
21. Schafer, 1956: 159.
22. Weinstein, 1979: 100.

23. Ennin describes the confiscation of a eunuch's immeasurable wealth during the subsequent persecutions of Wuzong. (See Reischauer, 1955: 235ff.)

24. Waley, 1948: 143. At the time, the fruit of Han's labor fell on barren ground, but in the next era many of the sentiments he expressed in his memorial were greeted sympathetically. After a year, and a letter of apology, Han was recalled to the capital.

CHAPTER XII

EMPEROR MUZONG

Muzong (r. 820-824) was a disappointment to the court.[1] His accession was due to the intervention of the eunuchs, who had now advanced to the higher levels of society. Advisers continually admonished Muzong not to spend so much time on pleasurable pursuits, especially hunting, polo, and sumptuous banquets. Despite these reproaches, a lavish building program was undertaken in Chang-an in 820, two "basilicas" were erected in the Great Luminous Park, and Daming Palace was extensively repaired. In 821, a 34-meter structure was added on to the Daming Palace. Owing to the poor financial condition of the country, the construction was severely criticized.[2] Because a third project that proposed enlarging Lotus Park involved extensive relocation of residences and cemeteries, the plan raised public objection and was halted in 822.[3]

Among the problems plaguing Muzong's short reign was the question of leadership in the northeast provinces. Additionally, the eunuchs, now a large component of the political government, were drawn into factional camps that were in perpetual conflict. It was during this reign when corruption in the exam system was so apparent that Bai Ju-yi, the poet official, was ordered to retest.[4] In 823 Muzong fell from a horse in a polo match, becoming an invalid; eunuchs ruled in his stead for the rest of the year until he died at the age of 29. Although Muzong was a follower of the Chan sect, making extravagant gifts to the Buddhist church, he was also responsive to the Taoists at court. Like the suspicious deaths of other Tang rulers, Muzong's demise has been viewed not as the result of the polo accident but as the consequence of imbibing alchemical concoctions in the hopes of achieving immortality.[5]

NOTES

1. Waley, 1949: 133.
2. Schafer, 1956: 161.
3. Schafer, 1956: 161.
4. Dalby, 1979: 640.
5. Weinstein, 1987: 106.

CHAPTER XIII

EMPEROR QINGZONG

At age 15, Qingzong (r. 824-826) succeeded to the throne. Apparently an indolent teenager, he habitually arrived late for court, and spent far too much time with the ladies and hunting. Like his predecessor, Qingzong also engaged in several extravagant building projects. In 825 he had a new basilica erected in the Daming palace; the painted panel decorations used lavish amounts of gold and silver foil.[1] A new pond with a royal hall was built in 826; in the same year, the Han palace of Wenyang was restored.[2]

Civil distress at the arrogant misuse of power by the eunuchs under Qingzong's mandate led a small group of rebellious men to storm the palace in an unprecedented protest. Within a short period of time, Qingzong, returning from a hunting expedition late at night, was killed in a drunken brawl; he died only having reached the age of 17.[3] The extraordinary circumstances of his death are explained as a eunuch plot.[4] In 827 his brother Wenzong ascended the throne.

There is but one entry in art history of an artist active in this reign, Zuo Quan, from Sichuan, who painted Buddhist, Taoist, and secular subjects. His work was found in Chengdu and Chang-an.[5] Here, as elsewhere, it is apparent that artists of the Tang were responsible for creating secular and religious works for both Taoist and Buddhist patrons. Slight adjustments in iconographic details were presumably the only characteristics that distinguished these works from one another.

NOTES

1. Schafer, 1956: 162.
2. Schafer, 1956: 163.
3. Waley, 1949: 168.
4. Dalby, 1979: 646.
5. Guo Ruo-xu, Soper, 1951: 23.

CHAPTER XIV

EMPEROR WENZONG

Emperor at 17, Wenzong (r. 826-840) was a serious-minded young man, determined to remedy the government. In an effort to reform imperial expenditures, household expenses were drastically cut, the number of concubines was reduced, and imperial decrees ordered "simplicity and sobriety in costume, makeup, ornamentation, carriages, and even conduct."[1] On alternate days the emperor held imperial audiences; resuming a long neglected practice, he made himself available to his officials. Wenzong was bitterly opposed to both the power of the eunuchs and the Buddhist establishment, which were interrelated spheres of influence. In 835, endeavoring to free himself of eunuch control, he took part in a plot--the Sweet Dew Incident--which failed disastrously.[2] It is said that after this defeat, Wenzong withdrew from the primary arena of political turmoil to the solace of wine. A patron of Confucian studies and a lover of poetry,[3] Wenzong sponsored many imperial activities that attempted to revive the artistic achievements of the past; such efforts mirrored the nostalgic mood that pervaded the late Tang. Wenzong's death has been attributed to an old illness.[4] Among the intrigues of the last part of his reign was the question of succession, which was exacerbated by the mysterious death of his son and designated heir. In the end, a eunuch faction successfully backed one of Emperor Muzong's sons, Wuzong.

In the particular case of Wenzong, who like other emperors vowed to strengthen the government, supported Confucian institutions, and achieve a stable and long-lasting reign, much more historical information was recorded. Like other such emperors, Wenzong was also a patron of the arts, which so often embodied Confucian ideals. In an effort to recapture the splendor of ancient times, Wenzong had two eighth-century buildings in Qujiang Park from the era of Xuanzong rebuilt; and he also had the pool dredged. Furthermore, in 841 reconstruction of Weiyang Palace (from the Han dynasty) was once again undertaken.[5] Like the emperors of the past, Wenzong was an antiquarian; his concerns were recorded by the art historian Zhu Qing-xuan:

> During the 827-836 era the emperor Wen Tsung had antiquarian and Confucian interests. He decided that the illustrations of Mao's edition of the Poetry Classics, which had been done by Wei Hsieh at the court of Ming Ti of the Chin dynasty, fell short of full accuracy in respect to plants, trees, birds and beasts, ancient sages, and rulers and subjects, and so ordered Hsiu-chi to make a new set. In every case the latter first checked the nomenclature against the classical text and then did as he thought best in developing the theme. Thus, whether he was showing the cut of headgear or the shapes of flora and fauna, he did not neglect to show in detail even the most ancient, nor fail to present clearly even the most obscure. Once he (did a screen with bamboo for the Wen ssu hall. On this the emperor composed a poem that runs:
>
> Here the subtle mind of a fine artist has revolved.
> Cunning at such a height seems truly inspired.
> When brought to be looked over near a window,
> Its tangled shadows merge, then grow light again.[6]

Later, the Song art historian Guo Ruo-xu recorded that in the year 828:

> Wen Tsung made a personal selection of those princes and officers whose services had been outstanding, as heads of Ministries, and directed his master to portray them in a pavilion on (lake) T'ai-i, where he examined them morning and night.[7]

One of the artists active during Wenzong's reign was the great portraitist Zhou Fang whose many accomplishments were recorded by the historians. Guo Ruo-xu offers a rather interesting anecdote casting Zhou Fang, a revered figure painter specializing in the depiction of women, in the role of a teacher. It is rare that Chinese artists are so portrayed. Zhou instructed Chen Xiu-ji for 20 years during which time Chen copied the works of master; he discussed and critiqued his efforts "so as to pass on the finer points of his own art."[8] This type of interest in the lives of artists is indicative of a time when the artist's role in society is increasingly prominent.

ARCHAEOLOGY

In accord with the numerous silver objects found in the late Tang, it is important to remember the new role these precious materials played as a commodity. Court historians were paid in silver vessels, as well as the traditional bolts of silk cloth, during Wenzong's reign.[9] But so far, no known examples of this type of official vessel have been found.

Certain themes common in Tang art repeatedly appear in the fine and applied arts: ladies in a garden, musical parties, foreigners, and scholars in a garden. The classic image of a scholar in a garden, for example, is cast on a bronze mirror inscribed with the date of 827; here the figures play music in a landscape setting. In other variants the characters drink or chat with friends.[10] (FIGURE 80) The subject of sages seated in a bamboo grove playing musical instruments was not a Tang innovation. Illustrated for centuries, the theme appeared on ancient Chinese mirrors as well as in tomb decor, like the fifth-century Nanjing tomb tiles.[11] But in the Tang this theme became ubiquitous, as is evident in the several types of decorative objects in the Shosoin collection in Japan. Among the contemporary objects in Japan are comparable mirrors as well as a marvelous lacquered musical instrument with silver and gold inlaid scenes of sages seated under a tree and playing the zither or drinking wine.[12] Although seemingly secular in its connotation, the image of sages in the woods relates to Taoist practices to prolong life.[13] In fact, playing the Chinese zither itself was considered to be a means of achieving immortality;[14] thus the lacquered instrument's decor is particularly apt. The depiction of a sage in a landscape is also present on a painted screen preserved in Toji, in Kyoto, which is believed to represent a more specific subject: the visit of a nobleman to the Chinese Tang-era poet Bai Ju-yi.[15] In the end the illustration of sages in the woods is remarkable for remaining relatively unchanged while having been adapted to various media and styles over a long period of time.

Not unrelated to these depictions of scholars in garden settings is the popular ninth-century pastime of gardening. Paralleling Wenzong's interest in the restoration of the gardens of Xuanzong's era, aristocrats and officials tended gardens in which they raised exotic blooms and wildlife. The minister Li De-yu's "natural garden" on his large estate was considered the finest of the age, with its "fantastic stones and ancient pines" and pavilion for viewing art.[16] There were wildlife preserves filled with both domestic fowl and exotic birds. Another official, Duan Cheng-shi, had a magnificent garden filled with flowering plants. Typical of this late-Tang era was the omnipresence of tree peonies; now the most beloved of blossoms, they filled gardens and decorated all kinds of articles. Many of the hairpins, boxes, cups, and plates were fashioned from precious materials. Depicted in the various stages from early bud to full, luxurious blossom, peonies are often shown with paired birds, a symbol of conjugal bliss; as such, these images are most frequently associated with women and adorn their personal articles. The peony paired with phoenixes on a gilt silver plate found in Yaoxian and ascribed to a slightly later era (847-60) is an excellent example. (FIGURE 91)

WENZONG'S TOMB

Wenzong's tomb was of the traditional Tang imperial type. The shendao reportedly still has a broken column, a stone lion, and a damaged figure of an official.[17]

BUDDHISM UNDER WENZONG

Wenzong made tremendous efforts to limit the growth of the Buddhist church.[18] Through a series of edicts the Buddhist community's growth was impaired and its activities were restricted. No new monasteries were allowed to be built. Ordinations were limited; the regulations for the registration of monks were tightened. However, further measures met resentment among the populace. Ambitious plans were under way to take down a palace icon when a typhoon hit the capital and frightened its residents. Because the populace believed the storm was divine retribution for anti-Buddhist activities, the order to remove the icon was revoked. Later, in 835, restrictive measures were enacted that attempted to purge the Buddhist church. As a result Buddhist monks were tested for literacy in the scriptures; those found incompetent were defrocked. Buddhist rituals and religious observances were banned from court events and disassociated from the imperial cult, especially the celebration of the emperor's birthday. These obstructive measures, evidence of the growing dissatisfaction with the Buddhist church, foreshadow dramatic events in the following reign.

BUDDHIST ART

Not much Buddhist art is attributed to Wenzong's reign.[19] Cave 101 at Dunhuang, dated 839, both preserves many of the iconographic formats prevalent in the earlier Tang caves at the site and presents innovative features as well. These new features may be of Tibetan derivation, for Dunhuang was under their dominion until 851. Tall narrative panels were painted on the rear wall behind the main iconic sculptures; they often contain scriptural illustrations. One of the popular narratives of this era is the ancient *Hungry Tiger Jataka*. The pair of Bodhisattvas, Wenshu and Samantabhadra, who are seated on their mounts (the lion and elephant, respectively) are painted on the walls flanking the rear niche. Compared with the middle Tang depictions of their entourage, with a child and a foreign groom attendant, as in Cave 148, in the later Tang a large retinue is shown. There are several kinds of divine beings, including guardian figures, multiple Bodhisattvas, and musicians as well as deities of horrific and distinctly demonic character, as in Cave 148.[20] Exotic in nature, with horns, fangs, multicolored skin, bulging muscles, and flaming hair, these members of the retinue are the Eight Classes of Being. Described in the scriptures as the audience of Shakyamuni, these beings now attend the Bodhisattvas as well. Although at Dunhuang they are interpreted more broadly, the sutras describe them as:

> Devas, or gods, Nagas or snake deities, Gandharvas or celestial musicians, Asuras, or Titans, Garudas, or monster birds, Kinnara, half-human half-bird musicians, and Mahogany deified reptiles. . .[21]

A more familiar icon is the forehall painting of the Thousand-eyed and Thousand-armed Guanyin. Also popular are the illustrations from scriptures represented on the side walls: The left wall images are drawn from the *Huayan Sutra*, the right has representations from the *Lotus Sutra* and the Paradise of Amitofu. The Vimalakirti and Wenshu debate rendered on the doorway wall is noteworthy for its inclusion of a Tibetan in the audience who replaces the image of the Chinese emperor. One surprising theme is the portrait of the donors flanking a dated inscription. Though much has been written about Tang portraiture, this depiction, one of the few extant examples, unfortunately reveals more about the costumes of the figures than their physiognomies.[22] Relatively large-scale, though still smaller than life-size, the image of the female donor is non-Chinese and dark-skinned. She is dressed in a long-sleeved gown with pale-blue skirt and aqua bodice and sleeves, a terra-cotta jacket, and a sheer, black scarf; each garment has a contrasting textile design. (FIGURE 81) The male figure, badly effaced, has light skin and is simply dressed in a long, round-collared gown. Both donors have an attendant; the young maid wears a round-collared terra-cotta dress with scattered floral print, tied at the waist with an aqua belt; the skirt has two slits in front.

NOTES

1. Schafer, 1956: 151.
2. Wright and Twitchett, 1973: 12; Dalby, 1979: 654ff.
3. Waley, 1948: 168.
4. Dalby, 1979: 658; earlier, in 831, the emperor had a "stroke" that affected his speech; there is enough in Tang politics to arouse suspicion about this illness and his subsequent death.
5. Schafer, 1956: 164.
6. TCMHL, Soper, 1958: 223.
7. Guo Ruo-xu, Soper, 1951: 9.
8. Chen Xiu-ji, who passed the classics exam, copied at least 60 works; TCMHL, Soper, 1958: 223.
9. Twitchett, 1992: 153. The practice began in 833; for later usage, see p. 156.
10. Meng Jia-rong, "Congtang Taihe Yuannian Dongyin Tanchuanshi Fanniuyin," *Wenwu*, 1984.7: 70-71.
11. Now in the Nanjing Museum, these tiles show six sages seated under a tree; each character is identified by name and holds an attribute. A. Soper, "A New Chinese Tomb Discovery: The Earliest Representation of an Famous Literary Theme," *Artibus Asiae*, 1961, vol. XXIV, no. 2: 79-86.
12. Hayashi, 1975: 20 and 129ff.
13. These include breathing, physical exercises, meditation, and proper diet.
14. R. H. Van Gulik, *The Lore of the Chinese Lute* (Tokyo, 1940, reprint, 1969): 51.
15. Akiyama, 1977: 69, fig. 71, says this is a Japanese copy after a Chinese original. Interestingly enough, this is believed to be a secular object that was appropriated for esoteric practices. Similarly the silver tea jar from Famen decorated with a sage in the landscape is also apparently a secular object used in esoteric ritual. (See chapter XVIII).
16. Schafer, 1956: 152.
17. Cheng, 1988: 131.
18. Weinstein, 1987: 106-114.
19. Guo Ruo-xu, Soper, 1951: 23, records but one Buddhist artist active during the Taiho era (827-836), Zhao Kong-yu, a native of Sichuan, who painted both Buddhist and Taoist subjects.
20. *Zhongguo Shiku: Dunhuang Maogaoku,* 5 vols. (Wenwu, 1987), vol. 4. Cave 172, pl. 15; Cave 148, pl. 34; Cave 159, pl. 80. Cave 172 and Cave 148 are designated mature Tang 712-781, Cave 148 is middle Tang (781-848).
21. Soper, 1959: 227.

22. These portraits have been identified as belonging to a family important in Dunhuang after the Tibetan occupation. (See *Zhongguo Shiku*: Dunhuang, vol. IV: pl. 101, p. 223.)

CHAPTER XV

EMPEROR WUZONG

Wuzong (r. 840-846), the third of Muzong's sons, owed his rise to the throne to the intervention of the eunuchs. Despite their role in his attaining the throne, he worked hard to diminish their power.[1] These attempts resulted in a considerable decrease in their influence: Though still powerful at court, the eunuchs' military activities were curtailed. Taking military control away from the eunuchs allowed more efficient administration of the armed forces. In times of military crisis, like the Uighur attacks of 842 or the serious uprising in Zhao-yi, the imperial army was able to quickly and successfully terminate the conflicts. Emperor Wuzong was fiercely anti-Buddhist; his measures, described below, seem aimed at annihilating the religion and its institutions, though financial considerations were paramount in causing the proscription. The emperor was wholly supportive of Taoism and sought to establish its primacy. In 841, he had several Taoist structures built, and in 843, a convent for a Taoist priestess was constructed; the grandest project of all came in 845, when the Sylph Terrace, 50 meters high, was erected. Its garden was filled with conifers and imported rocks.[2] A grand celebration marking the hundredth anniversary of the Taoist Palace of Greatest Clarity, built by Xuanxong, reflects the nostalgia of the era.[3] Guided by Taoist fanaticism, Emperor Wu, a Taoist in the manner of Dezong and Xianzong, imbibed alchemical elixirs; some believe it was these that first made him mad and then killed him.[4]

ARCHAEOLOGY

The tomb of an official, Li Cun, who died in 845, was discovered in Yanshi, Henan; it contained several kinds of artifacts, among them six white jade articles. Two are small jade sculptures of a sheep and a cow;[5] the other jades are small-scale utilitarian articles: a cup, a water jar with lid, a covered box, and an oblong plate. The lid of the box has a memorable, large floral design composed of one fully opened peony, reflecting the late-Tang delight in that flowering plant. Here, jade was adopted for the box form that had been made of gold in the middle Tang. The small, unadorned wine cup, with a four-lobed body supported by a low foot, was also derived from metallic prototypes. (FIGURE 82) Jade is the most precious of all materials to the Chinese, who, since neolithic times, admired its hardness and color. Associated with longevity since antiquity, its use as a funeral article was related to the belief in its ability to prevent putrefaction of the corpse.[6] By the late Tang, it seems that jade, admired for its inherent beauty, was used for small decorative objects. Three white porcelain pieces were also unearthed from the 845 tomb, including a wide-shouldered jar with a small mouth and lid and a porcelain spittoon with a broad, funnel top and bulbous body that resembles the one dated in Xianzong's reign.

A series of recently discovered miniature coffins shows a change in funeral practices. One example, dated to this reign by the presence of a coin of Wuzong's reign, is a boxed set--an inner coffin of iron and an outer one of stone.[7] The use of these long-lasting materials indicates that the ancient, indigenous desire to preserve something of the body was still a prevalent consideration.[8] Many of the themes that appear on this stone coffin, like the directional animals, have a long and continuous history. Originating in pre-Han funeral art, these images persevered through the Tang era, as the spirit animals on a silver coffin, from Jiangsu, attributed to the late seventh century demonstrate.[9] Narrative scenes are an important component of the coffin from Wuzong's era. One scene depicts an ancient Buddhist narrative, the *Dipamkara Story*: a young brahmin worships the Buddha. As a result of his piety, eons later, the brahmin was born as the Historic Buddha.[10] As a funerary decoration this story seems most unusual, but there is a certain logic in the theme of rich rewards for faith in the Buddha. A second miniature limestone coffin found in Gansu and ascribed to before 850, also presents a scene of the life of the Buddha. This reliquary, measuring 45.6 centimeters long, displays a syncretic approach to Buddhist and Taoist theology. On one side is the death of the Buddha, on the other, the assumption of the soul.[11] (FIGURE 83) Two other small coffers made of precious materials were found in 1985 in Shaanxi. The larger one, made of silver, has Buddhist figures modeled out of gold attached to the front, back, and sides. (FIGURE 84) Pearls and turquoise adorn its top, hang from the eaves, and are set into its stepped, gilt base. The fourth reliquary, lacking narrative themes, is made of gold, with pearl and jade flowers and lions.[12] It is somewhat ironic that a mortuary art that began as a Taoist form and reached its artistic maturity in the Six Dynasties, should be adapted for Buddhist use. The ancient function of the coffin was to protect the physical remains of the deceased from decomposition and to orient the soul in its postmortem assumption. Now a miniature coffin holds the post-cremation remains, in accord with Buddhist practice. In form and appearance, these coffers are unlike earlier Buddhist reliquaries, which were modeled on the Indian monument, the stupa, and its Eastern adaptation, the pagoda. The boxes, adapted by the Chinese, now imitate palatial architectural forms, with overhanging eaves and entranceway.

The narrative themes found on these reliquaries are indicative of the renewed interest in storytelling that took place in the late Tang. A revival of ancient Buddhist pictorial narratives is also visible among the murals of the cave-chapels of Dunhuang. There the *Hungry Tiger Jataka*, (one of the earliest stories to be portrayed) at the site after a lengthy period of absence, is seen again in the late-Tang Caves 101, 85, and 231. In the earliest phase of Chinese Buddhist art, narratives were preeminent; however, with the introduction of the icons of the Mahayanist pantheon, they fell into disuse. The resurgence of Buddhist storytelling is paralleled by the contemporary depiction of narrative details in the secular arts--murals and tomb figurines--as well as in the proliferation of short stories produced at this time.

Sumptuary laws from Wuzong's era limited the number of wooden images; previously, ceramic figurines were restricted. This statute represents the change of materials in funeral mingqi. Although inferior in craftsmanship and of perishable material, two wooden figures of the later Tang have been found. They are relatively crude and only roughly approximate the appearance of a human. Still, the late-Tang-style figure is in evidence: The female figure has a fleshy pear-shape face, hair piled on top of the crown of the head, and a dress with low-cut bodice, high waist, ample skirt, and voluminous sleeves in which the hands are placed. The male wears a round-necked belted garment, also with capacious sleeves; he has a similarly shaped head, and low, cloth cap.[13] (FIGURE 85)

WUZONG'S TOMB

Said to have been created in the typical Tang mode, Wuzong's tomb
path has two extant stone lions. Three of the six stone horses, one
column, six of the flying horses, and five officials are reported as
broken and toppled.[14] But a visit to the site evinced only the two
lions; both are poorly carved and small in size and stature. (FIGURE
86)

WUZONG AND BUDDHISM

Wuzong is remembered for his vicious persecution of Buddhism. His
reputation for cruelty was based on the many acts he sponsored to
extirpate the "foreign religion." Imperial decrees ordered the
dismantling of monasteries, the defrocking of hundreds of thousands
of monks and nuns (some were said to have been slaughtered), and the
melting down of metal icons. Detailed analysis of the edicts and
actions taken by Wenzong has shown that this period of annihilation
was not an overnight decision; a continuous effort to systematically
reduce the number and power of Buddhist institutions and
practitioners began as early as 830.[15] These measures, effectively
carried out in both the capital and provinces, were witnessed by the
Japanese monk Ennin, who chronicled the catastrophic results of the
edicts, until he was forced to return home.[16] By 844, a number of
small monasteries were closed. Older monks were transferred to
larger monasteries; younger ones were defrocked. In 845 all monks
under the age of 50 had to return to lay life. By August of that year,
260,500 monks were laicized, as were 2,000 Nestorians,
Zoroastrians, and Manicheans. Their 150,000 slaves were acquired by
the state. More than 4,600 temples and 40,000 private shrines,
chapels, and hermitages were destroyed.[17] Studies indicate that
economic considerations were primarily behind the persecution: The
financial burden of large numbers of monks exempt from tax and
government service, the monies required to sustain the religious
population, and the tax-exempt status of most temples was a serious
drain on the economy.[18] With similar zeal, Wuzong elevated the
Taoist church.

BUDDHIST ART

Sichuan was a sanctuary for political refugees of the Tang court;
twice it was a haven for its emperors. During this period many

eminent monks fled west seeking to escape the persecutions of the Wu regime. A cave dated by inscription to 845 at Danli Chigongshan is silent testimony to the fact that Buddhist projects were still undertaken. (FIGURE 87) This cave presents the Paradise of Amitofu, who is the central image; he is seated in meditative posture on top of an hourglass-shape throne. Flanking him are his two primary Bodhisattvas; now the attendants are nearly as large as the Buddha. Filling the background area are dozens of three-dimensional lotus flowers bearing reborn souls; the stems of their bases merge into one large vine that issues from the base of the central icon. Three stepped registers beneath the icons are replete with seated meditating Buddhas.[19] It is important to note the new halo motif of the main images; radiant points replace the earlier flame and lotus patterns. The Sixteen Visualizations of Amitofu are carved on the walls framing the niche.

NOTES

1. Waley, 1949: 199, Dalby, 1979: 646ff; Wright and Twitchett, 1973: 12.
2. Schafer, 1956: 164-165.
3. Schafer, 1987: 52.
4. Dalby, 1979: 663.
5. Zhongguo Shehui Kexueyuan Kaogu Yanjiusuo Henan dier Gongzuodui, "Henan Yanshi Xingyuancui de Liangzuo Tangmu," *Kaogu*, 1984.10: 910-914. Only the jade objects are illustrated by photograph, the others are represented by line drawings.
6. For an exemplary jade funeral suit from Mancheng, Hopei (from the second century B.C.E.). (See E. Capon, *Princes of Jade*, New York, 1973).
7. Chang Xu-zheng and Zhu Xue-shan,"Shandongsheng Huiminxian Chutu Dingguangfo Sheliguan," *Wenwu*, 1987.3: 60-62. The tomb is dated by the presence of coins from Wuzong's reign; Kaiyuan coins were also present.
8. It was this desire to preserve the body after death that led to various embalming practices; some were successful, as exemplified by the remains at the second-century B.C.E. tomb in Mawangdui, Hunan.
9. Liu Jian-guo, Yang Zai-nian, "Jiangsu Jurong Xingxiang Faxian Tangdai Tongguan Yinkuo," *Kaogu*, 1985.2: 182-184. This coffin, ascribed to Empress Wu's reign, is decorated with a dragon on the long sides.
10. Unfortunately this is not illustrated in the archaeological report; only rubbings of the four directional animals are represented.
11. (See Cheng Ming-chi, "Lingtai Sheli Shiguan," *Wenwu*, 1983.2: 48-52; see also Karetzky, 1988, for an analysis of the decorative program) The assumption of the soul is a popular Six Dynasties Taoist theme.
12. (See Wang, 1990: 276, fig. 6, for the larger reliquary, measuring 21 cm. long. It was unearthed at Qingshansi and is now in the Lintong Museum, Xian. (See p. 275, fig. 5, for the smaller one, which is 14 cm. long.)
13. *Han Tang Silu*, 1990: 104, fig. 133. Found in Qinghai, Xining, these wooden figures, with traces of painting, are ascribed to the Tang. They are now in the Qinghai Provincial Cultural Research Bureau.
14. Cheng, 1988: 131.
15. Weinstein, 1987: 114.
16. Reichauer, 1955: 217ff.
17. Schafer, 1956: 166.
18. Kenneth Ch'en, "The Economic Background of the Hui-Ch'ang Suppression of Buddhism," *Harvard Journal of Asian Studies*, vol. 19, 1956: 67-105.
19. *Zhongguo Meishu Quanji: Diaosubian, Sichuan Shiku Diaosu*: 23, pl. 67.

CHAPTER XVI

EMPEROR XUANZONG

The heir apparent to Wuzong was his uncle, Prince Kuang, who was backed by the eunuchs. Born in 810, Kuang was a sickly, retiring child who grew up in an apparently semi-autistic state. After he acceded to the throne, his persona underwent a dramatic change; he emerged the strong and determined ruler Xuanzong (r. 847-859).[1] Xuanzong's first act was to get rid of the old regime, particularly the Taoists who supported the Buddhist persecutions.[2] Harboring resentment of the three previous emperors (his nephews) for their role in the murder of his father, Emperor Xianzong, he ordered punishments to be meted out to them (posthumously) and to their accomplices.[3] Executions of supporters of the last reign of terror were summarily carried out. In short order the measures most repressive to Buddhism were repealed, restoring the Buddhist church to its former strength.

Although several efforts were directed to fiscal reform and to recodifying the law, the power of the dynasty was ebbing. Late in Xuanzong's reign the northwest was threatened by the Tanguts, semi-nomads of Tibetan descent. The Tanguts, rebelling against corrupt local Chinese officials, resisted Xuanzong's troops for five years. Trouble also prevailed in the southern provinces; unrest broke out in Annam (Vietnam) in 858. Due to abuse of power by local officials, garrison rebellions spread in the fertile Yangze valley. Independent Nanchao (Yunnan) attacked Sichuan at the end of the third decade of the ninth century, and later, from 858 to 866, the garrison mutinied. In the 850s, Nanchao joined forces with Annam, threatening China's southern borders. (It was not until 868 that the south would return to a relatively pacific state.) Xuanzong suddenly died, in 859, of poisoning caused by the alchemical substances he imbibed. As a result, problems arose with the succession, and once again eunuch factions had the opportunity to promote their candidates.

Antiquarian interest and a nostalgia for the past, characteristic of the ninth century and mirrored in the restoration activities of Wenzong, also appear in the several art historical essays written during Xuanzong's reign. Zhang Yan-yuan wrote his *Record of Famous Painting in History (Lidai Minghua Ji)* as well as a compendium on calligraphy.[4] Zhu Ching-xuan's *Celebrated Painters of the Tang (Tang Chao Ming Hua Lu)* was composed in the late 840s.[5] Visiting the capital after the destruction of Buddhist monuments in 845, Duan Zheng-shi transcribed his *A Vacation Glimpse of the T'ang Temples of Chang-an (Sidaji)*.[6] In addition, the Buddhist rebuilding begun under Xuanzong may also be seen as a manifestation of the evocation of the past and the desire to preserve its glories.

ARCHAEOLOGY

Ceramic figurines are not at all common in the mid-ninth century. However, in 1948 several figures were found in a tomb dated to the fourth year of Dazhong (850).[7] One is a portrayal of a camel and his Central Asian groom; the foreigner extends his hands before him, holding the reins (now lost) of the camel. In response to the pressure on the reins, the camel pulls its head back. One new feature is the large monster face modeled in shallow relief on the saddlebag. (FIGURE 88) The camel is nicely realized--there are textural contrasts between the areas of hair and the tufts of fur on the body, but the eighth-century exactness in rendering details and the overall portraitlike effect are lacking. These two pieces are not glazed; their only decoration is hand-painted. A second figurine from this tomb portrays a foreigner, an African man. (FIGURE 89) More crudely rendered than the others and looking like a cartoon, this character is painted black, with a mass of tightly curled hair.[8] Two additional figurines of Africans were found in the tomb belonging to Lady Pei.[9] It was apparently not uncommon to see such visitors here in the Tang, curly haired, black-skinned people arrived from India and Southeast Asia,[10] but there were also people from East Africa who were presented at court in the years 813 to 818.[11] Because of their exotic appearance, they were thought to have supernatural powers. One ninth-century historian remarked on their "nakedness" and on their "ability to tame ferocious beasts."[12] The theme of the African as mythic hero is also found in the literature of the time, for example the miraculous exploits of "The Kunlun Black Slave."

Lady Pei's mid-ninth-century tomb also contained several much larger female figurines, all of which are hand-painted. Considerably reduced in girth, the ladies are not yet slender, but the corpulence of the middle Tang era is gone. Wearing simply tailored garments with voluminous sleeves, their skirts taper at the feet, allowing the toes in their upturned slippers to show. (FIGURE 90) Tilting their heads, they resemble the middle Tang sculptures, but now the hairstyles, like the clothes, are subdued; a single topknot is worn at the crown. The ladies hold objects in their outstretched hands; one has a petal-shape plate with fruit, another holds a mirror.

Objects wrought of precious metals dated to this reign were found in a tomb dated from the Dazong era, 847 to 860, in Yaoxian county. Unearthed was a large silver six-lobed platter: The center of each lobe and the central areas have a raised peony design in gold.[13] (FIGURE 91) Of 23 tombs found in Jiangsu, six are dated by tomb records to this reign (one is dated 848, and another, 854).[14] Small, decorative gold objects like hair adornments, bronzes, and ceramics, including utilitarian earthenware pottery in a number of shapes--tall jars and bowls--were excavated. There were also porcelain cups, water jars for brushes, and the by now familiar spittoon. Two small, flower-shape pottery boxes found in these tombs imitate the style of golden boxes of an earlier era. Two late-Tang tombs excavated in Hebei, one dated by a tomb record to 856, similarly yielded several white porcelain pieces.[15] Among the finds were two small, delicate, refined bowls in the four-lobed shape; plain but for the incising around the rim, both are inscribed at the bottom with the character "Zhang," believed to be the name of either the artist or tomb master. (FIGURE 92) A third bowl, differing slightly in the configuration of the low foot, and a tall, long-necked ewer with a handle are similarly inscribed. By the mid-ninth century white porcelain was used for larger vessels like this tomb's tall, bulbous, covered jar; there was also a small covered bowl with a knobbed lid.

XUANZONG'S TOMB

Xuanzong's shendao, with the typical layout and themes of imperial Tang tombs, is in relatively good repair.[16] Lions from the four gates, a column, the winged horses, and one of the paired ostriches remain. Four of the stone horses are broken, but 13 of the officials are preserved. The carving style has degenerated considerably. The winged, stone horse, small and squat in proportion, is simply carved; its wings form flat bands that appear to be part of the bridle. The face, barely articulated, is a poor comparison to previous stone sculptures. A lion, partly eroded, is not at all fierce in its appearance; its posture is relaxed, and it no longer seems tensely alert.[17]

BUDDHISM UNDER XUANZONG

After the persecution of 845, there was a tremendous effort to restore Buddhism and its monuments. With the increasingly unstable political situation, adherents of the religion appealed to the Buddhist deities for protection of the throne and the solace of their paradises. In Chang-an an edict ordered that 16 temples be reopened, in adding to the four that were allowed to function during Wuzong's reign. Two monasteries were mandated in each prefecture, three in military headquarters. The use of metal for icons was prohibited due to the shortage of materials, and only wood, stone, or clay images were permitted to be made. By 847, consent was given to illustrious monks to reopen monasteries without regard for their location. Chi Xuan, an eminent monk humiliated in the previous era, was invited to court where he was honored. Restored temples were renamed, their new designations reflecting concern for the preservation of the dynasty, such as Paotangsi (protecting the Tang), Tangchansi (tranquillity of the Tang), and Yentangsi (prolongation of the Tang).[18] The art historian Guo Ruo-xu records that Fan Qiong, Chen Hao, and Peng Jian were active restoring Buddhist murals during the period 847 to 850; they painted at least 200 frescoes in Chengdu temples. Regrettably, he adds, much of this work was destroyed in the subsequent civil wars.[19] It has been pointed out that the rebellious uprisings at the end of the ninth century did as much, if not more, destruction to Buddhist art than the proscription.[20]

BUDDHIST ART

Five temples were restored at the important religious site of Wutaishan. Still extant is Foguansi, located at the foot of the five slopes; it was rebuilt in 857 after the original was destroyed during the period of persecution.[21] Organization of the main altar suggests the geographical structure of Wutaishan with its five terraces: There are five groups of deities and their entourages. At the center are three Buddhas (the Past, Present, and Future) with their six attendant

Bodhisattvas. Flanking these are Wenshu and Samantabhadra on their mounts, each with their own celestial attendants. Wenshu, as usual, is accompanied by a small child and a foreign monk; this innovative grouping spread throughout the Buddhist world.[22] Samantabhadra has two Bodhisattvas. At either end of the dais are huge Tianwang guardian figures.

Although the statues are in excellent condition, it is the murals of the Great Eastern Hall that truly merit attention. A burly, corpulent Guardian general no longer stands on the forces of evil but sits cross-legged. The demons, naked, with grotesque bodies and distorted heads, are now pinned down by the force of his knees. (FIGURE 93) Superb drawing renders the expressive, if misshapen, musculature and fearsome expressions of this figure in the act of conquest. The divine scarves of the Guardian King's headdress and armor flutter energetically. Standing nearby is a donor, a demure maiden, her delicacy a stunning contrast to the swarthy general. On top of her head are two elegant braids festooned with flowers; she wears a long-sleeved, voluminous garment with an apron, all drawn in vivid tones of red and aqua. (FIGURE 94) Another figure, a wild, demonic character with fangs and glowing aqua eyes, struts about in a leopard-skin loincloth, holding a sword in his hand. Here, too, the body's musculature is expressively drawn with sepia; shading accentuates the protruding muscles. Behind the ferocious character a conquered demon falls backward; a skeletal creature, his extraordinary anatomy is rendered in tones of red. The exaggerated realism and emotional content of these images are the hallmarks of late-Tang art.

NOTES

1. Waley, 1949: 212. Although the phonetic spelling of this emperor's reign is the same as the sixth emperor, the characters are entirely different.
2. Not much has been recorded about this emperor's reign owing to destruction of court documents during the turmoil at the end of the dynasty. (See Dalby, 1979: 673.)
3. According to Dalby, 1979: 670, Xuanzong even had the rituals at the imperial shrine for Emperor Muzong and his three sons downgraded.
4. Acker, 1954, and Amy McNair, "Fa shu yao lu, a Ninth-Century Compendium of Tests on Calligraphy," *T'ang Studies,* 1987, vol. 5: 69-83.
5. Soper, 1958: 212.
6. Soper, 1960: 15-38.
7. *Han Tang Sichou zhi Lu,* fig. 115, pp. 97 and 158, respectively. The tomb of Peishi is in Xiao Niang-zi, Jiali village in the district of Xian; the figurine is now in the Shaanxi Provincial Museum.
8. *Han Tang Sichou zhi Lu:* fig. 118, p. 97.
9. Also from the tomb of Peishi in Xiao Niang-zi. It is in the Shaanxi Provincial Museum. The ceramic ladies measure 30 cm. tall.
10. Ch'en, 1961: 282, points out that in addition to their dark-colored skin and curly hair, their short stature was considered remarkable. This may explain the small size of the African figurines in Lady Pei's tomb in relation to the other figures.
11. Schafer, 1962: 26-27.
12. Schafer, 1962: 26-27, noted that the historian Huilin's account is marked by bias in describing the barbaric nature of these "Indian" peoples.
13. Now in the Shaanxi Province Historical Museum.
14. Zhengjiang Bowuguan, "Jiangsu Zhengjiang Tang Mu," *Kaogu,* 1985.2: 131-148. A series of over 20 tombs are dated, by engraved steles, from the middle to late Tang. A tomb designated M14, dated 848, has yielded several small golden adornments; tomb M15 is dated 852, tomb M16, 854; and tomb M17, 865.
15. Li Zheng-qi, *Wenwu,* 1990.5: 21-27.
16. Cheng, 1988: 131.
17. Wang Ren-bo, 1990: 77, pl. 18: p. 65, pl. 16, respectively. The lion is now preserved in the Shaanxi Jingyangzhenling Lingyuan.
18. Weinstein, 1987: 138.
19. Soper, 1951: 24.
20. Weinstein, 1987: 148.
21. Shanxisheng Gujianzhu Baohu Yenjiu Suobian, *Foguansi he Dadongdian Tangwudai Bihua* (Beijing, 1983).

22. C. G. Kanda, "Kaikei's Statues of Manjusri and Four Attendants in the Abe no Monjuin," *Archives of Asian Art*, 1979, vol. XXXII: 21, discusses the evolution of the image of Wenshu (Manjusri) in Japan, but did not mention this temple.

CHAPTER XVII

EMPEROR YIZONG

Yizong (r. 860-874) was not a strong emperor, as he was only concerned with his own amusements. Even his ministers have been judged at fault, lacking the ability to effect innovative reforms.[1] Court appointments were made on the basis of personal favoritism or marriage with the imperial family, a practice heretofore avoided. This is one of the few times eunuchs and officials joined forces to oppose unmeritorious advancement.[2] Yizong is best remembered for his willful extravagance, which later in life was directed to Buddhist projects.

ARCHAEOLOGY

Among the fragments of murals from the tomb of a late Tang official, Yang Xuan-lue, dated 864, is an unusual portrait of a tall scholar in profile view, his two hands hidden in voluminous sleeves.[3] (FIGURE 95) Despite its ruinous condition the drawing of the figure suggests some of the later Tang painting techniques; the lines seem to be more varied. Both thick and thin lines describe the drapery, heavy beard, and widely opened eyes. In addition, the full profile pose foreshadows the Southern Song painter Liang Kai's idealized portrait of the poet Li Bo.[4] Other themes in the tomb murals include female attendants, male officials, and fragments of a lady and tree composition in the upper area of the wall. It appears that the image of the white crane seen here, a symbol of longevity and scholarship, replaced the earlier funeral tradition of painting one of the four spirit animals on each wall. A second tomb, belonging to the Wei family, is not dated, but its frescoes present a variety of themes indicative of this era.[5] In addition to the several portraits of young maidens and officials, two of the murals are remarkable in subject, if not in painting style. One portrays an outdoor banquet. (FIGURE 96) Although the festive party resembles those depicted in Han tomb murals, this composition differs in its organization of pictorial elements. Now dominating the center of the wall is a large table neatly set with dishes and cups; the guests are seated on benches along three sides of the table. The revellers are shown in a variety of postures, including storytelling, rapt attention, wine-drinking, and calling for refills. Among the maids and attendants who stand grouped on either side are an elderly man with a cane and long beard, youthful servants, a majordomo figure, and a woman and child. In the upper part of the composition are scudding clouds; in the lower right a rock is sketched. The entire mural is painted in delicate hues of green, tan, and red.

Depiction of a mother holding a child among the standing attendants, as in the Wei tomb fresco, appears elsewhere in the late Tang. This subject, whether mother and children or children at play, can be found among small-size ceramic figurines. One sculpture has a baby in a basin being bathed by a small child; (FIGURE 97) another shows a small, very well-articulated figurine of a standing child; and a third depicts a baby wrapped in bunting that is tied with three neat ribbons.[6] All suggest the appearance and the personality of an infant. Heretofore such scenes were thought to be unique to Song figure painters.[7]

Another mural from the Wei tombs employs the familiar format of a series of panels with paintings of ladies seated under trees. Although this mural has a passing resemblance to the images in the imperial tombs of the early eighth century, on closer inspection the pictorial elements--the setting and the feminine ideal--are noticeably altered. (FIGURE 98) Still portly and mature, the women are no longer obese as in the previous century; their garments are plain, their hairstyle is less extravagant. In relation to the landscape elements, particularly the trees, the ladies are much smaller. Their size has changed considerably in comparison to examples of the early Tang monumental style, where the figures fill the entire composition, as in the Feathered Ladies screen in the Shosoin. The ladies in the mural are seated in a convincing garden setting replete with decorative rocks, shrubs, and trees; their postures and attitudes as well as the props suggest a narrative content altogether absent in earlier examples. One figure warily looks out over her fan into the garden;

another, with bent head, plays what could be a plaintive tune on a lute, a theme celebrated in Tang poetry.[8] Similar in theme and mood is a painting ascribed to the late Tang in the Palace Museum in Taiwan, which depicts a gathering of palace women seated at a large central banquet table; as in the Wei family mural, various small dishes, cups, and other food containers are laid out. Several of the ladies have obviously drunk too much; uncertainly they return the cup to the table or stare blankly into the distance. With great concentration, others play musical instruments, such as the lute, flute, vertical pipes, and zither; one (standing) youthful servant plays the rhythmic bamboo clapper. Dressed in loose-fitting gowns with voluminous sleeves and delicate, thin scarves, the women have their hair piled in a topknot that falls to one side. Some wear ornate headpieces, and all are exotically made up with white-powdered brow and nose, red lips, and decorative rosettes painted on their foreheads. The ladies sit on backless, carved fruitwood chairs with sculpted legs and brocade pillows. A small, curled-up dog is asleep beneath the large inlaid table. Delicate hues of aqua, red, black (mostly for the hair), and brown dominate the composition. Although the figures do not differ too greatly from one another in physiognomy (there is more variety in their dresses), they are seated in various postures and seen from a multitude of angles, so that no two do the same thing. Some are seen in full rear view, and others are seen in frontal, full-profile, and three-quarter poses.

Among the few excavated tombs from this era two in the Hebei/Henan region yielded porcelains. This region is believed to be the place of manufacture of the luminous white Xingware long held to be an achievement of the Song era. A Hebei tomb dated 870 contained several white pieces--a bowl, a tall jar with broad shoulders, and two wine cups--in addition to an eight-lobed bronze mirror with flower and bird decor, and a round bronze mirror with four dragons in flight in the center. White porcelain vessels were also found in several other tombs at this site; however, they are not dated. The tomb of Li Yue (dated 869) in Henan had rather meager contents. Counted among the 17 burial objects were porcelain jars, ink slabs, a tall, broad-shouldered, lidded jar, and a smaller broad-shouldered jar with a pointed mountain-shape top.[9] These tall porcelain jars were quite popular in the later Tang; the mountain-shape top, which the Chinese call pagoda vase, is a new fashion.

YIZONG'S TOMB

It is reported that Yizong's tomb path was laid out in the manner of the previous Tang emperors. Of the extant sculptures two fragments of the stone horses remain, with three small lions, five of the small lions from the four gateways, and three partially destroyed stone men.[10]

BUDDHISM UNDER YIZONG

Yizong was an even greater supporter of Buddhism than his predecessor. Lavish amounts were spent on monasteries, temples, and events, such as the great feast at Anguosi in 871, to which 10,000 people were invited.[11] Occasions like the imperial birthday were also celebrated with huge vegetarian feasts; such events occurred frequently. Yizong established a nunnery in the palace; there, and elsewhere, platforms were set up for unlimited ordinations. Reviving the ceremony of the bone, the relic was brought to the capital from Famen and then sent to various temples for the people to worship. This occasion was celebrated by enthusiasts, who went so far in their devotional zeal as to cut off a finger.

BUDDHIST ART

One of the best-known documents dated to Yizong's reign is the earliest extant printed Buddhist text, one of the treasures from the Dunhuang Library from Cave 17. Certainly the technique of woodblock printing antedates this 868 scroll of the *Diamond Sutra*, with its frontispiece of the preaching Buddha surrounded by his divine retinue.[12] The invention of woodblock printing was derived from Buddhist practices. Support of the doctrine, by donations to the church, the performance of good works, and perpetuating the scriptures (through recitation and copying), was rewarded with the accumulation of spiritual merit. The desire to duplicate the scriptures more quickly and in greater numbers provided the stimulus for seeking a mechanical form of reproducing the sutras. This practice of copying the scriptures resulted in their proliferation and, as in this case, made their survival more likely.

FAMENSI

A magnificent and informative assembly of objects was found hidden in the basement of the Famen Temple, about 150 kilometers from the ancient capital of Chang-an. After an earthquake in the

1980s, the structure of the pagoda was damaged; during the restoration three underground chambers and a hidden niche were found filled with temple treasures.[13] The foundations of the temple date to the Tang, but epigraphical evidence establishes its existence as early as the Northern Wei period and describes the peculiar form of worship perpetuated at Famen: Every 30 years the basement of the temple was opened for ceremonies to assure the fertility of the land. The underground chambers, an area not used for any ritual purpose in other Buddhist pagodas, were laid out like an altar. Moreover, the arrangement of the objects in each of the subterranean rooms recreated a mandala, with the most important object, a bone relic, at the center; in the rear room, for example, guardian figures in protective postures surrounded it and vases, inscribed with the names of the four directions, were placed in the corners.

For the temple, its most valued possession is the finger bone relic of the Buddha which, according to legend, was sent to the temple by the proselytizing King Asoka of India. The relic was transferred to the capital several times for worship by Tang emperors beginning with Empress Wu. Four bones were found enshrined at Famen, but only one is considered a genuine relic. Nonetheless, all four of the bone relics were treated magisterially: encased in multiple precious boxes decorated with engraved Buddhist designs or embedded with pearls and gems. The case with the genuine bone, found hidden in a secret niche in the rear chamber, reflects Chinese attitudes to materials: The innermost box containing the bone was a miniature Chinese-style coffer made of jade, the most prized of all materials. (FIGURE 99) This in turn was placed in a crystal reliquary, the second most precious substance; then in sandalwood (now disintegrated), then in a gilt silver casket with an inscription;[14] and finally in an outer iron box. A second relic, found in the rear chamber, had a set of eight caskets dated to the later reign of Emperor Xizong; an inscribed tablet in the anteroom identified some of the articles.

Many of the precious bowls and objects found in the underground chambers were associated with the complex rites of esoteric Buddhist sects. According to the inventories, the cache can be grouped into several major categories: a series of precious utensils for a tea ceremony given by Yizong, a group of gifts given to Yizong on the occasion of his birthday, gifts from Xizong, and ritual objects and sculptures belonging to the temple. These objects were made out of various materials, such as gold, silver, embroidered fabric, glass, porcelain, and marble; the majority of the articles comprise silver vessels and esoteric utensils. Many of these were used for the rituals involved in transporting the relic to and from the capital, like the resplendent garments embroidered with Buddhist motifs in gold (FIGURE 100), solid-gold bowl, and traveling boxes.[15]

The delicate and refined sculpture of a kneeling Bodhisattva is an extraordinary piece of workmanship. The deity holds a lotus petal, on top of which is a miniature case with an inscribed tablet. (FIGURE 101) A 65-character-long inscription, dated 873, not only gives the reign, era, and date but states that the sculpture was made as a birthday gift for Yizong; in addition, it declares the emperor's intention to move the bone relic. A variety of techniques is employed: The figure is modeled out of silver; the crown, base, and cover are finely engraved gold; and the oversize lotus petal is wrought from silver with raised, gilt veins. Pearls and jewels adorn both the body and crown of the deity. The silver, hourglass-shape base has three parts. The upper section is modeled like a lotus flower with an engraved gilt image of a deity playing music on each petal. (FIGURE 102) The central section has the four Tianwang, each in its own petal-shape frame. At the base are eight esoteric deities seated in various postures, some with multiple hands and attributes; all have a large mandorla of flames. Sanskrit writing is seen in the area above these figures.

Decorative objects are plentiful, like the several covered boxes of silver or of gilt silver, one of which is naturalistically shaped and decorated to resemble a turtle. There are bowls made of silver and solid gold, numerically matched sets of silver and gilt plates, and numerous incense burners in a variety of styles and shapes. A round, silver, openwork incense burner has a mechanism inside that enables it to remain upright. The silver sphere, suspended from a link chain, is covered with floral designs and ten round, gilt insets engraved with bees and flowers. (FIGURE 103)

Silver and gold articles devoted to the tea ceremony, donated by Yizong, include cups and saucers, tea caddies, a grinder to pulverize the leaves, ladles, and a spice cellar. In the Tang one ate rather than drank tea. Tea drinking was introduced into China with the propagation of Buddhism; it was deemed an excellent aid in meditation. The *Classic of Tea*, written in the late eighth century by Lu Yu, discusses the various types of tea plants and advises on the methods of cultivation and harvesting and on the various types of porcelain most suitable for drinking tea. This text is evidence of the widespread adoption of tea drinking as a social custom. Whether or not it was part of Buddhist ritual is difficult to determine, but the prevalence of these objects at Famen suggests that the custom was still practiced. One remarkable silver tea caddy has tiny, engraved and gilt narrative scenes. Each area of the covered jar has a different design: On the pedestal are wave designs and a supporting lotus-petal base. (FIGURES 104, 105) The canister has five scenes of recreation in ogee-shape frames, among which are sages in a landscape setting playing music, chatting with one another, and playing a board game. The lid is shaped into lotus petals, each petal is carved with floral designs and inset with gilt animals in chase. At top is a lotus bud.

Thus the treasures of Famen attest to both the continued prominence of certain Buddhist temples and the production of magnificently wrought objects in luxurious media after the great persecution. In these two respects, the history of the later Tang has to be seriously amended. It can no longer be asserted that Buddhism and its art did not enjoy imperial sponsorship after 845, as the lavish finds donated by the late Tang emperors clearly prove they did. Also these magnificent gold and silver articles demonstrate that superior craftsmanship in metal objects continued long after the mid-eighth-century reign of Xuanzong.

It should be mentioned that such magnificent objects were not limited to imperial donations to the Famen Temple. A beautifully wrought five-lobed silver box, inscribed with the date 866, was found in a tomb in Lantiantang Yuyangjiagou, Shaanxi.[16] Replacing the ring background of earlier eras is a delicate vegetal pattern; embossed on the surface of the lobes are paired birds; at the center are two mythical phoenixes in flight.[17]

BUDDHIST PAINTING

The famous Dunhuang Cave 17, dated to 862, honored the eminent monk Hong Bian, who was overseer of the Buddhist clergy in the northwest after the recapture of Dunhuang from the Tibetans in 848.[18] It was his statue that must have once occupied the now empty dais.[19] (FIGURE 106) This rare portrait sculpture, which was found in another cave, has a hole in the back that held a silk bag containing the remains of ashes and bones. This Buddhist practice is similar to the Shanye clay tablets, which contain the ashes of deceased monks. The mural behind the sculpture provides a setting for the icon: two flanking figures and two trees in full blossom; hanging from one of the trees are a water bottle and a traveling bag. The figure on the left is a male attendant (or perhaps a donor); the one on the right, a nun, carries a large fan. Painted on the sides of the dais are traces of deer and the shoes of the priest. Although all of these efforts are treated naturalistically, they are no longer rendered with the exacting realism characteristic of the eighth century.

Several caves at Dunhuang are dated by inscription to the reign of Yizong. These caves are remarkable for their innovations in iconography and decor. For example, Cave 12, dated to 869, has one of the Buddhas of the Four Directions on each quadrant of the sloping sides of the tent-shape ceiling as well as the more usual placement on the side walls.[20] Another innovative appropriation of the ceiling is in Cave 161; here, an unusual image is painted of Manjusri with a thousand arms and a thousand begging bowls; this icon is a direct illustration of a scripture.[21] Cave 107 should be mentioned for its portrayal of a female donor; dated 871, its style clearly is in accord with the archaeological finds. (FIGURE 107) Full bodied, but less fulsome than in previous reigns, the donor has her hair modestly piled on top of her head. She wears a plain long gown with voluminous sleeves.[22] Most unusual is the fact that she turns to speak to another figure; previously, portraits of donors were more formal.

Several Buddhist caves in Sichuan, such as the site of Jaijiang, were in continuous use throughout the Tang.[23] One late-Tang niche has a rich sculptural treatment of the theme of Amitofu Buddha and his two Bodhisattvas. Each sits surrounded by rich architectural settings rendered in an ornate three-dimensional style. At another site, Qionglaixian, are images of Wenshu on his lion; others are also found in Sichuan.[24] The athletic guardian figure, dated 865, from the caves at Pujian Kandengshan Dafoku, is notable for its militaristic appearance. (FIGURE 108) With rippling muscles, the half-naked figure strikes a bold pose; one arm raised, his legs are in a martial stance, and his skirt and draperies flutter around him. Sharply turning his head, his face, horrific in its distortion, no longer looks human.[25]

NOTES

1. Peterson, 1979: 557.

2. Dalby, 1979: 712.

3. Yang Xuan-lue's tomb, Zaoyuancun, Xian; this mural fragment is currently housed in the Shaanxi Province Historical Museum. (See Yi Sheng-ping, 1991: 155-159, pls. 196-202. See also photo in Wang, 1990, pl. 6, p. 95.)

4. Sickman, 1974: pl. 183; Liang Kai's adaptation of this full-profile pose for the poet may have been a conscious quotation of a late-Tang portrait convention which, up until now, was unknown to modern viewers.

5. The Wei had been an important family since the beginning of the eighth century; their tomb is situated to the north of Weiqu, in Chang-an county, Shaanxi Province. (See Yi Sheng-ping, 1991: 160-165.) Some of these frescoes are also in the Shaanxi Province Historical Museum. The attribution to the late Tang is based on Yi.

6. Wang, 1990: 118, fig, 10. The figures were found in the eastern suburb in the tomb of Han Sen-zhai; they are now in the Xian City Cultural Research Center.

7. One example is the knickknack peddler, shown with several children attacking his displays. (See E. J. Liang, "Li Sung and Some Aspects of Southern Sung Figure Painting," *Artibus Asiae*, 1975, vol. XXXVI: 3ff). Another example is the famed Su Han-chen of the Southern Song, who was known for his portraits of children. (See Sickman, 1974: 244, fig. 168.)

8. Particularly Bai Ju-yi's famous poem, the "Lute Player." (See Waley, 1949: 105.)

9. Zhonguo Shehui, 1986: 451-454. This was the tomb of a poor official killed in a military coup; unfortunately, these tomb objects were not illustrated except for line drawings.

10. Cheng, 1988: 131. There are no illustrations of any extant sculptures.

11. Weinstein, 1987: 145-146.

12. The printed scroll is in the British Museum, inv. Or. 8210. It is over 16 feet long (see Frances Wood, *Chinese Illustration*, London, 1985: 2). An earlier printed piece of paper was found in a Korean temple, Pulkuk-sa in Kyong-ju, and is believed to antedate the temple's completion in 751. Characters employed in Wu Ze-tian's reign have led some to date the piece to the end of the seventh century. Other early evidence includes an eighth-century printed charm found in Japan. (See Denis Twitchett, *Printing and Publishing in Medieval China*, New York, 1977: 13ff.)

13. Nearly the entire issue of *Wen Wu*, 1988.10, is devoted to the Famen finds.

14. Zhu Qixin, "Buddhist Treasures from Famensi," *Orientations*, May 1990: 80, translates it as "This precious Han casket was respectfully made for the *sarira* of Shakyamuni as a tribute to the emperor."

15. Some of these objects, like the gold bowl and embroidered silks, were given by Yizong's successor Xizong and are discussed in Chapter XVIII.

16. Wang, 1990: pl. 9, p. 170-71.

17. A tomb in Henan dated to 869 identified by a tomb record as belonging to Li Yu contained several utilitarian bronze objects and a bronze mirror, though these are of inferior quality. See Zhongguo Shehui Kexueyaun Kaogu Yanjiusuo Henan dier Gongzuodui, "Henan Yanshi Xingyuancun de Liuzuo Jinian Tangmu," *Kaogu*, 1986.5: 429-431. The objects are reproduced by only a line drawing.

18. Cave 17 later served as a library; it was the location of the hidden cache of scrolls found at the beginning of the twentieth century.

19. Ma Shih-chang, "Quanyu Dunhuang Zangjingdong de Jige Wenti," *Wenwu*, 1978.12: 21-33. Dien: 1,788-1,791. The statue was found in another cave (365). It is assumed that it was moved and subsequently returned.

20. *Zhongguo Shiku: Dunhuang Mogaoku*, vol. 4: pls. 158-59, p. 228.

21. *Zhongguo Shiku: Dunhuang Mogaoku*, vol. 4: pls. 143-45, p. 227. Zhang in the LTMHJ mentions a painting of the subject, see Acker, 1954: 259.

22. *Zhongguo Shiku: Dunhuang Mogaoku*, vol. 4: pl. 171, p. 229.

23. Wang Xi-xiang and Zeng Deng-ren, "Sichuan Jiajiang Qianfoyan Moya Zaoxiang," *Wenwu*, 1992.2: 58-66.

24. Akiyama, 1972: pl. 170.

25. *Zhongguo Meishu Quanji: Diaosubian, Sichuan Shiku Diaosu*, vol. 12: pl. 58, p. 20.

CHAPTER XVIII

EMPEROR XIZONG

Succeeding to the throne at the age of 12, Xizong (r. 873-888) owed his accession to the intervention of the eunuch generals.[1] As a youth he was a typical boy, preoccupied with games, but at the age of 20, appreciating his power, he sought to rule directly. He proved to be a strong-willed but inexperienced emperor. The eunuchs were a dominant force in government and they were appointed to high-ranking positions once reserved only for officials, for eunuchs, an unprecedented height. The era was marked by severe famines and other hardships among the people, and although the imperial government sought to reduce the heavy tax burden, local officials did not comply with the remedial measures, and the populace suffered further hardships. Rebel bands ravaged areas throughout the empire, culminating in a mass revolt in 878, led by Huang Zhao, that challenged the central government. Despite intermittent success in warding off the bandit armies, Huang Zhao conquered Fukien and, in 879, the rebel army plundered the city of Canton murdering over 100,000 foreign merchants. After marching into Luoyang in 880, the rebels entered Chang-an, causing the emperor to flee to Sichuan. The emperor's retreat to a place far from the center of the empire disheartened many, who feared there was no chance for the restoration of the imperial government. Huang Zhao inaugurated a new dynasty, naming himself emperor, but his wanton massacre, in 882 in the capital, of over a thousand people, including civil officials, lost him any strong support. Rebels held Chang-an for two years, during which time the capital saw extreme carnage and destruction at the hands of the conquering forces. The occupation left the capital in a state of devastation from which it never recovered. After ten years of war, Huang Zhao was finally defeated; in 883, he committed suicide. In his stead, local militia, organized by rich landowners, established their hegemony; the empire, now broken up into provincial entities, was ravaged by bandits. Xizong returned to the capital in 883, but the city was again besieged by rebel bands, forcing the emperor to flee. The capital city was sacked once more. Attempts to set up a new dynasty by rebel factions failed and the court re-entered Chang-an in 886. Xizong died in 888 at the age of 27, and the throne passed to his son, who was a virtual puppet emperor, subject to the powerful influence of the eunuchs.

Though artifacts of this era are few, historical records attest to the continued production of art at court during these troubled times. The artist Chang Zong-yin (874-889), appointed to Hanlin College, was reputedly an excellent portraitist who painted Emperor Xizong and his courtiers.[2] One of his paintings for the Baoli Temple bore the title "Celestial Monarch Praying to a Stupa." Several artists accompanied Xizong to Sichuan (880 to 881), when he was forced to flee the capital. These included Lu Yao and Zhu Qian, originally natives of Chang-an, both skilled in Buddhist and Taoist subjects and Painters-in-attendance at Hanlin College. Their frescoes were in both Chang-an and Chengdu. Sun Yu, a native of Zhekiang, also a refugee in Sichuan, was known for his paintings of secular figures, dragons, pines and rocks, bamboo ink, celestial monarchs, and demon divinities. The landscape painter Chang Xun portrayed mountains and cliffs, dead pines and unusual rocks. His Zhongho-era (880-885) rendering of three landscapes in the Zhaoxuesi, a view of dawn, noon, and dusk, evoked Xizong's comments:

> Morning and twilight views have been ably handled by all masters of modern or ancient times; it is the noon view which is hard to depict (as poets tend to favor the other seasons at the expense of summer).[3]

BUDDHISM UNDER XIZONG

The burning of the scriptures during Emperor Wu's suppression of Buddhism had a devastating effect on the schools that were dependent on texts and their exegeses.[4] Thus the Faxian and Huayen schools fell into neglect. However, those beliefs dependent neither on the monastic life nor on scriptural traditions flourished, like that of the cult of the Western Paradise and the Chan sect. The meditative Chan school prided itself on the importance of self-realization without the aid of rituals and scriptures. Later Chan icons accordingly show their patriarchs burning wooden sculptures of the Buddha for warmth or tearing up the sutras. Esoteric temples, like Famen, apparently also thrived in the late Tang.

BUDDHIST ART

Xizong's patronage of and lavish gifts to the Famen Temple are recorded and dated 874 in an inventory inscribed on two stone steles in the forechamber. At the end of Xizong's reign in 888, the temple's underground rooms were closed. Among the articles given to the temple by Xizong were many objects--sets of plates for ritual offerings, incense burners, bracelets, a ceremonial staff and Ruyi scepter--associated with the esoteric rituals. Also dated to this emperor's reign is a set of eight boxes housing one of the bone relics. The smallest that held the bone, is a solid-gold one-story pagoda. (FIGURE 109) The next two boxes are silver and gold with floral designs of pearls and turquoise. The fourth box, made of gilt silver, has engraved designs, but the figures are slightly raised from the surface. Guanyin, the central icon, appears in the six-armed manifestation; important to note is the new posture of the Bodhisattva. One leg is up, bent at the knee; the other is bent beneath him. The head is tilted to the side and supported by one of the hands. (FIGURE 110) This posture, also seen in the northwestern regions of Pakistan and in Kashmir,[5] is probably of Guptan origin.[6] It also appears on small bronze icons of the late Tang; several of these are currently in the Shanghai Museum. (FIGURE 111) Surrounding figures include Bodhisattvas in prayer or presenting offerings; the other sides of the fourth box have similar divine attendants grouped around a central Buddha. The fifth box, of gilt silver, is designed in the same manner: Major icons are shown with their attendants. The sixth box is of plain silver. Each side of the seventh box, which is made of gold, has raised designs of the four Guardian Kings and their entourages; the guardians hold a weapon or an attribute in one hand and have a flaming halo behind them. (FIGURE 112) Among the retinue are armed warriors, grotesque soldiers, officials, and two small children holding offerings in either corner. The Guardian King sits on two repulsive representations of evil; the posture is also relatively new-- one leg is bent at the knee, the other is pendant. No longer standing on the personifications of evil and ignorance, the Guardian King sits crushing the demons beneath him. This pose was employed earlier at

Foguansi at Wutaishan. (FIGURE 93) At Famen, Guardian King figures in this posture also appear on a large marble box that held one of the reliquaries and was restored under Xizong, as well as on the four marble sculptures of the rear chamber. (FIGURE 113) The eighth box, made of sandalwood, is in fragmentary condition.

The celadon porcelain vessels mentioned in the inventory were an unusual find, for this type of ceramic was not believed to have been produced prior to the Song dynasty. Silver bands once adorned the feet and rim of the celadon bowls and jars. A long-necked jar with an octagonal bottom recalls Guanyin's jar filled with the waters of immortality. (FIGURE 114) It is not only the celadon-colored glaze but the simplicity of form that anticipate Song ceramics. Similarly plain is the solid-gold bowl that was used to transport the finger bone relic back to the temple. The bowl has an elegant shape, narrowing gradually from the wide lip. Its lack of decoration, except for its inscription to the Xiantong era, represents the aesthetic of restraint often celebrated in Song ceramics.

In addition to the several pieces of Western glass[7] found among the Famen treasures, there are glass tea bowls and saucers, which are evidence of the sinicization of the ancient Western art of glassblowing. The technology of glassmaking was known to the Chinese since the Zhou dynasty,[8] but it was not until the Tang that blown glass technology was perfected in China.[9] The eighth-century pharmacologist Chen Zang-qi still considered blown glass exotic:

> It is a jewel of Western countries, and is akin to jade and stones. It is born within the earth, and some say that it is water transformed after a thousand years; still this is not necessarily so.[10]

Tang sources record tribute gifts of glass coming from Kapisa, India; blue glass from Farghana; pink and blue from Tukhara; and red and green from Rome.[11]

Although Cave 161 at Dunhuang is not specifically dated to this reign, it is generally attributed to this period. Like the Six-armed Guanyin on the gilt silver casket from Famen, the Bodhisattva is seated in the new pose--left leg bent at the knee, the other foot resting on a lotus base. (FIGURE 115) At the site of rock-cut caves at Jaijiang in Sichuan the posture is also employed in the Thousand-armed image of Guanyin; the innumerable arms radiate around the figure, each holding an attribute. This posture is frequently associated with the Song era, but these examples make it clear that it was prevalent in the late Tang.

A large-scale Buddha from Sichuan, at Neijiangxiang Longshan, is dated 880, the time of Xizong's flight.[12] The extremely heavy figure sits in Western posture, his ponderous feet resting on lotus flowers. The treatment of the garment is slightly changed; there is a belt around the waist, and the shawl falls in triangular points over the legs. (FIGURE 116) From the site of Jiajiang Qianfoya is a large image of one of the Tianwang, Guardian of the North. Wearing a tall crown, the guardian stands with his legs spread in a martial stance, each foot trampling a demon; the arms are raised above his head; one holding his attribute, a reliquary, the other a sword. (FIGURE 117) His burly physique seems about to burst through his armor. These images have great weight and size. Their increased bulk seems to be an attempt to reinvigorate the figures with a sense of power.

NOTES

1. See Robert Somers, "The End of the Tang," *Cambridge History of China*, vol. III, 1979: 714-773.
2. Soper, 1951: 24.
3. Soper, 1951: 135, note 245, translates this entry from the *Xuan Ho Huapu*.
4. Weinstein, 1987: 146-150.
5. A similar piece from the Western Himalayas made of gilt copper is ascribed to the eighth century (see Klimburg, 1983: pl. 88, p. 175, but here the Bodhisattva Avalokitesvara has only two hands.)
6. This posture, *rajalilasana*, seen in Pala dynasty images, is found throughout the Buddhist world. It probably originated in the Guptan era, but the pensive Bodhisattva carved on Gandharan steles is also extremely similar. This posture also appears on clay pieces from eastern India. (See S. Huntington, *Leaves from the Bodhi Tree*, Dayton, 1990, fig. 55, p. 181, for a clay plaque ascribed to the eighth century; it is also seen in Java, ca. ninth century, see fig. 73, p. 231.)
7. There is a tall, yellow glass ewer, thought to be of fifth-century Eastern Roman manufacture and several brilliant, clear-blue plates with Near Eastern designs etched into their centers.
8. Colin A. Ronan, *The Shorter Science and Civilisation in China* (Cambridge, 1981), vol. 2: 356-357.
9. Schafer, 1963: 235-237.
10. Schafer, 1963: 236.
11. Schafer, 1963: 236.
12. *Zhongguo Meishu Quanji: Diaosubian, Sichuan Shiku Diaosu*, vol. 12: pl. 109, p. 35.

CHAPTER XIX

EMPEROR ZHAOZONG

Placed on the throne by eunuchs in 889 Emperor Zhaozong (r. 888-904) was a virtual puppet. When, in 895, provincial forces again threatened the imperial government, Zhaozong fled the capital, which, once again, was sacked by rebels. It was not until 898 that the emperor returned. During these insurrections, a provincial lord, Zhu Wen, gradually rose to power, and, in 904, had Emperor Zhaozong murdered. These recurrent civil wars at the end of the Tang destroyed cultural life and social institutions. The sad state of the capital was the subject of a lament by the poet Wei Zhuang:

Chang'an lies in mournful stillness, what does it now contain?
-- Ruined markets and desolate streets in which ears of wheat are sprouting. . . .
All the gaily coloured chariots with their ornamented wheels are scattered and gone,
Of the stately mansions with their vermilion gates less than half remain,
The Hanyuan Hall is the haunt of foxes and hares.[1]

Despite the chaos of Zhaozong's reign, according to Guo Ruo-xu's history of late Tang painters, several artists were still active. Zhao De-qi, a third-generation artist, painted portraits of a royal prince and his chariots and banners, as well as imperial consorts and concubines, in the era 898 to 901; he was appointed to Hanlin College by the emperor himself.[2] Ma Zhu-li, from Sichuan, whose specialty is not recorded, painted in the era 898 to 904 and Diao Guang-yin, active 901-04 was famous for compositions of dragons, bamboo and rocks, flowers and birds, and cats and rabbits.

One of the most famous and admired landscape artists of the era is Qing Hao. Although sometimes placed in the Five Dynasties period,[3] Qing Hao is listed in the Tang by both Guo Ruo-xu and the Song Imperial Painting inventory, *Xuan Ho Huapu*.[4]

> (A man of) wide learning and refinement and a lover of the past, good at painting landscapes. He compiled a one volume book, "Secrets of Landscapes," which was presented to the throne by a friend and has been preserved in the Imperial Library.[5]

Though reliable copies of his work are hard to come by, Qing Hao's famous essay on landscape painting has survived. This was not the first composition on the topic; extant texts by Zong Ping and Gu Kai-zhi date to the late fourth or early fifth century. Like these art historical texts, the essay is discursive on a number of topics, including the fine points of technique. Being later in date, it also addresses the questions of evaluating artists, traditions, and models of the past. The most significant difference is that Qing Hao's text is written from the first-person-narrative point of view, reading like a journal of his excursions in the countryside. For example, there is an encounter with a sage who encourages Qing Hao to pursue his art and gives him advice:

> Since you like to paint clouds and trees, mountain and streams, you must understand clearly the fundamentals of every natural object. When a tree grows, it follows the true nature which it receives from heaven. The true nature of a pine tree is as follows--it may grow curved, but never appear (sic) deformed and crooked. It looks sometimes dense and sometimes sparse, and neither blue nor green. Even as a tiny sapling it stands upright and aims to grow high, thus already showing its posture of independence and nobility. Even when its branches grow low, sideways or downwards, it never falls to the ground. . . .[6]

The sage goes on to describe the various species of trees. In these descriptions, the importance placed on observing and recording the true nature of living things anticipates the inspired achievements of Northern Song landscape painters, in particular the eleventh century-artist Guo Xi, who similarly wrote about painting landscapes. Thus Qing Hao is usually grouped with the artists of the later monumental landscape style, with their primary aesthetic of representational likeness.

NOTES

1. Schafer, 1963: 157-158, quotes Lionel Giles' translation of 1926.

2. Soper, 1951: 23.

3. For example, Cahill, 1980: 26, who says he was active at the end of the ninth and first half of the tenth century.

4. Soper, 1951: 136, quotes the *Xuanho Huapu*.

5. Soper, 1951: 136.

6. Shio Yen Shi and Susan Bush, *Early Chinese Texts on Painting* (New York, 1991): 146.

CHAPTER XX

EMPEROR ZHAO XUANDI

Zhu Wen, having murdered Zhaozong and most of his court, put the emperor's twelve year old son on the throne in 905. Zhao Xuandi (r. 905-907) was a nominal ruler for two years until Zhu Wen named himself emperor of the Liang Dynasty and brought a formal end to the Tang.

CONCLUSION

The image of the glorious Tang, which for years has suffered from a lack of extant materials has, now with the new archaeological evidence, become more comprehensive, though many important monuments are still beyond our knowledge. No longer limited to historical descriptions, third-hand copies, or vaguely attributed works of art, modern viewers can now examine multifarious examples of Tang painting, sculpture, decorative works, and ceramics in addition to the wealth of Buddhist art. Owing to the lucrative commerce of the silk road and sea routes and as a result of military expansion, a unique international culture was forged from diverse foreign influences and flourished in the major cities. Wealth produced from these activities enriched the imperial and aristocratic families as well as the merchants, all of whom spent vast sums on displays of affluence. Their patronage enabled the art of painting and the fine arts to expand and develop at a rapid rate.

All three of the chronological eras of the Tang--early, middle, and late--saw the continued production of a high level of art. The ideal of the emperor as a builder of cities, aesthete, collector of art, and literatus who enjoyed participating in calligraphy and poetry did much to maintain splendor at court and to cultivate choice artistic production in all aesthetic endeavors.

The intent of the analytic approach undertaken here--of placing the historical, religious, and artistic evidence in its chronological order-- is to convey a distinct portrait of each era. The period of the early Tang is marked by the influx of foreign influences and the formulation of an international style that adapted non-Chinese elements to create a new, cosmopolitan ideal evident not only in the funeral arts but also in Buddhist monuments. A secure and able

government saw the flourishing of the arts, whereby the idea of
naturalism was applied to all forms of pictorial expression as well as
in literary endeavor. In both tomb murals and figurines, activities
from aristocratic pastimes and court figures were prominent. In
Buddhist art foreign elements appeared in the iconography, the focus
of which was the historic Buddha, the Buddha of the Future, and the
Western Paradise.

Although marked by a central government periodically weakened by
the movement toward provincial independence in the middle Tang
period, this era offers artistic evidence that attests to the creativity of
the time. Replacing the naturalistic aesthetic ideal was a growing
interest in narrative depiction and the evocation of mood. Both the
literary and pictorial arts were concerned with the image of woman:
All of the arts sought to capture the ideal of feminine beauty. This is
no doubt related to the unique role played by female political figures.
Prevalent secondary artistic themes show people in outdoor settings--
seated in gardens, playing music, celebrating at banquets. Depictions
of the games and sports found in tomb murals of the earlier period
wane in popularity. Also, the perfection of the triglaze technique that
occupied artists at the beginning of the middle Tang period, gave way
to experimentation with porcelain. Lastly, recent finds provide new
evidence of the importance of the esoteric school of Buddhism in the
middle Tang, although the cult of the Western Paradise maintained its
strong appeal.

The late Tang brought even more troubled times, as the now
diminished empire suffered sporadic revolts that threatened the
existence of the dynasty. Though repeatedly quelled, chaotic and
widespread rebellions continued and finally in the final decades of the
ninth century, destroyed the central government. Yet even in this
environment, artistic creation persevered: Archaeological evidence
disproves the common assumption that high-level art languished.
Objects of surprisingly fine workmanship demonstrate the superior
craftsmanship produced in the late Tang. Court artists worked for the
emperor even in his exile from the capital city. A discernible nostalgic
mood pervaded the literature, including the writing of art histories,
and was manifested in the renovation of ancient monuments.
However, much of the art of the late Tang was innovative; it heralded
the artistic styles and techniques of the subsequent Song period.
Finally, although the mid-ninth century saw a destructive rage intent
on the extirpation of Buddhism, this persecution was not as successful
in destroying the religion as has previously been thought. In fact, the

short-lived proscription was followed by a large-scale effort to restore Buddhism that resulted in a renaissance of art and architecture.

Thus, in concert with historical and literary evidence, new pictorial material has been organized to view in a chronological fashion the achievements of the illustrious Tang, enhancing what was once only a sketch of its brilliance.

FIGURE 1. Equestrian figures, Mural, Li Shou Tomb, Jiaocun, San Yuan county, Shaanxi Province, dated 632.

FIGURE 2.   Rhinoceros, from Gaozu's Shendao, Shaanxi Provincial Museum.

FIGURE 3. Taizong's charger: Saluhsi, Sculpture, University of Philadelphia Museum.

FIGURE 4. Paradise of Amitabha, Mural, Dunhuang, Cave 341, top section of wall.

FIGURE 5. Paradise of Amitabha, Mural, Dunhuang, Cave 341, detail lotus pond.

FIGURE 6. Buddha and attendants, Mural, Dunhuang, Cave 57.

FIGURE 7. Bodhisattva Guanyin, Mural, Dunhuang, Cave 57, detail.

212   COURT ART OF THE TANG

FIGURE 8. Vimalakiriti and Wenshu Debate, Mural, Dunhuang, Cave 220, Audience of Wenshu: Chinese emperor, dated 642.

FIGURE 9. Vimalakiriti and Wenshu Debate, Mural, Dunhuang, Cave 220, audience of foreigners, detail.

FIGURE 10. Buddha group, Sculpture, Dunhuang, Cave 322.

FIGURE 11. Lady, Mural, Li Shuang Tomb, dated 668.

FIGURE 12. Lady, Mural, Jingshengcun 337, Taiyuan, Shanxi.

FIGURE 13. Dancing girl, Mural, Zhi Shi Geng-jie Tomb, Xian, dated 668.

FIGURE 14. Dancing girls, Mural, Li Ji tomb, Zhaoling, Xian,
dated 668.

FIGURE 15. White porcellaneous footed bowl, tomb in Hansenzhai, Xian dated 667.

FIGURE 16. Official, pottery figurine, Zheng Ren-tai Tomb, Liquan County, Shaanxi, dated 664.

FIGURE 17. Ceramic flask in Sasanian style with bird head, Shaanxi Provincial Museum.

FIGURE 18.   Foreign officials, Sculpture, Shendao, Qianling, Xian.

FIGURE 19. Guardian official, Sculpture, Shendao, Qianling, Xian.

FIGURE 20. Buddha, Sculpture, Fengxian Cave, Longmen, Luoyang, dated 672-675.

FIGURE 21. Guardian Sculpture, Fengxian Cave, Longmen, Luoyang, dated 672-675.

FIGURE 22. Amitofu, Sculpture, Cave of a Thousand Buddhas,
Longmen, Luoyang.

FIGURE 23. Eleven-headed Guanyin, Mural, Dunhuang, Cave 321.

FIGURE 24. Asura deity in audience of Vimalakirti, Mural,
Dunhuang, Cave 335, dated 686, detail.

FIGURE 25. Foreign dignitaries, Mural, Li Xian, Sanyuan county, Xian, dated 706.

FIGURE 26. Hunting, Mural, Li Xian's Tomb, Sanyuan county, Xian, dated 706.

FIGURE 27. Playing polo, Mural, Li Xian's Tomb, Sanyuan county, Xian, dated 706.

FIGURE 28.   Female attendants, Mural, Li Xian's Tomb, Sanyuan county, Xian, dated 706.

FIGURE 29. Jue gates, Mural, Li Zhong-ren's Tomb, Sanyuan
county, Xian, dated 706.

FIGURE 30. Hounds and Trainers, Mural, Li Zhong-ren's Tomb, Sanyuan county, Xian, dated 706.

FIGURE 31. Ceramic Figurine, Li Xian's Tomb, Sanyuan county, Xian, dated 706.

FIGURE 32. Equestrian, Ceramic figurine, Li Xian's Tomb, Sanyuan county, Xian, dated 706.

FIGURE 33. Equestrian, Ceramic figurine, Li Xian's Tomb, Sanyuan county, Xian, dated 706.

FIGURE 34. Ostrich, Sculpture, Shendao, Qiaoling.

FIGURE 35. Taoist trinity, Sculpture, Shanghai Museum, dated 740.

FIGURE 36.   Taoist trinity, Sculpture, Renshou Niujiaozhai, Sichuan.

FIGURE 37.   Landscape, Mural, Dunhuang, Cave 209, detail.

FIGURE 38.   Landscape, Mural, Dunhuang, Cave 321, detail.

FIGURE 39. Lady playing a game, Mural, Tomb 187, Astana, Turpan.

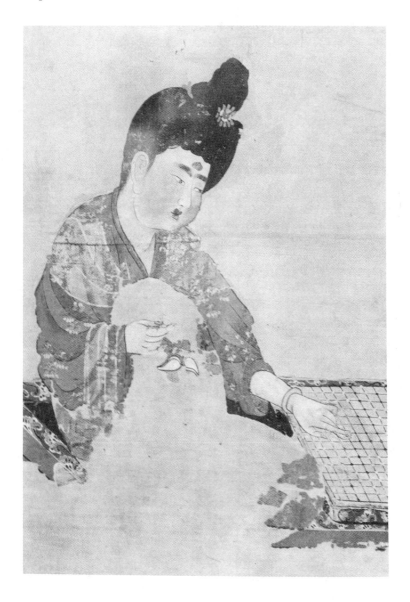

FIGURE 40. Middle-aged servant, Mural, Tomb of Lady Xue, Xianyang, Shensi, dated 710.

FIGURE 41. Dancer and musicians, Mural, Tomb of Su Si-xu, dated to 745.

FIGURE 42. Horses and grooms, Mural, Astana, Cave 188, Turpan, dated to 715.

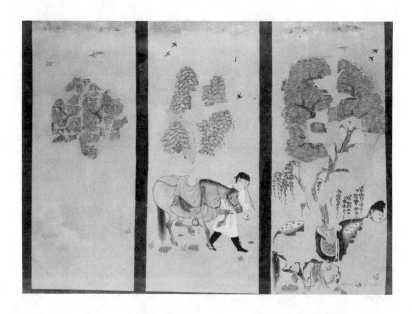

FIGURE 43. Female, Ceramic figurine, Tomb in Zhongbao, Xian.

FIGURE 44. Guardian, Ceramic figurine, Tomb in Zhongbao, Xian.

FIGURE 45. Camel, Ceramic figurine, Tomb in Zhongbao, Xian.

FIGURE 46. Female, Ceramic figurine, Tomb of Wu Shouzhong, dated 748.

FIGURE 47. Storyteller and musicians, Ceramic figurines, Tomb in Hongqing village.

FIGURE 48. Gold cup, Hejia Village, Xian.

FIGURE 49. Gilt silver clamshell box, Yanshi, Henan.

FIGURE 50. Bronze mirror with landscape theme, Xian.

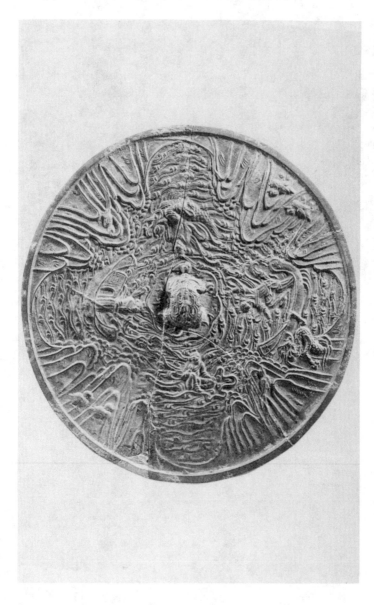

FIGURE 51. Flying Horse, Sculpture, Tailing, Shendao.

FIGURE 52.   Official's head, Sculpture Fragment, Tailing, Shendao.

FIGURE 53. Buddha and Bodhisattva, Sculpture, Cave XXI,
Tianlongshan, Shanxi

FIGURE 54. Buddha, Sculpture, Dunhuang, Cave 328.

FIGURE 55. Bodhisattvas, Sculpture, Dunhuang, Cave 328.

FIGURE 56. Guanyin, Mural, Dunhuang, Cave 45.

FIGURE 57. Mural Guanyin, Mural, Dunhuang, Cave 33.

FIGURE 58. Vimalakirti Debate, Mural, Dunhuang, Cave 103.

FIGURE 59. Thousand-armed Guanyin, Sculpture, Qiongxia, Shisunshan, Sichuan.

FIGURE 60. Tianwang Guardian Figure, Sculpture, Qiongxia, Shisunshan, Sichuan.

FIGURE 61. Bodhisattva, Sculpture Daming Palace, Xian, Shaanxi Provincial Museum

FIGURE 62. Official's head, Sculpture Fragment, Suzong's
Shendao, Jianling.

FIGURE 63. Silver lotus leaf plate, Dantu, Jiangsu.

FIGURE 64. Guardian, Sculpture, Pagoda, Anyang, Henan, dated 771.

FIGURE 65. Acala Vidyaraja (Fudo Myoo), Sculpture, Anguosi, Shaanxi Provincial Museum.

FIGURE 66. Eleven-headed Guanyin, Sculpture, Xian.

FIGURE 67. Manjusri, Sculpture, Foguansi, Wutaishan.

FIGURE 68.   Guardian figure, Sculpture, Qiongxia Shisunshan, Sichuan, dated 768.

FIGURE 69. Western Paradise, Mural, Dunhuang, Cave 148, dated 775.

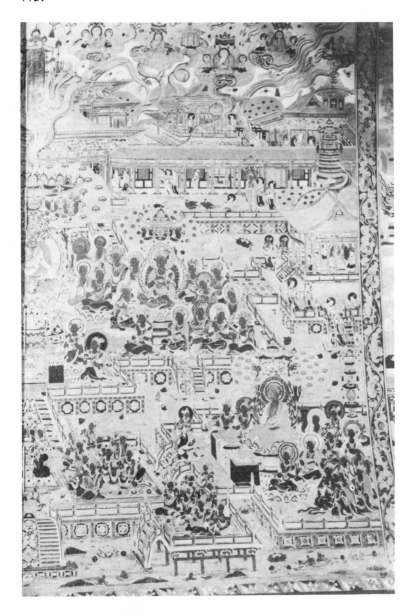

FIGURE 70. Female figure, Mural, Princess Tangan Tomb,
Wangjiafen, Xian, dated to 784.

FIGURE 71. Female head, Ceramic Sculpture, Princess Tangan Tomb, Wangjiafen, Xian, dated to 784.

FIGURE 72. Copper plate with phoenix and peonies, Jengdizhai, Shaanxi Province Historical Museum, dated 785.

FIGURE 73. Mandala, Bronze plaque, Xian, Shaanxi Museum, dated 796.

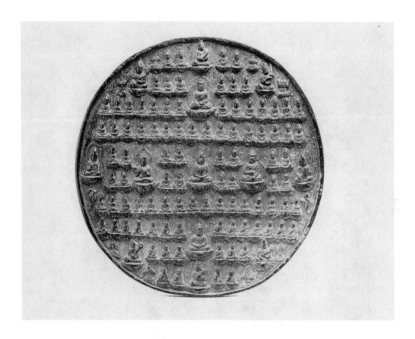

FIGURE 74. Buddha and Eighteen Lohans, Clay plaque, Xian.

FIGURE 75. Mandala, Silk Painting, from Xian.

FIGURE 76. Buddha Group with Wenshu and Samantabhadra, Sculpture, Nanchansi, Wutaishan, dated 782.

FIGURE 77. Guardian Figure, Sculpture, Wanfosi, Sichuan.

FIGURE 78. Thousand-Armed Guanyin, Sculpture, Sanlizhoushan, niche 64, Sichuan.

FIGURE 79. Horse, Sculpture, Xianzong Shendao.

FIGURE 80. Bronze mirror, dated 827.

FIGURE 81. Donors, Mural, Dunhuang, Cave 231, dated 839.

FIGURE 82. Jade box, Li Cun Tomb, Yanshi, Henan, dated 845.

FIGURE 83. Death of the Buddha, Stone Coffer, from Lingtai, Gansu, dated 850.

FIGURE 84. Silver and gold coffer from Shaanxi.

FIGURE 85. Wooden figurines, from Qinghai, Xining.

FIGURE 86. Tomb lion, Sculpture, Wuzong Shendao.

FIGURE 87. Paradise of Amitofu, Sculpture, Danli Jigongshan, Sichuan, dated 845.

FIGURE 88. Camel and groom, Ceramic figures, Peishi Xiao Niang-zi Tomb, Jiali village, Xian, dated 850.

FIGURE 89. African, Ceramic figurine, Peishi Xiao Niang-zi Tomb, Jiali village, dated 850.

FIGURE 90. Female, Ceramic figurine, Peishi Xiao Niang-zi Tomb, Jiali village, dated 850.

FIGURE 91. Silver plate, Yaoxian county, Shaanxi Province
Historical Museum, dated 847-860.

FIGURE 92. Porcelain dishes, Tomb in Lincheng, Hebei, dated 856.

FIGURE 93. Tianwang, Mural, Foguansi, Wutaishan, dated 857.

FIGURE 94. Demon, Mural, Foguansi, Wutaishan, dated 857.

FIGURE 95. Official, Mural, Yang Xuan-lue Tomb, dated 864.

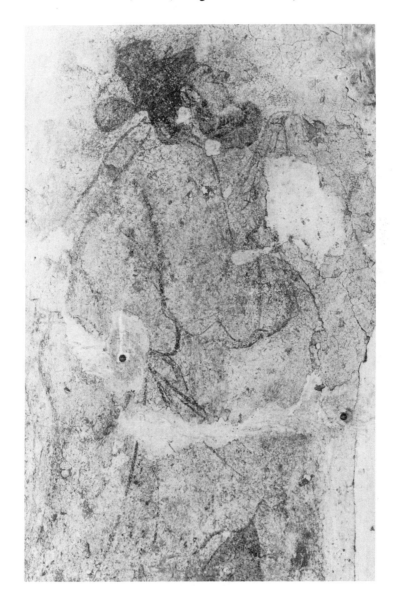

FIGURE 96.   Banquet, Mural, Wei Family Tomb, Xian.

FIGURE 97.   Children Bathing, Ceramic Figurine, Shaanxi Province
Historical Museum.

FIGURE 98. Women in a garden, Mural, Wei Family Tombs, Xian.

FIGURE 99. Jade reliquary coffer, Famensi, Xian.

FIGURE 100. Embroidered silk, Famensi, Xian.

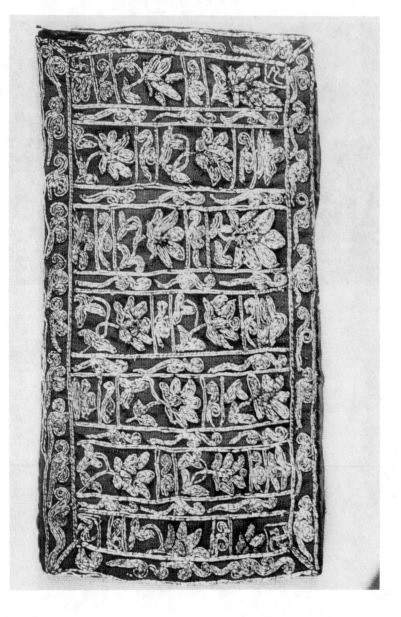

FIGURE 101. Gilt silver Bodhisattva, Sculpture, Famensi, Xian.

FIGURE 102. Gilt silver Bodhisattva, Sculpture, Famensi, detail.

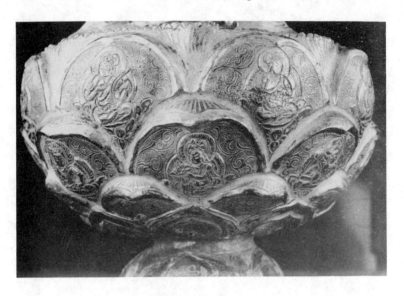

FIGURE 103. Gilt Silver Incense Burner, Famensi, Xian.

FIGURE 104. Gilt Silver Tea Jar, Famensi, Xian.

FIGURE 105. Gilt Silver Tea Jar, Famensi, Xian, detail.

FIGURE 106. Portrait Huang Bian, Clay Sculpture, Dunhuang, Cave 17, dated 869.

FIGURE 107. Donors, Mural, Dunhuang, Cave 107, dated 871.

FIGURE 108. Athletic Guardian, Sculpture, Pujian Kandengshan, Dafoku, Sichuan, dated 865.

FIGURE 109. Nested Boxes, Famensi, Xian

FIGURE 110. Nested Boxes, Six-armed Guanyin, Famensi, Xian, detail.

FIGURE 111. Guanyin, Bronze Sculpture, Shanghai Museum.

FIGURE 112. Guardian King, Nested Boxes, Famensi, Xian, detail.

FIGURE 113. Guardian King, Marble Sculpture, Famensi, Xian.

FIGURE 114. Celadon porcelain vase, Famensi, Xian.

FIGURE 115. Bodhisattva, Mural, Dunhuang, Cave 161.

FIGURE 116. Buddha, Sculpture, Neijiangxiang Longshan, Sichuan, dated 880.

FIGURE 117. Guardian, Sculpture, Jiajiang, Sichuan.

GLOSSARY

AMITABHA Sanskrit name of the Buddha of Infinite Light, Buddha of the Western Paradise (Amitofu in Chinese).

AMITOFU Buddha of Infinite Light, Buddha of the Western Paradise (Amitabha in Sanskrit).

AVALOKITESVARA Sanskrit name of attendant Bodhisattva to Amitofu, Bodhisattva of Compassion (Guanyin in Chinese).

CHANG-AN Ancient capital of Tang, now called Xian in Shaanxi Province.

DVARAPALA Sanskrit name of Buddhist divine guardians shown as athletic warriors nude to the waist.

ESOTERIC BUDDHISM Later school of Buddhism centered on the practice of a secret doctrine communicated by utilizing sacred diagrams (mandalas), chants (mantras), icons, and ritual implements.

FAMEN Temple in outskirts of Xian and site of recent finds.

GUANYIN Attendant Bodhisattva to Amitofu, Bodhisattva of Compassion (Avalokitesvara in Sanskrit).

HINAYANA Early school of Buddhism focused on the philosophical doctrine of self-discipline and meditation.

LOKAPALAS Buddhist heavenly Guardian Kings of the Four Directions (Tianwang in Chinese).

LOHAN Enlightened one (Arhat in Sanskrit).

LUOYANG Ancient second capital of the Tang, in Henan Province.

MAHAYANA Later school of Buddhism centering on expanded pantheon of innumerable deities.

MAITREYA Sanskrit name of the Buddha of the Future (Milo in Chinese).

MANDALA Diagram of the cosmic forces of the universe, with strict adherence to symmetry and hierarchy, the most powerful beings at center.

MANDORLA Body halo.

MANJUSRI Sanskrit name of the Bodhisattva of Wisdom (Wenshu in Chinese).

MILO Buddha of the Future, (Maitreya in Sanskrit).

MUDRA Special hand gesture of deities.

PAGODA Buddhist towered structure containing relics (Stupa in Sanskrit).

SAMANTABHADRA Bodhisattva paired with Manjusri.

SANCAI Three color glaze technique.

SHAKYAMUNI Historic Buddha who lived in the sixth century B.C.E. and formulated the Buddhist philosophy.

SHENDAO Processional path leading to tomb with paired animals placed along the periphery.

SHOSOIN Japanese imperial repository in Nara housing objects in the possession of the emperor Shomu, sealed after his death in the mid-ninth century.

STUPA Buddhist monument of mound of earth erected over relics of the Buddha.

SUTRAS Buddhist scriptures.

TANTRIC BUDDHISM Later doctrine that incorporates elements of Hinduism and esoteric Buddhism and is dependant on ritual and diagrams to communicate teachings.

TAOISM Ancient native philosophical-religious system of thought in China.

TIAN WANG Heavenly Guardians of the Four Directions shown crowned as kings (Lokapala in Sanskrit).

VIMALAKIRTI Sagacious Chinese scholar prominent in scripture of the same name, who debates with the Bodhisattva of Wisdom.

WENSHU Bodhisattva of Wisdom, (Manjusri in Sanskrit), cult at Wutaishan.

WUTAISHAN Five mountain peaks in Shanxi Province, home of Wenshu, site of many temples and monasteries.

BIBLIOGRAPHY

Acker, William. *Some T'ang and pre T'ang Texts*, Leiden, 1954.

Akiyama, T. *Japanese Painting*, Geneva, 1977.

Akiyama, T., and Matsubara, S. *Arts of China: Buddhist Cave Temples*, translated by A. C. Soper, Tokyo, 1968.

Benn, Charles. "Religious Aspects of Hsuan Tsung's Taoist Ideology," *Buddhist and Taoist Practice in Medieval Chinese Society*, Hawaii, 1987: 127-145.

Birnbaum, Raoul. *The Healing Buddha*, Boulder, 1979.

---------------- *Studies on the Mysteries of Manjusri, Journal of Chinese Religions*, 1983.

Boyd, A. *Chinese Architecture*, London, 1962.

Bingham, Woodbridge. *The Founding of the T'ang*, New York, 1970.

Bower, Virginia. "Polo in Tang China: Sport and Art," *Asian Art* (Winter, 1991) 23-47.

Bynner, Witter. *The Jade Mountain* (Three hundred poems of the T'ang), New York, 1959.

Cahill, James. *An Index to Early Chinese Painters*, Berkeley, 1980.

Cahill, Suzanne. "Night-Shining White: Traces of a T'ang Dynasty Horse in Two Media," *T'ang Studies* (1986) vol. 4: 91-95.

---------------- "Reflections, Disputes, and Warnings: Three Medieval Chinese Poems about the Eight Horses of King Mu," *T'ang Studies* (1987) vol. 5: 87-94

---------------- "The Word Made Bronze: Inscriptions on Medieval Chinese Bronze Mirrors," *Archives of Asian Art* (1986) vol. XXXIX: 62-69.

Camman, Schuyler. "Lion and Grapevine Patterns on Chinese Bronze Mirrors," *Artibus Asiae* (1952) vol. XVI: 266 ff.

---------------- "Significant Patterns on Bronze Chinese Mirrors," *Archives of Asian Art* (1955) vol. IX: 43 ff.

Capon, Edmund. *Princes of Jade*, New York, 1973.

Chang, H. C. *Chinese Literature 2: Nature Poetry*, New York, 1977.

Chang Yen-yuan, *Li T'ai Ming Hua Chi* (History of Famous Painters), translated by W. Acker, *Some T'ang and pre T'ang Texts*, Leiden, 1954.

Chappell, David. "Chinese Buddhist Interpretations of the Pure Lands," *Buddhist and Taoist Studies* I, Hawaii, 1978: 23-50.

Ch'en, Kenneth. "The Economic Background of the Hui-Ch'ang Suppression of Buddhism," *Harvard Journal of Asian Studies*, (1956) vol. 19: 67-105.

-------------- *Buddhism in China*, Princeton, 1972.
-------------- *The Chinese Transformation of Buddhism*, Princeton, 1975.
Ch'en Shou-yi. *Chinese Literature*, New York, 1961.
Chin Wen. "Two Underground Galleries of Tang Dynasty Murals," *New Archaeological Finds in China*, Part II, Beijing, 1978: 94-102.
Coomaraswamy, Ananda. *History of India and Indonesian Art*, New York, reprint 1965.
Chu Ching-hsuan. *T'ang Ch'ao Ming Hua Lu* (Celebrated Painters of the T'ang), translated by A. Soper, "T'ang Ch'ao ming hua lu of the T'ang Dynasty by Chu Ching-hsuan of T'ang," *Artibus Asiae* (1958) vol. XXI: 200ff.
Chow, Tse-tsung, ed. *Wen-Lin*, Wisconsin, 1966.
Chung, S. P. "A Study of the Daming Palace: Documentary Sources and Recent Excavations," *Artibus Asiae* (1990) vol. L: 23ff.
Columbia University Exhibition of Art of the T'ang Dynasty and its Antecedents from the Sackler Collection, New York, 1967.
Cooney, Eleanor, and Altieri, Daniel. *The Court of the Lion*, New York, 1989.
Cooper, Arthur. *Li Po And Tu Fu*, New York, 1973.
Creel, Herrlee G. "The Role of the Horse in Chinese History," *What is Taoism*, Chicago, 1970.
Dalby, Michael. "Court Politics in Late T'ang Times," *Cambridge History of China*, vol. 3, Cambridge, 1979: 561-681.
Dawson, Raymond. *Imperial China*, London, 1972.
Dien, Albert. *Chinese Archaeological Abstracts*, Post Han: vol. 4, California, 1985.
Dumoulin, S. J. *A History of Zen Buddhism*, Boston, 1963.
Eberhard, Wolfram. *A History of China*, Berkeley, 1966.
Eliot, Charles. *Japanese Buddhism*, London, 1935.
Fan Pen Chen. "Problems of Chinese Historiography As Seen in the Official Records on Yang Kuei-fei," *Tang Studies* (1990-91) vol. 8-9: 83-96.
Fitzgerald, C. P. *Li Che-min*, Paris, 1935.
-------------- *Empress Wu*, London, 1968.
Fong, Mary. "Four Chinese Royal Tombs in the the Early Eighth Century," *Artibus Asiae* (1973) vol. XXXV: 300ff.
-------------- "Tang Tomb Murals Reviewed in the Light of Tang Texts on Painting," *Artibus Asiae* (1984) vol. XLV: 35ff.

-------------- "Wu Daozi's Legacy in the Popular Door Gods
(menshen) Qin Shu-bao and Yu chi-gong," *Archives of Asian Art*
(1989) vol. XLII: 6-24.
-------------- "Antecedents of Sui Tang Burial Practices in Shaanxi,"
Artibus Asiae (1991) vol. LI: 147-199.
Fontein, Jan, and Wu Tung. *Han Tang Murals*, Boston, 1976.
Frankel, Hans. *The Flowering Plum and the Palace Lady:
Interpretations of Chinese Poetry*, New London, 1976.
Goldberg, S. "Court Calligraphy of the Early Tang Dynasty," *Artibus
Asiae* (1989) vol. XLIX: 189-237.
Goodrich, L. Carrington. *A Short History of the Chinese People*, New
York, 1963.
Graham, A. C. *Poems of the Late Tang*, Britain, 1970.
Guisso, R. W. L. *Wu Tse t'ien and the Politics of Legitimization in
T'ang China*, Western Washington University, 1978.
-------------- "The Reigns of Wu, Chung-tsung and Jui-tsung,"
Cambridge History of China, Cambridge, 1979.
Gyllensvard, Bo. *Chinese Gold, Silver and Porcelain: The Kempe
Collection*, New York 1979.
Harper, Donald. "The Analects Jade Candle: A Classic of T'ang
Drinking Custom," *T'ang Studies* (1986) 4: 60-91.
Hartman, Charles. *Han Yu and the T'ang Search for Unity*, Princeton,
1986.
Hayashi, R. *The Silk Road and the Shoso-in*, Tokyo, 1975.
He Jian-guo, Zhang Yan-ying, and Guo You-ming. *Hair Fashions of
Tang Dynasty Women*, Hong Kong, 1987.
Herbert, P. A. *Under the Brilliant Emperor*, Canberra, Australia,
1978.
Ho, Judy. "The Perpetuation of an Ancient Model," *Archives of Asian
Art* (1988) vol. XLI: 32-50.
Howard, A. F. "The Development of Chinese Buddhist Sculpture
from Wei to T'ang," *Chinese Buddhist Sculpture from Wei through
the T'ang*, Taiwan, 1983: 1-36.
-------------- "Buddhist Sculpture of Pujiang Sichuan, a Mirror of the
Direct Link between Southwest China and India and High Tang,"
Archives of Asian Art (1984) vol. XLII: 49-61.
-------------- "In Support of a New Chronology for the Kizil Mural
Paitings," *Archives of Asian Art* (1991) vol. XLIV: 68-83.
Huntington, Susan. *Leaves from the Bodhi Tree*, Dayton, 1990.
I Ching. *Chinese Monks in India*, translated by L. Lahiri, New Delhi,
1986.

Kanda, C. G. "Kaikei's Statues of Manjusri and Four Attendants in the Abe no Monjuin," *Archives of Asian Art* (1979) vol. XXXII: 9-26.

Karetzky, P. E. "A Scene of the Taoist Afterlife on a Sixth Century Sarcophagus Discovered in Loyang," *Artibus Asiae* (1983) vol. XLIV: 5-20.

--------------- "Foreigners in Tang and pre-Tang Painting," *Oriental Art*, London, (1984) vol. XXX: 160-166.

--------------- "Scenes of the Life of the Buddha and the Rites of Pilgrimage," *Oriental Art*, London, (1987) vol. XXXIII: 268-274.

--------------- "Scene of the Parinirvana on a Recently Excavated Stone Reliquary of the Tang Dynasty," *East and West*, Rome, (1988) vol. 38: 215-230 ff.

Keene, Donald. *An Anthology of Japanese Literature*, New York, 1960.

Kelly, Clarence. *Chinese Gold and Silver in American Collections*, Dayton, 1984.

Kirkland, J. Russell. "The Last Grand Master at the T'ang Imperial Court: Li Han-kuang and T'ang Hsuan-tsung," *T'ang Studies* (1986) 4: 43-67.

--------------- "Huang Ling-wei: A Taoist Priestess in T'ang China," *Journal of Chinese Religions* (1991) 19: 47-73.

Klimburg-Salter, D. *The Silk Route and the Diamond Path*, Los Angeles, 1982.

Klopsch, Volker. "Lo Pin-wang's Survival: Traces of a Legend," *T'ang Studies* (1988) 6: 77-97.

Kroll, Paul. "Po Chu-i's 'Song of Lasting Regret' a New Translation," *Tang Studies* (1990-91) 8-9: 97-105.

Kuwayama, George. "The Sculptural Development of Funerary Figures," *The Quest for Eternity*, Los Angeles, 1986.

Lahiri, Latika, *Chinese Monks in India*, New Delhi, 1986.

Liang, E. J. "Li Sung and Some Aspects of Southern Sung Figure Painting," *Artibus Asiae* (1975) vol. XXXVI: 3 ff.

Liu, James. *The Chinese Knight Errant*, London, 1964.

--------------- "Ambiguities in Li Shang-yin's Poetry," *Wen Lin*, ed. Chow, Wisconsin, 1968: 65-85.

Lin Yutang. *Famous Chinese Short Stories*, London, 1953.

Loewe, Michael. *Ways to Paradise*, London, 1979.

Ma, Y. W., and Lau, J. *Traditional Chinese Stories*, New York 1978.

Mahler, Jane Gaston. *Westerners Among the Figurines of the T'ang Dynasty of China*, Rome, 1959.

McNair, Amy. "Fa shu yao lu, a Ninth century Compendium of Tests on Calligraphy," *T'ang Studies* (1987) vol. 5: 69-83.

--------------- "Early Tang Imperial Patronage at Longmen," *Ars Orientalis* (1994) XXIV: 65-81.

Medley, Margaret. *Chinese Metalwork and Chinese Ceramics*, London, 1972.

-------------- *The Chinese Potter*, Ithica, 1976.

-------------- *T'ang Pottery and Porcelain*, London, 1981.

-------------- "Tang Gold and Silver," *Pottery and Metal work in T'ang China, Colloquies on Art and Archaeology in Asia*, no. 1, London, 1970: 16-22.

Murals of Li Xian, Peking, 1974.

Melikian-Chirvani, Assadullah Souren. "Iranian Silver and its Influence in T'ang China," *Pottery and Metal work in T'ang China, Colloquies on Art and Archaeology in Asia*, no. 1, London, 1970: 9-13.

Mino, Yutaka. *The Great Eastern Temple*, (Todaiji), Chicago, 1986.

Murase, Miyeko. "Kuan-yin As Savior of Men," *Artibus Asiae* (1971) vol. XXXIII: 39-73.

Nienhauser, W. "Han Yu, Liu Tsung-Yuan, and Boundaries of Literati Piety," *Journal of Chinese Religion* (1991) 19: 75-98.

Oriental Ceramic Society. *Arts of the T'ang Dynasty*, London, 1955.

Paludan, Ann. *The Chinese Spirit Road*, New Haven, 1991.

Pas, Julian. "The Life and Thought of Shan Tao," *Buddhist and Taoist Practice in Medieval Chinese Society, Buddhist and Taoist Studies II*, Hawaii, 1987: 65-84.

Payne, Robert. *The White Pony*, New York, 1947.

Peterson, C. A. "Court and Province in mid and late T'ang," *Cambridge History of China*, Cambridge, 1979.

Perry, John. *Essays on T'ang Society*, Leiden 1976.

Prodam, Mario. *Art of the T'ang Potter*, London, 1960.

Pulleyblank, Edwin. *The Background of the Rebellion of Lu shan*, London, 1966.

--------------- "The An Lu-Shan Rebellion in Later T'ang China," *Essays on T'ang Society*, ed. Perry, Leiden, 1976: 33-60.

Rawson, Jessica. *The Silver Ornament on Chinese Silver of the Tang Dynasty*, British Museum Occasional Paper no. 40, 1982.

Reischauer, Edwin. "Notes on T'ang Dynasty Sea Routes," *Harvard Journal of Asian Studies* (1940): 142-164

--------------- *Ennin's Travels in T'ang China*, New York, 1955, two volumes.

Rhie, Marilyn. "A T'ang Period Stele Inscription and Cave XXI at T'ien-Lung Shan," *Archives of Asian Art* (1974-75) vol. XXVIII: 6 ff.

Robinson, G. W. *Poems of Wang Wei*, Great Britain, 1973.

Ronan, Colin, A. *The Shorter Science and Civilisation in China*, Cambridge, 1981, three volumes.

Saehyang, P. C. "Hsing Ch'ing Kung: Some New Findings on the Plan of Emperor Hsuan tsung's Private Palace," *Archives of Asian Art* (1991) vol. XLIV: 53-67.

Schafer, Edward. *The Golden Peaches of Samarkand*, Berkeley, 1962.

--------------- "The Last Years of Ch'ang-an," *Oriens Extremis* (1963) vol. 10: 33-171.

--------------- *The Vermilion Bird*, Berkeley, 1967

--------------- *Pacing the Void*, Berkeley, 1977.

--------------- *The Divine Woman*, San Francisco, 1980.

--------------- "The Dance of the Purple Culmen," *T'ang Studies* (1987) 5: 45-69.

Sherman, John, *Mannerism*, Great Britain, 1967.

Shi Ping-ting. "A Brief Discussion on the Jingbian Buddhist Illustrations at Dunhuang," *Orientations* (1992) vol. 23: 61-63.

Shi Wei-xiang. "High Art in the Mogao Caves," *Orientations* (1992) vol. 23: 49-51.

Sickman, Larwence. *Art and Architecture of China*, Maryland, 1974.

Singer, Paul. *Chinese Gold and Silver*, China Institute, New York, 1972.

Soothill, William. *The Hall of Light*, London, 1961.

Soper, A. C. *T'u Hua Chien-wen Chih, Kuo Jo Hsu's Experiences in Painting*, Washington, D. C., 1951.

--------------- *"T'ang Ch'ao Ming Hua Lu* of the T'ang Dynasty by Chu Ching-hsuan of T'ang," *Artibus Asiae* (1958) vol. XXI: 204ff.

--------------- *Literary Evidence for Early Buddhist Art in China*, Ascona, 1959.

--------------- "A T'ang Parinirvana Stele," *Artibus Asiae* (1959) vol. XXII: 159ff.

--------------- "A Vacation Glimpse of the T'ang Temples of Ch'ang-an," *Artibus Asiae* (1960) vol. XXIII: 15-38.

--------------- "A New Chinese Tomb Discovery: The Earliest Representation of an Famous Literary Theme," *Artibus Asiae* (1961) vol. XXIV. 2: 79-86.

--------------- "Yen Li-pen, Yen Li-te, Yen P'i, Yen Ch'ing: Three Generations in Three Dynasties," *Artibus Asiae* (1991) vol. LI: 199-207.

Soper, A. C. and Sickman, L. *Art and Architecture of China*, Maryland, 1974.

Steinhardt, N. S. "The Mizong of Qinglongsi: Space, Ritual and Classicism in Tang Architecture," *Archives of Asian Art* (1991) vol. XLIV: 27-50.

Sullivan, Michael. *The Arts of China*, Berkeley, 1982.

Swart, Paula, and Till, Barry. "The Xiudingsi Pagoda," *Orientations* (May, 1990): 64-76.

Tay, C. N. "Kuan Yin: The Cult of Half Asia," *History of Religions*, (1976) vol. 16.2: 247-277.

Temple, Robert. *The Genius of China*, New York, 1985.

Thompson, Nancy. "The Evolution of the Lion and Grapevine Mirror," *Artibus Asiae* (1967) vol. XXIX: 24-54.

Tomita, Ken. "Yen Li-pen's Portraits of the Emperor's Scroll," *Bulletin of the Museum of Fine Arts, Boston* (1932), vol. 30. 177ff.

Tregear, Mary et al. *Arts of China*, vol. I, Tokyo, 1968.

Twitchett, Denis. "The Fragment of the T'ang Ordinances of the Department of Waterways Discovered at Tunhuang," *Asia Major* (1957) N.S. VI, part 1: 23-79.

--------------- "Introduction," *Perspectives on the T'ang*, ed. A. Wright and D. Twitchett, New Haven, 1973: 1-43.

--------------- "The Composition of the T'ang Ruling Class," ed. A. Wright, *Perspectives of the T'ang*, New Haven, 1973: 65 ff.

--------------- Varied Patterns of Provincial Autonomy in the T'ang Dynasty," ed. Perry, *Essays on the T'ang*, Leiden, 1976: 90-109.

--------------- *Printing and Publishing in Medieval China*, New York, 1977.

--------------- *The Writing of Offical History Under the T'ang*, New York, 1992.

Twitchett, Denis, and Fairbanks, J. *The Cambridge History of China*, Cambridge, 1979, (ten volumes), vol. 3, part I.

Twitchett, Denis, and Wechsler, Howard. "Kao Tsung and the Empress Wu: the inheritor and the usurper," *Cambridge History of China*, Cambridge 1979, vol. III.

Van Gulik, R. H. *The Lore of the Chinese Lute*, Tokyo, 1940, reprint 1969.

Van Slyke, L. P. *Yangtze*, Stanford, 1988.

Vanderstappen, H. and Rhie, M. "The Sculpture of T'ien-lung shan: Reconstruction and Dating," *Artibus Asiae* (1965) vol. XXVII: 208ff.

Waley, Arthur. *Introduction to the Study of Chinese Painting*, London, 1921.

--------------- *A Catalogue of Paintings Recovered from Dunhuang by Sir A. Stein*, London, 1931.
--------------- *The Life and Times of Po Chu I*, London, 1949.
--------------- *The Real Tripitika*, London, 1952.
--------------- *Li Po*, New York, 1969.
Wang Chonren. *Recent Discoveries in Chinese Archaeology*, Beijing, 1984.
Wang Zhen-ping. "Tang Maritime Trade," *Asia Major* (1991) vol. 4: 7-38.
Watson, Burton. *Cold Mountain*, New York, 1970.
Watson, William. "On T'ang Soft-Glazed Pottery," *Pottery and Metal work in T'ang China, Colloquies on Art and Archaeology in Asia*, no. 1, London, 1970: 35-42.
--------------- *Mahayanist Art after A.D. 900, Colloquies on Art and Archaeology in Asia*, no. 2, London, 1971.
--------------- "Divisions of T'ang Decorative Style," *Chinese Painting and the Decorative Style, Colloquies on Art and Archaeology in Asia*, no. 5, London, 1975: 1-22.
--------------- *Art of Dynastic China*, New York, 1979.
--------------- *Tang and Liao Ceramics*, New York, 1982.
Weber, Charles. "The Spirit Path in Chinese Funerary Practice," *Oriental Art* (1978) vol. XXIV: 171ff.
Wechsler, Howard. *Mirror of Heaven: Wei Cheng at the Court of T'ang T'ai Tsung*, New Haven, 1974.
--------------- "T'ai Tsung the consolidator," *Cambridge History of China*, vol. III, Cambridge, 1979.
--------------- *Offerings of Jade and Silk*, Yale, 1985.
Wechsler, Howard and Twitchett, Denis. "Kao Tsung and the Empress Wu: the inheritor and the usurper," *Cambridge History of China*, Cambridge, 1979, vol. III.
Wechsler, Howard, "The Confucian Impact on Early T'ang Decision-Making," *T'oung Pao* (1980) vol. LVI: 3-40.
Weinstein, Stanley. "Imperial Patronage in T'ang Buddhism," *Perspectives on the T'ang*, Wright ed., New Haven, 1973: 291 ff.
--------------- *Buddhism Under the T'ang*, New York, 1987.
Welch, Holmes. *Taoism*, Boston, 1967.
Whitfield, Roderick. "The Lohan in China," *Mahayanist Art after A.D. 900*, Colloquies on Art and Archaeology in Asia, no. 2, London, 1972: 96-101.
Whitfield, Roderick, and Farrer Anne. *Caves of the Thousand Buddhas*, New York, 1990.

Wilhelm, Hellmut, and Knechtges, David. "T'ang T'ai-tsung's Poetry," *Tang Studies* (1987) 5 : 1-23.
Williams, J. "Sarnath Scenes of the Buddha's Life," *Ars Orientalis* (1975) vol. X: 171 ff.
Wood, Frances. *Chinese Illustration*, London, 1985.
Wright, Arthur. *Buddhism in Chinese History*, Stanford, 1959.
--------------- "Introduction," *Perspectives on the T'ang*, ed. A. Wright and D. Twitchett, New Haven, 1973: 1-43.
--------------- "T'ang T'ai-Tsung and Buddhism," *Perspectives on the T'ang*, ed. A. Wright and D. Twitchett, New Haven, 1973: 239-265.
--------------- "T'ang T'ai Tsung: The Man and The Persona," *Essays on T'ang Society*, ed. John Perry, Leiden, 1976: 17-32.
--------------- *The Sui Dynasty*, New York, 1978.
Wu Hung. "Reborn in Paradise: A Case Study of the Dunhuang Sutra Painting and its Religious Ritual and Artistic Context," *Orientations*, (1992) vol. 23: 52-60.
Yang Xian-yi. *Poetry and Prose of the Tang and Song*, Beijing, 1990.
Yang Xian-yi and Gladys Yang. *The Dragon King's Daughter*, Bejing, 1954.
Yu Chun-fang. "Feminine Images of Kuan-yin," *Journal of Chinese Religions* (1990) 18: 61-89.
Zhou Xun. *Five Thousand Years of Chinese Costumes*, Hong Kong, 1984.
Zhu Jing-xuan. *Tang Chao Ming Hua Lu,* ca. 840s.
Zhu Qi-xin. "Buddhist Treasures from Famensi," *Orientations* (May 1990): 77-83.
Zwalf, W. *Buddhism*, Britain, 1985.

CHINESE ARCHAEOLOGICAL MATERIAL

Beijingshi Wenwu Gongzuodui. "Beijingshi Faxiande Bazuo Tangmu," *Kaogu* (1980) 6: 498-505.
Changan Guibao, Xian, 1985.
Chang Xu-zheng and Zhu Xue-shan. "Shandongsheng Huiminxian Chutu Dingguangfo Sheliguan," *Wenwu* (1987) 3: 60-62.
Changzhishi Bowuguan. "Changzhixian Songjiazhuang Tangdai Fancheng Fufu mu," *Wenwu* (1989) 5: 58-65.
--------------- "Changzhishi Xijiao Tangdai Lidu, Songjiajin mu," *Wenwu* (1989) 6: 44-50.
Changzhishi Bowuguan. "Shanxi Changzhishi Tangdai Fengkuo mu," *Wenwu* (1989) 6: 51-57.
Chen An-li and Ma Ying-zhong. "Xian Wangjiafen Tangdai Tangangongzhu mu," *Wenwu* (1991) 9: 16-26.

Cheng Mingchi. "Lingtai Sheli Shiguan," *Wenwu* (1983) 2: 48-52.

Cheng Zheng and Li Hui. *Tang Shiba Ling Shike*, Shaanxi, 1988.

Cheng Xue-hua. "Tang Tiejin Huacai Shike Zaoxiang," *Wenwu* (1961) 7: 21-31.

Dantu Xianwenjiaoju Zhengjiang Bowuguan. "Jiangsu Dantu Dingmaoqiao Chuti Tangdai Ginto Jiaocang," *Wenwu* (1982) 11: 15-28.

Duan Peng-qi. "Xian Nanjiao Hejiatcun Tangdai Jinyin Qixiaoyi," *Kaogu* (1980) 6: 536-541 and 543.

Gansusheng Wenwu Gongzuoyendui. *Qingyang Beikusi*, Beijing, 1985.

310 Guodao Mengjin Kaogusuo. "Luoyang Mengjin Shaanxitou Tangmu," *Wenwu* (1992) 3: 1 ff.

Han Tang Bi Hua, Beijing, 1974.

Han Tang Sichou zhi Lu Wenwu Qinghua, Shaanxi, 1990.

Han Wei. *Zhaoling Wenwu Qinghua*, Shaanxi Bowuguan, 1991.

Hebei Lincheng Xingci Yan Zhixiaozu. "Tangdai Xingyao Yi Diaocha baogao," *Wenwu* (1981) 9: 37-43.

Henansheng Gudai Jianzhu Baohu Yanjiusuo. "Henan Anyang Lingguansi Tangdai Shuang Shitai," *Wenwu* (1986) 3: 70-79.

-------------- "Junxian Qianfodong Shiku Diaocha," *Wenwu* (1992) 1: 31-39.

Hou Yi. "Tangdai Laojiau Shizaoxiang Changyangtianzun," *Wenwu* (1991) 12: 42-47.

Hunan Bowuguan. "Hunan Changsha Xianjiahu Tangmu Fajue Jianbao," *Kaogu* (1980) 6: 506 ff.

Kuanchengxian Wenwu Baohuguanlisuo. "Hebei Kuancheng Chudi Liangjian Tangdai Yinqi," *Kaogu* (1985) 9: 857-8.

Li Hui-bing. "Tangdai Xingyao Yaozhi Kaocha yu Chubu Tantao," *Wenwu* (1981) 9: 44-48.

Li Yu-zheng and Guan Shuang-xi (Shaanxi Bowuguan). "Xian Xijiao Chutu Tangdai Shouxie Jingzhou Juanhua," *Wenwu* (1984) 7: 50-52.

Li Zheng, Shi Yun-zheng, Li Lan-ke. "Hebei, Lincheng Chizuo Tang mu," *Wenwu* (1990) 5: 21-27.

Li Zhi-yan. "Tangdai Ciyao Gaikuang yu Tangci de Fenqi," *Wenwu* (1972) 3: 38-48.

Linruxian Bowuguan. "Henan Linruxian Faxian Yizuo Tangmu," *Kaogu*, (1988) 2: 186-7.

Lindongxian Bowuguan. "Shaanxi Lintong Xingjiacui Faxian Tangdai Liujintong Zaoxiang Jiaozang," *Wenwu* (1985) 4: 1-8.

Liu Chi-yuan, *Chengdu Wanfosi Shike Yishu*, Beijing, 1958.

Lo Jiu-gao, Liu Jian-guo. "Dantu Dingmaoqiao Chuti Tangdai Jinto Shixi," *Wenwu* (1982) 11: 28-33.

Lu Chiu Kao. *Tangdai Jinyinqi*, Xian, 1991.

Lu Zhao-yin. "Cong kaogu Faxiankan Tangdai de Jinyin "Jinfeng" zhi Jing," *Kaogu* (1983) 2: 173-9.

Luoyangshi Wenwu Gongzuodui. "Luoyang Tang Shen Hui he Shangsheng Tataji Qingli," *Wenwu* (1992) 3: 64-67 and 75.

--------------- "Luoyang Chudi Houtang Diaoyin Jingzhou," *Wenwu*, 1992.3: 96ff.

Ma Shih-chang. "Quanyu Dunhuang Zangjingdong de jige Wenti," *Wenwu* (1978) 12: 21-33.

Meng Jia-rong. "Congtang Taihe Yuannian Dongyin Tanchuanshi 'Fanniuyin'," *Wenwu* (1984) 7: 70-71.

Shaanxisheng Bowuguan. "Tang Zheng Ren-tai mu Fachu Jianbao," *Wenwu* (1972).7: 33-44.

--------------- "Xian Nanjiao Hejiacun Faxian Tangmu," *Wenwu* (1972) 1: 30-42.

--------------- "Tang Li Shou mu Fachu Jianbao," *Wenwu* (1974) 9: 71-88.

--------------- *Tang Mu Pihua Jinbu*, Xian, 1989.

Shaanxisheng Kaogu Yanjiusuo Tongchuan Gongzuozhan. "Tongchuan Huangbao Faxian Tangsancai Zuofang he Yaolu," *Wenwu*, 1987.3: 23-31 and 37.

--------------- "Taiyuan Jingshengcun 337 hao Tangdai Bihua Mu," *Wenwu* (1990) 12: 11-15.

Shaanxisheng Wenwu Guanli Weiyuanhui. "Xian Xijiao Zhongbaocun Tangmu Qingli Jianbao," *Kaogu* (1960) 3: 34-38.

Shaanxi Taoyong Jinghua, Xian, 1986.

Shaanxi Xian Wenwu Guanli Weiyuanhui, Liquanxian Zhaoling Wenguansuo." Tang Ashina Zongmu Fajue Jianbao," *Kaogu* (1977) 2: 132-138.

Shaanxi Xian Wenwu Guanhui Zhaoling Wenguansuo. "Tang Lingquan Gongzhu Chutu de Muzhi he Zhaoshu," *Wenwu* (1977) 10: 50-59.

Shanxisheng Gujianzhu Baohu Yenjiu Suobian. *Foguansi he Dadongdian Tangwudai Bihua*, Beijing, 1983.

Sun Ji. "Tangdai de Maju yu mashi," *Wenwu*, 1981.10: 82-88.

--------------- "Tangdai Funu de Fuzhuang yu Huazhuang," *Wenwu*, 1984.4: 57-69.

Tangdai Yishu, Xian, 1991

Tang Mu Pi Hua Jijin, Shaanxi Provincial Museum, Xian, 1988.

"Tang Zheng Rentai mu Fajue Jianbao," *Wenwu* (1972) 7: 33-44.

Wang Ren-bo. *Sui Tang Wen Hua*, Shanghai, 1990.

Wang Xi-xiang and Zeng Deng-ren. "Sichuan Jiajiang Qianfoyan Moya Zaoxiang," *Wenwu* (1992) 2: 58-66.

Wutaishan, Wenwu Press, 1984.

"Xian Xijiao Zhongbaocun Tangmu Qingli Jianbao," *Kaogu* (1960) 3: 34-38.

Xiaoga Diqu Bowuguan, Anluxian Bowuguan. "Anluwang Dishan Tang Wuwangnu Yangshi mu," *Wenwu* (1985) 2: 83-93.

Yangzhou Bowuguan."Yangzhou Situmiaozhen Qingli yizuo Tangmu zang," *Kaogu* (1985) 9: 859-860.

Yi Shen-pin and Han Wei. *Tangmu Pihua Jijin*, Shaanxi, 1991.

Yichuanxian Wenwuguan. "Henan Yichuan Faxian yizuo Tangmu," *Kaogu* (1985) 5: 459.

Yun Shi, Zhaoling Wenwuguan Lisuo. "Zhaoling Pei Zangmu Diaochaoji," *Wenwu* (1977) 10: 33-40.

Zhang Yihua. "Xijiang Xiruichang Faxian de Tangdai Foju," *Wenwu* (1992) 3: 68-70.

Zhengjiang Bowuguan. "Jiangsu Zhengjiang Tangmu," *Kaogu* (1985) 2: 131-148.

Zhongguo Meishu Quanji: Diaosubian, Sichuan Shiku Diaosu, vol. 12, ed. Li Ji-sheng, Beijing, 1988.

Zhongguo Meishu Quanji: Diaosubian, Gongxian, Tianlongshan, Anyang, vol. 13, ed. Ding Ming-yi, Beijing, 1989.

Zhongguo Meishu Quanji: Maijishandeng Shiku Bihua, vol. 17, ed. Huang Yu-xiang, Beijing, 1987.

Zhongguo Shehui Kexueyuan Kaogu Yanjiusuo Henan Dier Gongzuodui. "Henan Yanshi Xingyuancui de Liangzuo Tangmu," *Kaogu* (1984) 10: 904-914.

-------------- "Henan Yanshi Xingyuancun de Liuzuo Jinian Tangmu," *Kaogu* (1986) 5: 429-431.

Zhongguo Shehui Kexueyuan Kaogu Yanjiusuo Xian Tangcheng Gongzuodui. "Tang Changan Ximingsi Yizhi Fajue Jianbao," *Kaogu* (1990) 1: 45-55.

Zhongguo Shiku: Gongxian Shikusi, Wenwu and Heibonsha Presses, Japan, 1983.

Zhongguo Shiku: Dunhuang Mogaoku, five volumes, Wenwu, 1987.

JAPANESE

Chugoku Sekkutsu Tonko Bakkokutsu, five volumes, Heibonsha, 1980-82.

Horyuji Tojirukuroodo Bukkyobunka, Tokyo, 1988.

Matsubara, Saburo. "Tang Buddhist Sculpture in the Mid Eighth Century," *Bijitsu Kenkyu* (1968) vol. 257 : 11-30.

Nara Kokoritsu Hakubutsukan. *Shosoin-ten*, Nara, 1988.

Toji Homotsuden. *Toji no Myo Ohzo*, Toji, 1988.

Toshodaiji, Nara, 1985.

INDEX